CARVED BY EXPERIENCE

CARVED BY EXPERIENCE

Vipassanā, Psychoanalysis, and the Mind Investigating Itself

Michal Barnea-Astrog

KARNAC

First published in 2017 by
Karnac Books Ltd
118 Finchley Road, London NW3 5HT

British Library Cataloguing in Publication Data

A C.I.P. for this book is available from the British Library

ISBN 978 1 78220 450 3

Edited, designed and produced by The Studio Publishing Services Ltd
www.publishingservicesuk.co.uk
email: studio@publishingservicesuk.co.uk

www.karnacbooks.com

CONTENTS

ACKNOWLEDGEMENTS AND PERMISSIONS

My thanks to Yaron and to those who generously and in various ways gave advice, support and help: Dana Amir, Tamar Apel, Eilona Ariel, Oded Barnea, Ronny Barnea, Smadar Barnea, Tamar Bialik, Yigal Borochovsky, Itai Breuer, Alex Cherniak, Yarden Dar, Paul R. Fleischman, Roni Gelbfish, Liora Grossman, Mirjam Hadar Meerschwam, Yuval Noah Harari, William Hart, Tammy Hershkovitz, Axel Hoffer, Ran Mayroz, Bob Milone, Esther Pelled, Jacob Raz, Carlo Strenger, and Galit Yaari.

Thanks also to those who shared their stories with me.

Permissions

Excerpt from Abadi, S. (2003). Between the frontier and the network. *International Journal of Psychoanalysis, 84*: 221–234, reproduced by kind permission of John Wiley & Sons.

Excerpt from Money-Kyrle, R. E. (1956). Normal counter-transference and some of its deviations. *International Journal of Psychoanalysis, 37*: 360–366, reproduced by kind permission of John Wiley & Sons.

Excepts from Racker, H. (1968). Transference and countertransference. *International Psycho-Analytic Library*, *73*: 1–196. Reprinted London: Hogarth Press and the Institute of Psychoanalysis, 1988. Reproduced by kind permission of the Institute of Psychoanalysis.

Twelve lines *Selected Poems: Rumi* (1995), translated by Coleman Barks. (Penguin Books, 2004). Copyright © C. Coleman Barks, 1995. Reproduced by kind permission of Penguin and Coleman Barks.

ABOUT THE AUTHOR

Michal Barnea-Astrog, PhD, is a researcher in the field of psycho-analysis and Buddhism, a senior Hakomi trainer, and a therapist in private practice. She studied the Refined Hakomi Method in the UK, and is the founder and head of the Three-Year Hakomi Training in Israel. She teaches at the East Asian Studies Department at Tel Aviv University, and is a dedicated Vipassanā meditator.

*To Satya Narayan Goenka, who showed me the way
and to those who follow it—wise, humble, and devoted—
whose love accompanies me every single day.*

ABBREVIATIONS FOR REFERENCED WORKS

Dhp   Dhammapada
DN   Dīgha Nikāya
Iti   Itivuttaka
MN   Majjhima Nikāya
SN   Saṃyutta Nikāya
VIS   Vissudhimagga

To all those who tremble with the world.

The mental action

We are used to thinking about desire and hate as momentous mental events, as good material for a dramatic film, or as key actors in our own personal drama. However, desire and hate occur incessantly in our minds, at more subtle and less obvious levels. A person wakes up in the morning after too short a night, his head aches, and all he can think about is the end of the day, when he'll be able to lie back and rest a bit. He takes that first sip of coffee, and his whole body says, "Oh, that's good!" Someone praises him for a job well done; filled with pride and satisfaction he thinks to himself, "After all, it was worth the effort." Back home, his wife glares at him for being late, and he winces guiltily.

You cannot complain, thank God, you have everything you need, but you cannot wait until you have finished with the mortgage and can begin living. You are happy to be a mother, but you cannot wait until the little one starts sleeping through the night, until he does not need you so much, until you can go back to work full time, until this nightmare of adolescence is over and he looks you in the eyes again, until he comes home from college for a holiday, until he stops fooling around and finds himself someone nice to settle down with. You hold your new granddaughter in your arms, and she smiles. "This is it," you think. "This is happiness, and nothing else in this world matters." Two weeks later, she is in hospital with pneumonia, and you toss and turn in bed all night, worried sick, unable to close your eyes. You find a lump in your breast and your entire world collapses. You manage to recover and the horizon seems open once more. You nurse your father on his deathbed, feeling his pain, feeling your pain, treasuring moments of grace and holding on to memories, regretting what never was and mourning what will never be.

What makes the mind so fickle, so dependent on circumstances? What are those forces it is subject to, rising and falling, soaring high only to plunge down again? There is a lot more than desire and hate here, you might say. There is fatigue, pain, anger and pleasure, the pride of accomplishment, frustration, regret, joy and sadness, longing and fear, worry and bereavement. That is true, but at the root of all these lies something far more elementary and profound: the mental action that craves the pleasant and welcomes it, resents the unpleasant and pushes it away. This habitual reaction is responsible for all the drama and turmoil in our lives, running us by default as long as it is not interrupted by an alternative. How is this reaction related to misery and happiness? Is it possible not to rely on it, and what would be left if it were to be taken out of the equation? This book offers an in-depth examination of this reactive infrastructure we are all subject to: its nature, the way of being and the basic premises it involves, the results it produces for the person subject to it and for their human environment, and its potential interruption—as a process, and as an existential alternative.

Preferring and pushing away

Freud describes the pursuit of pleasure and the avoidance of pain as predominant tendencies guiding mental life, which he perceives as directed by two principles: the pleasure principle and the reality principle. Mental life governed by the pleasure principle is driven by craving: it strives to gain pleasure and avoid anything which might cause unpleasure (Freud, 1911b). The reality principle is a derivative of the former, taking it one step further. At first glance, it seems to oppose the movement towards pleasure: it takes reality into account, and enables adaptation to it, utilises thought and judgement processes, protects from harm, and allows the delay of gratification. Neverthe-less, it is, in fact, enslaved to the pleasure principle, designed to serve and preserve it, only delaying immediate gratification for the sake of a more rewarding (or a more certain) return at a later time (Freud, 1911b). From the very beginning of a person's life and for its entire duration, according to Buddhist thought, the mind sorts every object it encounters into pleasant and unpleasant, accepted and rejected, and reacts accordingly:

> When he sees a form with his eye, he is infatuated with pleasing forms and gets upset over unpleasing forms. He dwells with body-mindful-ness unestablished, with a limited mind. . . . when he hears a sound with his ear, he is infatuated with pleasing sounds, and gets upset over unpleasing sounds. . . . When he smells a scent with his nose, he is infatuated with pleasing scents, and gets upset over unpleasing scents. . . . when he tastes a flavour with his tongue, he is infatuated with pleasing flavours, and gets upset over unpleasing flavours. . . . When he senses a touch with his body, he is infatuated with pleasing touch, and gets upset over unpleasing touch . . . (MN 38: 409)[1]

The dependency characterising this behaviour is so extreme that, to the extent that we are all subject to it, we are "normative" addicts—addicted to the pleasant and the pleasurable. But, as the mind finds pleasure in its own reactions, too, our addiction is not only related to what seems to be pleasant. It seeks out this moment-to-moment drama, the movement between compliance and resistance, between craving and rejecting; this movement fuels mental activity, which, in turn, feeds and incites it. Therefore, as strange as it might seem to some of us, pleasure derives not only from the pleasant, but from the very craving for it, too, as well as from the unpleasant and the hate we develop toward it (MN 38).

Thus, when I find myself repeatedly going over parts of a conver-sation I had, I find that I do so because that bit of conversation gave rise to pleasant sensations I want more of, pleasant sensations that are re-created every time those related words and images run through my mind. Either that, or the conversation evoked some unpleasant sensa-tions, and some unconscious part of me assumes that by repeating the scene internally, it will be able to gain some control over them, and, thus, change them and do away with the unwanted experience they cause. It is also possible, on a deeper level, that my mind will cling to, and fuel, the memory of an event that brought about an unpleasant, distressing, or painful experience, because it relishes those very acts of clinging and inciting on which it is so dependent.

The more drastic examples of addiction life provides us with make it obvious that addiction involves a great deal of suffering. In a certain sense, however, the difference between an addiction to drugs, alcohol, gambling, or self-harm and an ordinary normative addiction, is not a substantial one. Since the basic human addiction is not to the objects themselves, but to the sensations they generate and the craving these evoke, any addiction is the addiction to the pleasant and the hate of the absence thereof, and any addiction manifests as a clinging to whatever it is that gives rise to pleasantness and does away with unpleasantness, even if it is only temporary and takes a heavy toll. The Buddha's teaching calls this kind of addiction "thirst", and the chronic entanglement in it *saṃsāra*. (There is, of course, much more to say about the term *saṃsāra*, the chain of becoming, in which ignorance leads to craving and all the suffering life and death entail, and this will be extensively discussed later.) The Buddha's teaching differentiates between the mental actions of "hate" and "aversion" and those of "desire" and "greed", but it also indicates their common quality: craving, which, like physical thirst, is even more elementary and acute than hunger. The word "thirst" vividly illustrates the suffering inherent in the internal oscillations between rejection and attraction: on the one hand, striving to draw the beloved–pleasant closer, to appropriate it, to make it last longer, and obtain more of it, and, on the other hand, striving to distance the hated–unpleasant, be rid of it, or bring about its cessation. Once again, what appear to be two extremes, worlds apart from each other, are actually two sides of the same coin: hating something is the flip side of the desire to get rid of that same thing (and attain a complementary state), and desiring something is the flip side of hating the absence thereof.

 An addict is no longer his or her own master, but has succumbed to something external, or, more precisely, to the influence that external thing has on his or her body and mind. If that "thing" does not happen to be available when needed, the addict will be subject to the mental and physical anguish caused by its absence; when it is within reach, then the pleasure it provides is bound to be transient and short-lived, soon to be lost again. The addict is flung, experientially, between extreme highs and lows over which he or she has no control, and this addiction sustains itself: never completely and continuously satisfied, never exhausted, never ending by itself. To lesser degrees, we are all subject to this enslavement, flung between highs and lows, carried away by the vicissitudes and fluctuations of our lives.

Passing misery around

While we are being tossed around in the drama of our lives, some of the suffering involved in the process trickles out. This is equally true in extreme psychological states, and in simpler, everyday situations, although the intensity of suffering and the mental "materials" or contents spilling out differ from one case to another. When we are with someone who suffers from severe anxiety, we are likely to experience various sensations, feelings, thoughts, and states of mind. We ourselves might suffer extreme or mild anxiety accompanied by corresponding thoughts and physical sensations, or we might shut out the person we are with altogether, and disengage from them emotionally. We might be filled with criticism or anger toward them, or, alternatively, with love and empathy; we may sense an urge to get away as quickly as possible, or, conversely, compelled to stay. When a charged and tense atmosphere greets us on entering a conference room or sitting down to a family meal, we might begin to feel tense, restless, and impatient ourselves. Some of us will try to interpret and analyse the situation in an attempt to understand it, others will attempt to take control of the situation in order to try to change it, and yet others will experience helplessness or a vague, disturbing unease. Either way, an atmosphere saturated with misery of any kind has an actual influence on those it envelops. What is this atmosphere? And how does one person's suffering—his or her fear, anger, or sadness—defuse, infiltrate, or otherwise transfer into the minds of others around him or her, affect them, and even become their own?

Different disciplines in the world of psychology refer to the manner in which mental contents pass from one person to another. Social psychology studies phenomena named "emotional transmission" or "emotional contagion" and has found that people transmit feelings and their related behaviours to others with whom they regularly interact. This occurs between spouses, between parents and children, between work and home (Larson & Almeida, 1999), among friends (Mauss et al., 2001), and within large social networks (Hill et al., 2010). Neuropsychology explains these reciprocal relations with concepts such as "mirror neurons" (Cozolino, 2006; Di Pellegrino et al., 1992; Iacoboni et al., 2001; Jeannerod, 2001), and "resonance" (Lewis, et al., 2001; Platek, 2003; Rizzolatti et al., 1999), also finding that "emotions are contagious" (Lewis, et al., 2001, pp. 64–65). "Our experience of the world is constructed around the notion of the isolated self," says Cozolino, "And it is from this perspective that western science has explored the brain" (2006, p. 3). However, he adds, even though we cherish the concept of individuality and adhere to it, our interdependency on each other is the unquestionable reality of our existence. In fact, we continuously regulate each other's internal biological states (Cozolino, 2006, p. 3). Like neurons in the brain, which communicate with each other by means of chemicals secreted into the gap between them—the synapse—we, too, communicate with each other, from brain to brain, through the gap between us—the "social synapse" (Cozolino, 2006, pp. 4–5). And just as the communication between neurons affects their internal biochemistry and sets in motion processes which cause them to undergo structural changes, so, too, do we affect each other's biological states, and, in the long run, through multiple experiences, the manner in which our brains are structured and moulded (Cozolino, 2006, p. 5). Hence, "There are no single brains" (p. 6).

If there are no single and isolated brains, then there are no single and isolated minds. "There is no such thing as an infant" (apart from his mother), says Winnicott (1960, p. 587), and Ogden (1994, p. 4) adds that there is no such thing as a patient apart from his relationship with his analyst, and there is no such thing as an analyst apart from his relationship with his patient. Psychoanalysis describes the lack of mental separateness existing between people by using a family of concepts originating from the dynamics of projection (i.e., projection, projective and introjective identification, transference, and countertransference; also relevant is the term "selfobject", which I shall not discuss here). Projection stems from the basic conditioning due to which we desire pleasure and reject pain. This conditioning establishes a way of being that relates to the unpleasant as unwanted and therefore strives to dispose of it. According to Freud, when one comes into contact with an object in the world, the "pleasure-ego" judges it as either good or bad, useful or harmful:

> Expressed in the language of the oldest—the oral—instinctual impulses, the judgement is: 'I should like to eat this', or 'I should like to spit it out'; and, put more generally: 'I should like to take this into myself and to keep that out.' That is to say: 'It shall be inside me' or 'it shall be outside me'. (Freud, 1925h, p. 237)

This pleasure-ego judges every object either as worthy of ingesting, or as undesirable, and intended for keeping out. It "wants to introject into itself everything that is good and to eject from itself everything that is bad" (Freud, 1925h, p. 237), creating a sense of identity between what is bad, what is alien to the ego, and what is external. In effect, this primitive behaviour, which Freud attributes to the "original plea-sure-ego", remains active within us throughout our lives, adhering to the following rule: that which is deemed "good" or "useful", along with anything the subject wants to internalise, is related to pleasant sensations, and that which is perceived as "bad" or "harmful", along with anything the subject wants to keep out, is related to unpleasant sensations.

When someone cannot bear a certain psychological component in himself, he might project it into others he is in touch with. He might unconsciously try to rid himself of certain distressing feelings (with which he has no conscious contact) by causing another person to feel them, in his stead, and perhaps even process them for him, as well. For example, a woman ("the projector") can behave in a way that disgusts her colleagues, thus generating feelings toward her that are similar to those she feels toward herself—feelings she has carried since childhood, when she was subtly but systematically rejected by her parents. Another person could treat his wife with scorn and contempt, thus making her feel shame and humiliation similar to his own feelings in the presence of his father. A third might speak inces-santly and monotonously about insignificant matters, thus moving his therapist to an almost mechanical impassiveness, and even temporar-ily impacting her ability to feel or think deeply—experiences he himself is subject to and is unable to bear and digest.

What often happens then, is that the "object of projection" (the person into whom these experiences were projected) starts feeling some version of the unpleasant mental content within him- or herself, usually without being aware of the process that evoked it. Then he or she has to face the suffering engendered by this mental content, and if that is impossible to handle, they will probably react in ways that will fuel a blind cycle of reactions in themselves, in the projector, and in the mutual exchanges between them. Those whose colleague's behaviour evoked their disgust might react with revulsion towards her, thus replicating her original feeling of rejection. The woman whose spouse treats her contemptuously might react aggressively, or, alternatively, she might start disparaging herself, and behave in an ingratiating and placating manner, thus increasing her partner's contempt toward her. The therapist whose ability to think and feel has been temporarily compromised might seem impervious and detached, thus, perhaps, re-creating an unhealthy interpersonal environment similar to that which her patient experienced in his childhood.

However, projection is also expressed in ways far more subtle than these (although even in its more apparent instances, it usually sneaks in and goes unnoticed, hence its strength). If we observe ourselves honestly while carrying out simple, supposedly innocent mundane actions, such as shaking our head or sighing, we will find that they often carry a projective quality, that is, an attempt to get rid (in fantasy) of something unwanted. In the case of shaking our head, by physically dislodging it; in the case of a sigh, by expelling it with our breath. (Of course, there are other times when shaking our heads or sighing express other moods or states, such as satisfaction.) I think

that this is the heart of the matter: craving and desire, as well as rejection or hate, incessantly appear in the mind at varying levels of intensity, and as long as they are there, as long as the movement between preference and rejection, originating in the addiction to the pleasant, takes place in the mind, the tendency to project exists in it, too. Thus, the longing for pleasure and the rejection of pain are woven into the most basic infrastructure of the mental process, and are naturally bound to bring about a kind of "non-ecological" conduct: that of a mind that mistakenly thinks of itself as isolated, and, therefore, acts as an "intrapersonal economy" (Pelled, 2005, p. 54); that of a mind that perceives the internal as "self", which must be guarded, and the human environment as external and separate from it; that of a mind that assumes that the "outside" human environment, as such, is an appropriate place for disposing of everything unwanted, regardless of the effect it has on both the individuals composing this external human environment, as well as on the self, which lives in this very environment and takes it back in.

We have this drive to crave pleasure + reject pain.

Moreover this lives within a vacuum of ourselves.

However in our being pushed for pleasure, we project whose desires externally . influence those around us.

If we examine these processes carefully, we see how an act that is mental or internal by nature, has, in fact, actual and tangible results in the world. We can see how it constructs the manner in which the subject perceives the world, interprets it, and experiences it, and then reacts to it in ways which fuel his or her own habitual patterns of mental activity. We can also see how it takes part in the complex processes through which minds exchange their contents, influence and mould each other. This is why the Buddhist teachings define mental action as being of the utmost importance, and formulate the following relationship: if our mental action is rooted in craving, it will generate suffering for us, and, by its very nature, will also spread suffering further afield, to others; if our mental action is free of craving, it will not generate suffering at all, and, instead, will contribute to unravelling it.

Yehuda Amichai, the renowned Israeli poet, wrote,

> Sometimes pus,
> sometimes poetry—
> Always something is excreted,
> always pain.
>
> (1996, p. 6)

For Amichai, both pus and poetry are a means for exuding suffering. In the first case, the suffering is secreted as it is, raw and undigested; in the second, it has been transformed. This is the way experience carves our lives, depending on the nature of our mental actions: there is no thirst without suffering, and there is no suffering that is not "excreted" one way or another into the environment. A person can transform his or her pain only to the extent to which they are capable of tolerating and digesting it, and only to the degree that they are able to free themselves from the addiction to sensation and to craving can they be liberated from subjugation to the pleasure principle, from the urge to project, and from suffering itself.

* * *

Throughout the chapters of this book, by means of theoretical discussion and personal stories, the way our mental actions carve us will unfold. I have chosen to explore the subject mainly from two very different perspectives, each of which has carefully studied the human

Freeing yourself from the addiction to sensation

mind: Buddhist thought, as presented in the *suttas* (*sūtras*) of the Pāli Canon, the writings documenting the discourses of the man who lived in India about 2,600 years ago, known as the Buddha, and psychoanalytical thought, which, of course, is not monolithic at all, and shall be presented here through the wealth of literature concerning projective mechanisms. Occasionally, touches of other fields of knowledge, such as neuroscience and quantum physics, have found their way in as well, and are briefly discussed in very specific contexts, where I felt they can enrich the discussion without oversimplifying it.

All ideas and thoughts presented are accompanied by real-life examples and personal stories, including those of long-time Vipassanā students and teachers of various ages and different walks of life, who were kind enough to share with me, in a series of interviews, their vicissitudes on the Buddhist path. Among the various meditation techniques derived from the Buddha's teachings, many are called "Vipassanā". All the people whose stories are told here under their (fictitious) first names practise a particular form of Vipassanā, as taught for the past fifty years by Satya Narayan Goenka, following his Burmese teacher, Sayagyi U Ba Khin. Some of the profound mental processes they have gone through are offered in the form of case descriptions, examined from a perspective based on both psychoanalytic and Buddhist terminologies. With the help of this theoretical–experiential blend, I describe the impact of projection on the perception of reality, and its role in generating the feeling of being a solid and separate self; I examine the nature of the inter-psychic boundaries, and the ways in which suffering is transferred from one person to another; I explore the self-perpetuating nature of misery, and, finally, the possibility of digesting and transforming it, and even eradicating it through awareness, non-preference, and non-reaction.

CHAPTER ONE

Projection and projective identification: on the impulse to expel

When you scream
My inside screams out at me, too
Along with you.

The whole world crashes loud,
A crash continuous, flooding the arteries of thought.
Anger-bricks scatter, insufferable, into space, explode
As you explode in me.

When you grow calm
The world comes back together.
Once more we can admire
A praying mantis.
The bits of mud a pair of split-tailed birds solicitously stuck
Somehow having chosen us,
To build their nest with.

(Barnea-Astrog)

The me in you, the you in me

When she first mentioned projective identification, Melanie Klein cast a heavy stone into the waters of clinical thinking. Even today, seventy years on, the ripples can still be felt. What is projective identification and why is it still so perplexing? It is, I believe, because it touches on a very tender core buried deep in the primal, uncharted (or partially charted) layers of our psyche. Moreover, it questions some very basic assumptions, underlying our perceptions of ourselves and the world, whose feeble grip on reality and internal contradiction we are unaware of. About the first question—what is projective identification?—Meltzer wrote this: "We are still in the process of discovering what projective identification 'means', not that Mrs. Klein meant all that in 1946, consciously or otherwise" (2008[1978], p. 309). It is not my intention to try and cover all of the concept's various nuances here: I do not claim to have fully grasped them myself nor would I want to unnecessarily strain the reader. Still, I hope that the illustrations and examples I offer, as well as my theoretical discussions, will gradually illuminate the phenomenon and its fascinating implications on the life of the psyche. For now, though, some preliminary clarifications are in order.

When an infant is born she encounters a world far more demanding than the one in the womb in which she dwelled until then. In terms of the body, she now must breathe independently, take in air. She faces the reality of hunger and must suck milk and digest it. She must cope with attacks from the outside, such as viruses and bacteria, from which she was mostly protected inside the womb. No longer is she held in a watery ambience, tightly enfolded. Moving the body or just holding it is an effort and the possibilities are limited. In this exacting environment, in which the infant, being severed—at least to some extent—from her mother's body, must find herself anew, she will naturally experience suffering, mental as well as physical. Of course, she has experienced suffering before birth, but this change— some call it traumatic—brings along more complexities and suffering. This, in part, is related to the fact that in this new environment she meets the person inside of whom she lived until now: her mother. And this mother, who no longer continuously nourishes her through placenta and umbilicus, transforms into a not always satisfying object. The baby's needs are no longer met immediately or fully, and negative feelings (not exclusively) develop towards this object whom she perceives to be responsible. And for the mind, being as it is, right from the very start sensation entails thirst and thirst entails sensation. The infant's negative feelings arouse powerful anxiety, which grows even more intense when she imagines the punishment and revenge that will follow. Together with the initial anxiety associated with the trauma of birth and her frustrated needs, all this now faces the infant (Hinshelwood, 1991; Klein, 1946).

So, the infant suffers forms of distress evoked by outside sources and distress that originates within, body pain and mental pain, none of which she can process independently in the absence of the yet-to-evolve ability to hold them in consciousness or think (about) them. How does the infant's immature psyche cope with this bewildering reality? Where can she take the pains that visit her at random, indistinct as yet? The assumption is that the infantile psyche tries to simplify the complex reality while also exporting its pains to a place where they may be digested and clarified. This, according to Klein and her successors, is achieved when the psyche splits (in fantasy) internal and external reality into "good" and "bad" parts (Mitchell & Black, 1995). While in early reality there is one maternal object—or breast—which at times nourishes and generates pleasant sensations by appeasing hunger or other types of suffering, and at other times is absent and causes frustration, the infant, instead of perceiving one alternatingly satisfying and frustrating object, perceives a "good breast" and a "bad breast". Here is the prototype of the splitting mode, which is subsequently applied to all components of experience. On the same lines, the infant also splits her own mental components, with the positive feelings directed at the good breast, and the negative feelings becoming attached to the bad breast. Splitting makes order in chaos, but it lacks mental coherence without the act of projection which takes care of redistributing the components of reality so that bad goes with bad and good with good.

Let us take a step back and consider projection as a defence mechanism, as it was conceived prior to Klein. For Freud, though its defensive function is only one part of the story (see Chapter Three), projection originates in the psyche's way of fending off inner excitation that causes excessive displeasure. Instead of perceiving it as internal—which it is—the psyche "chooses" to experience the excitation as coming from outside, and hence as something against which it might raise the same barrier it usually puts up against excess external stimuli (Freud, 1920g). The psyche, acting on an unconscious assumption that this will allow it to escape them, thus renders a painful stimulus or danger coming from within as though they came from outside. It then projects its own materials on to an object, thereby attributing information coming from the unconscious to the mechanism of conscious perception in a way that confuses between inner process and outer reality (Freud, 1912–1913). A person, for instance, might be utterly convinced that his brother or colleague envies him though it is he himself who, unconsciously, envies them. Another person might blame someone of undermining her efforts or trying to destroy something, while the destructive, sabotaging forces actually arise from within herself.

For Klein, too, the infant who feels hate against what she perceives as the bad breast (absent, frustrating), projects the bad feeling on to it, and then experiences the breast—which has absorbed the projected hate—as even more bad. The infant does this to protect the ideal image of the good breast on to which she projects the loving parts of herself. These latter parts, then, remain pure in fantasy, uncontaminated and unthreatened by hate and frustration. At this point, however, as Klein describes the first three months of the infant's mental life, the notion of "projective identification" emerges, presenting clinical thought with another possible projective dynamics. Here, in addition to projection *on to* an object—of internal materials onto something external—there is the possibility to project *into it*. In addition to Freud's fantasmatic expulsion of unwanted impulses, Klein posits the projection, as well, of parts of the self whose presence, due to the primitive anxieties the infant suffers at the first stages of life, she cannot tolerate. The discussion about this possibility has become one of the most productive ones in contemporary psychoanalytic discourse (Bell, 2001), leaving its marks on many construals of intra- and interpersonal processes.

Klein (1946) defined projective identification (a term Weiss used in 1925 without perusing it much (Spillius et al., 2011)) as the unconscious act of disposing of split off parts of the self into another person, in analogy to biological processes of bodily discharge. She believed that along with actual excrements, experienced as harmful and expelled in hatred, split-off, bad parts of the self are projected *into* the mother. Consequently,

In so far as the mother comes to contain the bad parts of the self, she is not felt to be a separate individual but is felt to be the bad self. Much of the hatred against parts of the self is now directed towards the mother. This leads to a particular form of identification which establishes the prototype of an aggressive object-relation. (p. 102)

Expressed not only in the form of hate, aggression is also reflected in the fact that the bad self-parts projected into the mother, are meant to hurt her and take control over her from within (Klein, 1946). Once projected, these bits of badness can generate a sense of persecution and danger that seem to originate outside, and when they are subsequently re-internalised they trigger a sense of threat from internal destructiveness (Klein, 1946). Thus, a vicious circle comes into being: her internal anxieties drive the infant to use splitting and projection, and once she deploys the latter they feed further into the anxieties. The other side of splitting is that the infant also projects good aspects of herself into her mother. When this happens, rather than being experienced as toxic, the discharge takes on the meaning of a *gift*, resulting in a good object that entertains loving relations with a good self.

This is how the infant's unconsolidated mind copes when confronting difficulties: it uses splitting, projection, denial, and idealisation. It splits bad from good, within itself and in the object; it expels the bad in order to keep safe from it, or it projects the good into the object so as to turn it into an ideal, all-good object which is carefully isolated from all evil; it clings to the ideal object to deny the bad object, the frustrating situation, and the part of itself that maintains relations with the bad object (Klein, 1946). Facing reality, the infantile mind uses a strategy based on the reorganisation of self-parts and object-parts, whose logic is that good and bad must be separated by means of splitting, that it is easier to have control over something that has been internalised, and that what has been projected will never return (Ogden, 1986). While, according to Klein, splitting and projection are necessary to healthy development, they must keep in balance: in the early stages of life, splitting is responsible for keeping the good object, whose internalisation is crucial to the consolidation of the self and the development of the ability to love (excessive envy will not allow internalisation of the good object) (Klein, 1975c), but when there is too much splitting the self is bound to grow weak and depleted (Klein, 1946). Similarly, the mutualities between internalisation and projection constitute object relations (Klein, 1946), but this is true only for as

when something feels discarded / 2 internalise it.

long as they are in balance: overemphasis on one of them results in pathology, as for instance excessive projection of a hostile inner world, in the grip of persecutory anxieties, will issue in the internalisation of such a world.

Klein called this mental reality, with its characteristic primitive anxieties, its defence mechanisms, and object relations, "the paranoid–schizoid position": "paranoid" for the persecutory anxiety it involves; "schizoid" for the act of splitting from which it emanates, "position" because while first manifesting itself in the first three months of life, it remains active as a form of mental organisation which one enters and leaves, alternately. When, around her fourth month, the infant starts to process the "depressive position" (with its more complex perception of reality and its reduced deployment of splitting and projection), the paranoid–schizoid position remains an active layer of her mental life. And, to some extent and in varying degrees, it will be present throughout the rest of her—that is, our—life: all of our life.

We all shift, internally, between this position and others (that is, the depressive position and the autistic–contiguous position, which is a third, even more primitive, mode of experience defined by Ogden (2004a), than the paranoid–schizoid position). But some of us resort to the paranoid–schizoid position more than others. Take a woman, for instance, who, whenever she meets a man she finds attractive, tends to be totally captivated. Projecting all that is good on to him, she turns him into her ideal man: she exalts his brightness, denies his downsides, and ignores the frustration and pain he is likely to cause her just because he is in the world and happens to interact with her. Splitting him, she also splits herself, so that when she is with him or thinks of him, she is also in the company of her own loving and loved aspects, and that makes her feel good about herself. She loves and is being loved. She "loves him", that is, she "loves herself"; he is "the perfect man", that is, so far, his image has not brushed against reality.

However, the real, complex world is very unlike the fantasised split one, and interactions in the real world do not, at the best of times, compare with the always satisfying fantasised interactions. Sooner or later, the man will say something, will do or fail to do something, and it will clash head on with the woman's splitting–projective--idealising–denying fantasy. At that very moment, the man will change from white to black, from an angel into a devil, from blessing to catastrophe: the splitting–projective–idealising–denying bubble is

Projective identification is based on the processes of splitting

(good + bad)

doomed to burst, and usually it happens with a big bang, leaving casualties in its wake. We encounter this dynamic in a variety of inter-personal situations: between two adolescent girlfriends, between patient and therapist, between student and teacher, between a member of the group and the group leader, between a person and an idea, religion, or institution. It is the direct outcome of the internal organisation of those who participate in it, and the huge gaps inherent in the situation: between the black-and-white perspective typical of this position and actual reality, and between reality as it is and subjects' ability to absorb and digest it. This should not imply that this internal organisation and digesting ability are static things: fluctuations of degree occur from time to time, and more comprehensive changes might take place during adolescence, as a result of therapy, or as the outcome of deep meditative processes—as I will show.

Even though projective identification largely originates in the paranoid–schizoid position, which is based on processes of splitting, the envy, greed, and denial typical of the manic defences of the depressive position are also important factors in its emergence (Klein, 1975b). When we quickly mumble a spell against the evil eye, or say something like "touch wood", it is against this envy and greed that we (magically) try to defend ourselves. They are experienced as mysterious forces, looking at all that is good in us through an evil eye, trying to rob us of it—or simply destroy it. These same forces, which are none other than self-parts or mental components, use projective identification in order to achieve this from within by invading, that is, the object, which is none other than ourselves or our fellow human.

Container for projections

There is a natural continuity between the concept of projection before the notion of "projective identification" and after it, but the latter opened the way to a new idea. This is the notion that projection is not only directed at an internal representation of an object—the infant's image of the breast; the woman's image of the man—but can also involve a real movement of mental materials from infant to mother, from the projecting subject to its object, from one person to another. (I will further explore and elaborate this notion in Chapter Five.) Even though Klein, here, explicitly referred only to the infant's fantasy life, her very formulations, describing the process as a projection "into", already hold the seeds for understanding it as an interpersonal process *par excellence*.

Bion (1962b) took this and developed it into a sophisticated model of container and contained, with the latter referring to the projected mental materials, and the former to the mother or the object, the mental locus of their projection. By means of this model, he showed the fundamental nature of the process of exchange which projective identification constitutes in the formation and development of the psyche—whether healthy or pathological—and the extent to which it also expresses a form of communication: direct, raw, unmediated communication in which one person passes his mental contents into another and causes the latter to feel with him. Like Klein, Bion (1962b) believed that infants have an omnipotent fantasy of being able, temporarily, to split off unwanted parts of their personality and to deposit them in an object. Whereas Klein explicitly related to the infant's fantasies, Bion conceived of the subject, from the earliest stages of life, as having the ability to evoke in the mother feelings he himself does not want, or feelings he would want her to experience either with or instead of him (1962b). That is, Bion showed how the one who projects, by means of complex processes, can trigger in the object of projection feelings that accord with what was projected in the fantasy (Bell, 2001). If projection is an actual act, an interpersonal event in which mental processes of exchange really take place, then the mother, as "container" into which self-parts or experiences are projected, plays a fundamental role in the process.

At birth, the human infant's dependence on her surroundings is so great that it would be hard to claim they are autonomous. "Mother–infant" is how Winnicott referred to these two, tied together in this form of dependence, thus referring to them as one inseparable entity. To briefly revert to the environment into which an infant is born, it seems she has the basic physical equipment to begin life within it: if born healthy and at full-term, the infant's lungs will be ready for breathing, her digestive system will be able to cope with breast milk or its substitutes, and her immune system will be working reasonably well, as suits her relatively sheltered situation. Yet, she is immature. Take, for instance, the immune system. Since her immune system is far from mature, the infant is under constant threat of microscopic enemies from without. In the modern world, medical science helps to reduce this risk greatly and to camouflage it. Still, antibodies and other nutrients that the infant receives through the breast milk play an important role in her body's struggle with illness and its ability to grow strong (Horta et al., 2007; Sadeharju et al., 2007).

Let us for a moment set aside the sustaining components of breast milk and the psychological aspects of body contact and holding it involves (which, we know, improve the infant's general health in the long term), and just consider what happens to an infant who is fighting a present illness by means of the antibodies his body generates. (It does not seem realistic for research to isolate the effects of the mental *vs.* the physical factors of breastfeeding. Research, anyhow, has found a positive correlation between breastfeeding (in general) and mental health, intelligence, and cognitive achievement (see, for instance, Horta et al., 2007; Kramer et al., 2008; Oddy et al., 2010.)) When the infant is ill, or is exposed to some virus, the mother, who is nearby, is likely to catch the virus herself. She might also stay healthy thanks to her immune system, but, either way, her body, if it functions well, will produce the appropriate antibodies and pass them on to her baby via her breast milk. Better equipped to cope with the environment, the mother breathes in (or otherwise absorbs) the harmful factor and subsequently passes to her infant, as best as she can, the elements that will help his body to cope with it. Unwittingly, the infant thus infects the mother with his bodily afflictions many times over. The baby puts the source of illness into her and she gives back what it takes to deal with it. The infant's digestive system is not fully grown either at the start of life. This is why he often suffers from belly-aches. Interestingly this phenomenon occurs mainly in the first three or four months of life, a period that parallels the phase Klein associated with the paranoid–schizoid position, a time during which the infant's ability to "digest" reality is only beginning to evolve. In this period, the baby is unable to bite, chew, and digest the common foods of his surroundings. One might say that the mother eats that food for him, digests it, extracting whatever the body needs, then presents it to her child in the form of the breast milk that he is able to take in.

Like these physical systems, the infant's emotional digestive system is nowhere near being complete. His ability, therefore, to cope with the reality ingested—presently and in the future—is largely dependent on how the mother processes it inside herself before passing it back to her baby in a manageable form, and with the added resources required to deal with it. Gradually, through countless experiences, these latter will become part of the baby and serve for the rest of his life. In the absence of the mother's immune and digestive systems (or of their traditional and modern alternatives), the infant is lost. Without her—or other primary carers'—emotional digestive system, too, the infant's psyche will be lost. So, to the extent that the mother is responsible for supplying her baby with the means to successfully cope with physical challenges, she is also responsible for providing him with the tools to deal with material ingested by the mind:

> The milk, we may assume with a degree of conviction we cannot feel about love, is received and dealt with by the alimentary canal; what receives and deals with the love? . . . It may be useful to suppose that there exists in reality a psycho-somatic breast and an infantile psycho-somatic alimentary canal corresponding to the breast. (Bion, 1962b, pp. 33–34)

and that "The mental component, love, security, anxiety, as distinct from the somatic requires a process analogous to digestion" (Bion, 1962b, p. 35). This mental mode of digestion Bion called "reverie" and defined as

> that state of mind which is open to the reception of any "objects" from the loved object and is therefore capable of reception of the infant's projective identifications whether they are felt by the infant to be good or bad. (Bion, 1962b, p. 36)[1]

Whenever the infant experiences something intolerable—stomach-aches, hunger, fear of his own projected aggression, the terror of not being properly held or of slipping from wakefulness into sleep—he tries to evacuate it into the object. An infant might, for instance, scream it—like the girl in the poem at the opening of this chapter—into his mother. What does "scream it into his mother" mean? It means that now *she* is the one experiencing the sense of destruction which he feels but cannot grasp, think, or digest; that *she* now undergoes the momentary collapse of the world, which only seems to go on forever; that *she* experiences—with her mind and body—her baby's inability to think, the flooding of the arteries of thought. This means that she feels the insufferableness of all these things. (There are other ways of coping with primitive mental challenges. The terrors of having no envelope, of leaking out, or of endlessly falling into space are, in fact, considered to be more primitive, and the mechanisms that are supposed to deal with them are likely to be different forms of developing a "second skin" (Bick, 1968; Symington, 1985).) When the infant projects these bad and unprocessed sensations into a good object, which functions successfully as a container, they transform in the process and are returned to her: she can then take them back inside because they have become tolerable materials (Bion, 1962b). This is how, through her reverie (in addition to more physical ways), the mother expresses her love; this is how she takes in the sources of suffering which her baby implants in her and passes them back together with what the latter needs in order to cope; this is how she chews her baby's experiences and returns them in their milky, digestible form. In time, the infant internalises this activity, and the reality-digesting mechanism then becomes part of herself (Bion, 1962b).

One mother's immune system obviously is not identical to that of another, and the same goes for the digestive system; moreover, mothers live in very different, ever-changing environments. While one has a lot of antibodies against a certain illness, another does not; one has plenty of vitamin B12 and iron, while another is a little anaemic; one catches flu and the other does not. Neither are infants dentical in their ability to be nourished and immunised. Similarly, a mother's emotional digestive system may be more or less functional, and the baby's ability to be in touch with reality (whether internal or external), too, will vary in degree and quality. Either way, the ability to use projective identification and the presence of a mother who is able to constitute a container for these projections and to digest them by means of reverie are part of normative human development (Bion, 1962b).

The fact that the word "container" is used to refer to this function of the mother might be confusing: this container is not an inanimate object, or empty or static, and the mechanism denoted by the pair container–contained is a living thing rather than a rigid structure (Bion, 1962b): "Container and contained are susceptible of conjunction and permeation by emotion. Thus conjoined or permeated or both they change in a manner usually described as growth" (1962b, p. 90). A container is not a "thing", but a process (Ogden, 2004a), and when container–contained relations are as they should be, they lead to mental growth in mother and infant alike (Bion, 1962b). For the mother (and for anyone who serves as a container to projective identifications) it is an opportunity to move beyond herself, to expand and loosen her self-boundaries, because when the other enters her she experiences herself as an other to herself (Ogden, 2004a). Container– contained relations, in the case of the baby, develop the latter's ability to take in sensory impressions and to be conscious of them, and this contributes to the maturation of the ability to think (Bion, 1962b). It is through them that the infant can "emerge from the closed system of his internal psychological world", "to move beyond himself" (Ogden, 1986, p. 34), and to make the transition from the paranoid–schizoid to the depressive position (Ogden, 1986).

This process comes to grief when the mother is unable to tolerate, contain, and process the baby's distress on his behalf, or when the baby projects excessively and persistently. What happens when the infant struggles to split off something intolerable which he cannot contain, and the mother—into whom the baby tries to projects it—fails to recognise its right to enter her, or, alternatively, falls victim to the anxiety the projected part evokes in her (Bion, 1959)? The infant's projective identification, then, could escalate and become pathological, and trying not to experience the intolerable feelings and thoughts, the child might find himself almost entirely depleted of his psyche (Spillius, 1992). The mother–container might then transform into a "negative container", or an "obstructive object", consisting of the infant's anxieties and representations of the mother who rejects his projections. Much like an immune system that turns against the very body it is supposed to protect, and like a faulty digestive system which does not properly break down and process food which, as a result, turns toxic, this container fails to contain, and, in addition, actively attacks links that are vital to the infant, whether internal or external (Bion, 1959; 1962a; Grotstein, 1995). When this happens the infant is unable to examine her feelings within the context of a containing, strong enough personality. This negatively affects the curiosity on which learning has to rely, leading to serious developmental disorder. The management of mental life, too, becomes unbearable and causes the infant to hate all feelings and the external reality associated with them. This hatred leads to the projective identification of the entire perceptual mechanism (Bion, 1959), and to the expulsion of the mechanism of conscious awareness of (both inner and outer) reality as well as that of incipient verbal thinking (Bion, 1956). If the infant needs a mental place in which the unprocessed components of experience can undergo transformation and this place turns out to be blocked, closed, or perforated, or if the processes inside it are pathological or dysfunctional, then the components of her experience cannot be dealt with as they should, in order to become part of the infant's evolving personality, which can then turn into a site capable of taking in more components of experience. Instead of this, they are rejected. If the baby appeals to the mother's emotional digestive system and the latter turns out to be too dysfunctional, then the parts of reality (outer or inner) the baby encounters remain partly undigested, and, hence, disconnected, unusable, and harmful. The personality, in such conditions, might turn away from reality that, in the absence of a way to digest it, becomes toxic: being under attack, it, in turn, attacks.

Why project? Basic assumptions and unconscious motivations

Someone who projects mental components into another person might be guided by a variety of unconscious motives: she might feel impelled to remove and evacuate an undesirable feeling or a part of the self; she might have a fantasy that by implanting these self-parts in the other she will be able to control that person, or she might want to communicate unprocessed experiences by making the other feel what she herself is unable to feel or express otherwise (Klein, 1946; Spillius, 1992). So, for instance, a person who often feels unable to make sense of what is going on, one for whom everything tends to happen too fast and too confusingly, could adopt an unintelligible, rapid, awkward style of speaking, either too soft or too confused. This will then trigger in the other person an experience of perplexity that is similar to his own. This is one example of projective identification as a mode of communication: what is projected takes the form of a feeling or a state of mind that the object of the projection "must" now experience himself. Once this feeling or state of mind has been evoked, the other person may reject it, close himself off to it, react in anger, impatiently, or experience helplessness, for instance, or he might, alternatively, use it in order to encounter within himself the inner world of the owner of the original feeling. Evacuation through projective identification can be observed, for instance, in a person who, very early on in life, has learnt to associate the emergence of meaning with loss, which will make it likely for her to "empty" into someone (such as a therapist or a teacher) her ability to make sense, to leave it to them, while she herself sticks to a way of thinking that does not link parts of experience into a significant whole. A simple illustration of an attempt to control by means of projective identification is a man who uses a variety of behaviors to make his partner feel that she is hurting him; she then feels guilty and tries to compensate him, which he uses to his own advantage. This will count as projective identification only in so far as the manipulation described is unconscious.

Considering the interpersonal aspect of projective identification, all of these motivations may be present, to various extents, in each instance, the only question being which of them predominates. In this context, every act of projection into an object involves an evacuation (in fantasy) of what is intolerable, includes a degree of aggression, and an attempt to induce an emotional, cognitive, or behavioural reaction in the recipient which the recipient himself would not have experienced if it was not for the act of projection. When projection and projective identification are thought of as the same thing (projective identification being an extension and enrichment of projection), then projective identification does not have to include an interpersonal aspect, and so not every instance of it entails behaviours unconsciously intended to influence the recipient of projection (Spillius et al., 2011). Either way, even when the projector is mainly motivated by the need to discharge or to control, rather than by the need to communicate, it is still up to the object of the projection (provided he is conscious of the process) to make use of the projected materials so as to understand the experience of the projector "from within".

The tendency to project enfolds a number of unconscious, and partly clashing, assumptions. I shall try to portray the inner logic that seems to guide the mind when projecting. One assumption is that there exists an essential subjective entity, the self, and that it exists separately from everything and everyone else (which function as its objects). Further assumptions are that while the self is fixed and solid, it is, nevertheless, possible to cross the boundaries (which seem to blend in projective identification) between it and others; and that the parts of which self and other are composed are not so fixed, and can, therefore, be destroyed. I choose to formulate these assumptions as I do because every mental act has a point: even when it is unconscious or seems irrational. Thus, it is only provided that the subject experiences himself as an essential and continuous phenomenon that it makes (psychic, unconscious) sense to try to split the good–pleasant from the bad–unpleasant with the aim of consorting with the pleasant and with that which creates pleasantness, to preserve it and include it as part of what that individual considers his self. Only if he experiences himself as essentially distinct from others, yet also as being able to temporarily merge with, and transfer parts to, these others, only then the act of projection (which is so deeply grounded in notions of inside and outside and is all about the relocation of mental materials from what is perceived as internal to what is perceived as external) makes sense. Only if the inner parts composing the self are experienced as destructible does it make sense to try to rid oneself of what is unpleasant into the other. And it is only if the self is a solid and separate entity that it makes sense to keep good parts of that self and of objects away from bad parts, wishing to protect the good parts from the bad that threaten to destroy them.

Coexisting as well as alternating in projective identification, these basic assumptions add up to what the Buddha's teaching would have referred to as two possible ways of apprehending self and world: an eternalist and a nihilist view.[2] In the first, phenomena (all parts and features of the self as well as of objects) are constant, independent, and separate; one could say in possession of an eternal essential core. The second view assumes that since all and everything is doomed to perish, any distinctive features are annulled: as a result they themselves, as well as any actions relating to them, are meaningless to begin with. These two views form, according to Buddhism, the basis of desire and hate: if the self's mental contents and the functions that constitute it are stable and essential, and if the self is a stable and essential entity, then it will strive to accumulate as much as possible of what it perceives as pleasant, good, or desirable, and cast off as much as possible of what it perceives as unpleasant, bad, or undesirable. This is why the self yearns. If self and other (human and non-human) are stable and essential, then the removal of the undesirable from the perceived domain of the self is possible and effective. The nihilist angle, moreover, implies that such a removal will have neither negative effects nor moral implications. If, therefore, aggression, guilt, or fear arise in the subject's mind and she is unable to become conscious of them, responsible for them, tolerate and process them, and, instead, she unconsciously projects them into another person, she does this unaware of the suffering she inflicts on the latter or, less frequently, from an unconscious intention to destroy this person or dominate him from within.

Psychoanalysis, as well as other forms of psychotherapy rooted in psychoanalytic knowledge, offer elaborate ways for growing conscious of these mental contents and processes, and for developing the ability to cope with them. Buddhist thought has its own practices enabling this, designed to achieve somewhat different purposes. Without going into comprehensive explanations about psychotherapeutic and Buddhist techniques, which is beyond the scope of this book, I shall gradually explore a few core issues regarding both, in relation to the dynamics of projection.

One can look through Buddhist eyes at the same processes psychoanalysis calls "split" and "projection" and at the operations of the mind underlying them. Pāli Canon thought indicates a few fundamental functions and qualities of mental reality, and Vipassanā meditation offers to investigate them through experience. Those who examine themselves by using Vipassanā meditation actually examine their mental activities, gradually claiming more responsibility for them. As they become conscious of the effects of these activities on themselves and their surroundings, their world view gradually recedes from the above two extremes: the eternal and the nihilistic.

CHAPTER TWO

Vipassanā meditation as the investigation of mental action

As we move from psychoanalysis to Buddhism, it seems quite appropriate to quote the following words from Ernest Jones:

To ascertain what exactly comprise the irreducible mental elements, particularly those of a dynamic nature, constitutes in my opinion one of our most fascinating final aims. These elements would necessarily have a somatic and probably a neurological equivalent, and in that way we should by scientific method have closely narrowed the age-old gap between mind and body. I venture to predict that then the antithesis which has baffled all the philosophers will be found to be based on an illusion. In other words, I do not think that the mind really exists as an entity—possibly a startling thing for a psychologist to say. When we talk of the mind influencing the body or the body influencing the mind we are merely using a convenient shorthand for a more cumbrous phrase such as "phenomena which in the present state of our knowledge we can describe only in terms that are customarily called 'mental' (emotions, phantasies, etc.), appear to stand in a chronological causative sequence to others which at present we can refer to only in somatic phraseology". (1946, pp. 11–12)

On entering the conceptual world the Pāli Canon presents us with, and even more so when we encounter the practices it entails, the issues Jones raises are greatly clarified. Here, the basic mental foundations or the formative functions and elements of what we call "the mind" are revealed: their somatic equivalents, or, rather, their transient and mutually conditioned bodily correlates, and the other way around; the illusory nature of the dichotomies separating mental from physical, and self from non-self, identifying any one of these as essential entities; the gap between superficial reality, which manifests itself as a solid mass, and the deep particulate reality that comes to light on the former's dismantling; the realisation that we should treat the expressions by means of which we think about the mind-and-matter phenomenon as nothing more than a convenient shorthand.

Analysis, synthesis, and the process of becoming

Vipassanā is the in-depth and unmediated investigation of the mind-and-matter phenomenon we usually refer to as "I". Rather than an investigation in the intellectual sense of the word, however, this is a direct experiential investigation in which certain aspects of the mind are trained to objectively examine themselves as well as other, interacting, aspects of the so-called self. The use of "objectively" here, ostensibly dubious in the context of an examination carried out by observational means that are part of the observing subject, refers to the fact that the self, in this case, constitutes the object of meditation. It also refers to the fact that the main aim of this exercise is to develop an impartial or unbiased approach toward this object of investigation.

About 2,600 years ago, in India, a man called Siddhattha Gotama, engaging in such unmediated investigation of his own, discovered a system of fundamental truths concerning the nature of the above mentioned mind-and-matter phenomenon. His process of investigation was not intended to satisfy intellectual curiosity or to achieve status—it probed the mystery of suffering, its cause, and the way out of it. We are more familiar with this man as "the Buddha", the enlightened or the awakened one. The results of his penetrating analysis offer a complete picture of this mind–matter phenomenon's mode of operation (in constant relation to its surroundings) by detailing both its various constitutive parts and the complex relations they entertain with each other. One may understand this picture as being composed of an analytical, or dissecting, aspect and a synthetic, or connecting, one (Nyanatiloka, 1997; Thera, 1998[1949]).

The analytical aspect breaks the mind-and-matter phenomenon down into the various functions operating it: consciousness, perception, sensation, reaction, and matter (the physical or corporeal element, the body). These five functions are called "the five aggregates", or *khandhā*. According to the Buddha, none of these functions possesses an essential or stable core, and the self resides neither in any one of them, nor in any combination between them, nor in any other dimension beyond them. Hence, the analytical aspect is directed towards a non-eternalist view, a view that encompasses emptiness: realisation that the self, rather than an essential and stable phenomenon (SN 22.59), is a subjective experience, or, on the absolute level, a construct or illusion. The Buddha continued breaking down the psycho–physical phenomenon into many scores of elements which are all similarly devoid of an essential core; they are all, in the Buddha's words, *anattā*, "not-self".

The synthetic aspect maps the relations between the various functions or factors of the mind-and-matter phenomenon (which, from now on, I will often refer to as "the subject", not because it is an essential entity, but because it experiences itself subjectively, or as the "self", again, because it experiences itself as such). It suggests another facet of the absence of essential selfhood: the inseparability of the individual phenomenon's components and its dependency on what it perceives as being extraneous to it. The five factors that I have just described entertain mutual relations, which together create our experience of subjectivity. Simply viewed (a more detailed analysis yields dozens of elements), this is the process they generate, incessantly occurring in us all: the mind-and-matter phenomenon is equipped with sense organs, sense doors through which the mind encounters the world. Any object (a form, a sound, a scent, a taste, something tangible, or a mental object such as a thought or a memory) touching one of the sense doors is cognised by its respective part of consciousness: the eye consciousness cognises visual objects, etc. Then perception arises, *re*-cognises the object based on past experiences with similar objects, labels it and evaluates it as "good" or "bad", desirable or undesirable. As a result, pleasant or unpleasant sensations arise in the body. Following these, a mental reaction is evoked: if the sensations are pleasant, the mind welcomes them, craves them, wishing they will last; if the sensations are unpleasant, the mind resents them, tries to push them away, wishing they will stop. This process is not a linear one, and it advances along different routes simultaneously. It is clear, for example, that the perceiving–evaluating function is moulded by past events, and by the sensations and reactions they subsequently evoked; yet, at the same time, it is clear that its present activity (interpretation, evaluation) will influence future experiences with related objects.

Another set of non-linear interdependent factors—in a sense incorporating the one just described—consists, in its standard version, of twelve links. It explains, among other things, how the subjective perspective comes into being, how it affects the continued becoming of the one who sees through it, and how the two are related to a distorted perception of reality and to misery. This is the chain:

> From ignorance as a condition, reaction arises. From reaction [and the habitual patterns it forms] as a condition, consciousness arises. From consciousness as a condition, [the] mind-and-matter [phenomenon] arises. From [the] mind-and-matter [phenomenon] as a condition, the six sense spheres arise. From the six sense spheres as a condition, contact [with mental and material objects] arises. From contact [with mental and material objects] as a condition, sensation arises. From sensation as a condition, craving [and aversion] arises. From craving [and aversion] as a condition, clinging arises. From clinging as a condition, [the process of] becoming arises. From [the process of] becoming as a condition, birth arises. From birth as a condition, aging and death arise, along with sorrow, lamentation, physical and mental pain, and tribulations. Thus arises this entire mass of suffering. (MN 38: 404)

(Similar to the analytic aspect, the synthetic analysis presents additional systems, with their various interrelated modes of becoming. The ones mentioned above are the more relevant systems to the present discussion.)

If the emergence of each and every factor depends on another as its immediate condition, on a whole mosaic of factors, in fact, that must obtain at a given moment in time for it to appear, and if, once this constellation passes, it too will disappear, then there is no alone-standing essential independent entity, no soul that exists apart from the body once the latter ceases and moves on to another existence, no pure consciousness which endures unchanging as all other components of the psyche transform, or any other "eternalist" variation on this theme, one that assumes continuity of any type of self-core. A nihilist viewpoint, however, by no means follows: this is not about negating reality or the specific attributes of its phenomena—human or otherwise. The importance of the actions of living beings in this reality is by no means rejected, and neither is their impact viewed as being limited to the time slot that starts with the creature's birth (or its generation at the moment of conception) and ends with its death. Quite the contrary, actually: if the physical depends on the mental, and the mental on the physical, if the internal depends on the external and the external on the internal, if perception depends on reaction and reaction on perception, and if both depend on sensation, which, in its turn, feeds on them, arises out of them, if suffering depends on ignorance, and if death arises out of life whose very becoming depends on clinging—then every action matters, every action has an effect.

The position stated by the Buddha contradicts, therefore, these two extremes: he who acts, reaps, and the one acts, the other reaps (VIS XVII: 24). Instead, it draws a third path, a "middle path", suggesting a thorough investigation of phenomena, with all of their specific outlines, components, and internal interactions, on the understanding that they are impermanent, bound up with suffering, and lack any substantial separate nucleus, that they are constantly becoming in an endless dynamic process for as long as no opposing activity (or, rather, non-activity) intervenes. This type of relation is called "conditioned arising" and it reflects a principle to which all phenomena are subject: everything that exists depends on the circumstances. Whatever comes into being does so as a result of causal connections, not in isolation. No phenomenon arises of itself, from some inner essence, for a certain purpose, or, alternatively, by coincidence:

> Each transient entity, emerging into the present out of the stream of events bearing down from the past, absorbs into itself the causal influx of the past, to which it must be responsive. During its phase of presence it exercises its own distinctive function with the support of its conditions, expressing thereby its own immediacy of being. And then, with the completion of its actuality, it is swept away by the universal impermanence to become itself a condition determinant of the future. (Bodhi, 1995)

Every moment in reality, whether external or internal, arises from the specific accumulation of factors that past actions have generated.

Every moment in reality, whether external or internal, forms a complex of factors that join the accumulation of specific conditions from which the future unfolds. Each moment of consciousness, and, therefore, each mental action, is a juncture between the past that feeds it and the future that it, in turn, feeds. This is why the mental action is considered so important: through the infinity of complex causalities, it participates in creating the reality that follows it.

As it creates reality, the principle of conditioned arising follows a rule whereby anything that emerges from ignorance is marked by craving and leads to suffering. In order to persist, this active process needs fuel, and this is supplied by the *saṅkhāra*: the mental reaction. Briefly, this rich concept relates both to our reaction towards what is pleasant or unpleasant—the inner movement of attraction or repulsion which very rapidly transforms into craving or hate—as well as to the habits, patterns, and residues that form when such a reaction is repeated time and again. When we are subject to these reactions, we are governed by forces characterised by will and intentionality. We usually identify with these forces, think of them as our own, and lean on them to move us through life. We are under the impression that they are a source of strength, and that without them we will remain weak and passive. However, for the most part, they are not really "our" will and intentionality; we are not their masters. Actually, they are the will and intention of the *saṅkhāra*s, which activate us from within. These reactions—desire and greed, aversion and hate—are "volitional", not in the sense that someone decides whether or not he obtains or chooses them, but because will or drive is at their root. They have "intentionality" not in the exalted sense of that word, but in so far as they instigate a (internal) motion with a direction: towards the pleasant and away from the unpleasant. Due to this directed volitional impetus, the *saṅkhāra*s are a productive factor: "'They form the formed' thus they are formations" (VIS XVIII: 44). These formations are nothing but our habits, our typical characteristics, our personality (its beautiful and its ugly sides), and the reality of our lives for better and for worse. Everything that arises in the individual arises in this way, through reactive mental action. Everything the individual wants to break free from can only be shed in this way: by not producing a reactive mental action, by unforming the habits and residues that prescribe further mental reactions.

Another notion that underlines the importance of mental action is the familiar concept of *karma*, or, in the Pāli language that this book uses to render Buddhist concepts: *kamma*. Other than is commonly and mistakenly believed, *kamma* refers to action rather than to fate: bodily action, verbal action, but, foremost, mental action, which underlies and directs all verbal or physical action. A man who pushes his son hard, causing him to fall back a split second before he would have run into the road, and another man who, in an act of drunken aggression, gives his son a shove, and causes him to fall—these men, while performing the very same physical act, do it with absolutely different intentions. The first loves, cares, and protects; the second man's consciousness is clouded by alcohol and rage. According to the Buddha's teaching, it is the mental act whose nature determines its own results for the one who performs it. So, even if both men pushed a loved one, caused him to fall and hurt himself, still the outcome of the first man's act—which was wholesome in terms of its intentionality—will be good (for the one who did the pushing), and the result of the second man's act, bad. What are good outcomes and what are bad outcomes in this context? It will suffice for now to say that good outcomes are associated with happiness and freedom, while bad outcomes are tied to the chains of suffering. From this perspective, mental action is key, and, if it is wholesome, then it will naturally lead to wholesome verbal and physical actions. To revert to the becoming of suffering, much as mental action feeds it when it is associated with blind reactions of craving and aversion, it also has the power, when lucid and non-reactive, to interrupt suffering, thereby withholding the fuel it needs in order to continue becoming. Here is how it is usually formulated in the *suttas*:

> If ignorance is eradicated and completely ceases, reaction [and the habitual patterns it forms] ceases. If reaction ceases, consciousness ceases. If consciousness ceases, [the] mind-and-matter [phenomenon] ceases. If [the] mind-and-matter [phenomenon] ceases, the six sense spheres cease. If the six sense spheres cease, contact [with mental and material objects] ceases. If contact [with mental and material objects] ceases, sensation ceases. If sensation ceases, craving [and aversion] cease. If craving [and aversion] cease, clinging ceases. If clinging ceases, [the process of] becoming ceases. If [the process of] becoming ceases, birth ceases. If birth ceases, aging and death cease, along with sorrow, lamentation, physical and mental pain, and tribulations. Thus ceases this entire mass of suffering. (MN 38: 404)

How should we understand mental action if it is the key to both suffering and liberation from it? Where does it originate and to what does it react? Like the Buddha, many schools of thought and teachers, in his own times and before him, identified craving as the direct reason for suffering. In the attempt to remove it and neutralise its influence, many pointed at objects of desire as the culprits. One of the Buddha's great innovations in understanding mental processes was his discovery of the role of sensations: he found that it is bodily sensations to which craving is directed, that they are its true and immediate objects. In both systems of psycho–physical factors described here, sensation takes a key position. In the first (the five functions model), sensation is what is followed by mental reaction (*saṅkhāra*); in the second (the twelve links model), it is what is followed by craving. In both cases, sensation is what the mind reacts to with desire or hate: with relishing and greed or with the wish to expel. So, the Buddha noted, if one wants to find the cause of suffering and to remove its very roots, one must attend to the plane of sensations and study it (Goenka, 1990).

Vipassanā meditation as it is taught by Goenka aims to elucidate and reveal the following two intersections: the one between sensation and the mind's tendentious reaction to it, and the one in which the present moment of consciousness is informed by past conditionings, on the one hand, and informs the becoming of future moments, on the other. For this purpose, it suggests a thorough and meticulous investigation of the entire field of sensations by systematically directing attention to each and every sensation as it arises in each and every part of the body.

This focus on bodily sensations should not imply a turning away from all other mental materials that make us human, but since a physical sensation accompanies every physical and mental event, then, through observing the body's sensations, one can observe the entire mind-and-matter phenomenon (Goenka, 1990, p. 6). Certainly, this is not to say that this is the only existing method to study the mind. It also does not imply a dichotomy between the mental and the physical: since sensation (Pāli: vedanā), as mentioned, is a mental factor in its own right. Below is a first example of someone coping with mental material—anxiety in this case—by bringing systematic attention to his bodily sensations.

Joel

Joel, a young psychologist, came for his first Vipassanā course with a variety of mental encumbrances, the most severe of which were related to a whole spectrum of fears, general anxiety, and panic attacks. He was told that all of these—the anxiety that still dominated his life as well as the panic attacks he had suffered in the past but which had abated in recent years—were likely to reappear and rise to the surface in the process. That is just what happened. Joel described it in the following way.

"Each time my anxiety arose I would pay attention to the intolerable sensations it brought along. It would begin with a sudden and very fast plunge, starting around my face and then sliding down to my lower belly and pelvis. Then immediately my heart would be pounding fast and forcefully, and I felt a kind of storm stirring up in my stomach and chest. Streams of cold air would wash over my arms and legs as all warmth escaped, and a kind of lump would form in my throat, a lump that, during breaks, would turn into serious bouts of weeping. There was a sense of a sort of tiny, stinging bubbles moving rapidly through all of my body, up to my teeth. In addition to all this there were fear and self-pity, anger that I projected on to some external force, supposedly keeping me there, and intense emotional torment that was haplessly trying to find a way out through crying. I could see with my own eyes how all these internal reactions arose as a way to get rid of pain, and how instead they actually intensified and prolonged it. I could see how the physical sensations that came with the anxiety triggered negative emotional and intellectual reactions against them, and how these further stimulated the overwhelming sensations, which in turn hiked up my thoughts and feelings. I had a strong urge to escape but, at the same time, a feeling that there was no way out. I touched the very heart of the anxiety that was, in those days, stamped on each and every cell of my body and caused me great suffering."

Following many hours of this type of observation, Joel began to feel he was becoming an "expert" on his anxiety. He was getting acquainted with all its varieties and forms, each and every part of it. It became familiar material; from an overwhelming, shapeless, and indiscriminate lump that would take over and carry him off, it turned into a dynamic phenomenon which he was able to experience without being overly affected or identified. He began seeing it for what it was: tiny sensory–emotional–intellectual particles which came and went rapidly, continuously interacting with each other, sooner or later making space for other sensations and mental phenomena to appear, signalling that the present wave of anxiety had subsided.

If he wanted to continue on this first, extremely tempestuous, course, and the ones to follow in the first years of his meditation practice, Joel had to struggle to tolerate the full, undiluted brunt of his anxiety, as well as the urge to escape which his anxiety and panic naturally evoked. Not giving in and not abandoning the practice, he was able to move ahead in a way that allowed him to start dissolving the anxiety he carried so deep within, until he reached a point at which he felt it was "leaving all the cells of my body".

Observing sensations

Merely observing physical sensations cannot achieve what Vipassanā meditation strives for. In the kind of Vipassanā discussed here, and, of course, also in the way the Buddha explains it in his discourses, attention to sensations is a necessary condition but it does not suffice. A certain type of understanding must come along with this attention for it to be effective: the understanding that sensations are impermanent. Much like Joel, someone who observes his sensations as he is being flooded by a wave of anxiety will immediately feel how, as his breath accelerates and his heartbeat increases, heat and energy flow towards the centre of his body while it leaves his arms and legs, which grow cold and limp. Looking inward while angry, one finds that, together with increased heartbeat and breathing, sensations of heat appear in the face, chest, and arms, especially the hands. All these characteristic sensations can be observed "from the outside" by means of body heat measuring equipment. Figure 1 is a graphic representation of the outcomes of a study that examined average body heat distribution for a variety of emotional states (Nummenmaa et al., 2013).

However, in our case, observation is done without intervening equipment, without the intervention, even, of the imagination or interpretation (Goenka, 2010): "observing sensations in sensations", or "observing sensations within the framework of sensations" (DN 22; Goenka, 1998, p. 26), as the Buddha formulated it. If the person who

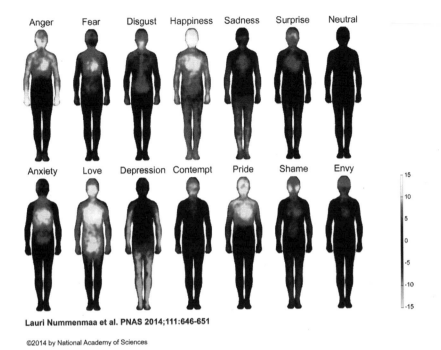

Figure 1. Bodily topography of basic (upper) and non-basic (lower) emotions associated with words. Reproduced by permission.

looks inward when anxious or angry would examine himself more deeply, he would discover a world of sensations much more subtle and detailed than the one offered by the above body heat map—something more like what Joel described. If he is aware of these sensations and examines them, he will see that they change from one moment to the next. If he systematically scans all parts of his body, not missing out on any spot, he will also notice the less intense sensations that appear elsewhere in his body. That is to say: he might register that it is not only anger or anxiety that occur in him right now—that he *is* not entirely "anger" or "anxiety". He will find that these less clamorous sensations, too, keep changing from moment to moment.

If this person will continue scrutinising his body like this, he will find that the solidity of these acute sensations accompanying the states of anger and anxiety dissolves. He will find that underneath each and every sensation, underlying each pain, pressure, spasm, impenetrability, cold, or intense heat, there is a constant flow of subtle sensations which appear for a fraction of a second only to subside and pass, a flow of sensations which experientially render the motion of the particles of matter which continues as long as the body is alive. This is the stage at which he will be able to perceive the ever-changing nature of sensations at an even more subtle, profound level. The moment-to-moment awareness of sensations, along with the realisation of their transient nature, helps to cultivate a balanced approach towards them, an approach that is marked by neither craving nor aversion, neither desire nor hate. If something pleasant arises only in order to pass away, then what is the point of craving it? If something painful comes up only to disappear, is it really necessary to try and dispose of it? The intellectual understanding of this idea cannot undo the mind's fundamental tendency to crave and to reject; experiential realisation, however, aims precisely at this.

We experience the world (internal and external alike) through our body and consciousness, through our perception and interpretation, through our sensations and habitual reactions. With all or some of these we identify, all or some of these we disown, or, we alternatively experience ourselves as being subjected to them: "I am what I feel", or "I am my consciousness but not my body", or "I undergo sensations and reactions, they happen to me". When a person experiences again and again, systematically, profoundly, and subtly, how bodily sensations change and, as a result, also how the other components of experience arise and vanish, something in these identifications and disavowals begins to shift. Something in the mind's default reaction starts to crack and become questionable in the face of the particulate reality that now becomes a present experience.

This is how Vipassanā proposes to conduct the two facets of the investigation of subjective experience—the analytical and the synthetic: the solid self dissolves in the process to gradually be replaced by a world of elements, functions, and minuscule particles appearing and disappearing in infinite interactions. Never in isolation, never arbitrary, always as a result of actions in the immediate and more remote past, even when they cannot be identified or named at any given moment in time. In the course of this process, mental actions—many of which were unconscious and, hence, automatic and rigid—become accessible and open to examination. Because the "unconscious" part of the mind is in constant touch with physical sensations and reacts to them, when non-selective attention is given to every point on and in the body and to each emergent sensation, whether pleasant or not, coarse or subtle, clear or vague, this constitutes a rather far-reaching act of non-neglect, non-disavowal, and non-ignoring of everything that happens in both the physical and mental domains. This systematic work aims to break through the usual barrier between conscious and unconscious. It is meant to transform the unconscious (that is, the process whereby one part of the mind registers the objects it encounters, another part identifies and assesses them, another part, as a result, starts to flow as a sensation, and another reacts to that sensation with greed or with a wish to expel) into something accessible, conscious, and clear.

Those who experience the processes that occur in their mind in this manner engage in mental activity that is the opposite of projection, splitting, denial, and repression. They have made the choice to be in full and precise contact with their experience and are trying to learn how to process it within the framework of their own body and mind, not striving to be rid of it, to close themselves to it, or to cast it off into others. They have a conscious, direct experience of the impulse to expel, and, at the same time, they practise not to go on generating it.

Of course, not everyone who starts practising Vipassanā starts from the same mental infrastructure and with the same resources. The stories presented here are examples of the classic course, so to speak, that the process tends to take when things work reasonably well. Still, there are other routes it might take. Many people who start on the path of Vipassanā take only a few initial steps and leave it before they reach deep into their minds and enjoy the more profound, long-lasting, results. Others continue the effort, but for some reason fail to comprehend and follow the few basic guidelines essential for beneficial practise. Deluded and diverted by illusive habit patterns, they are (temporarily, perhaps) unable to dissolve the causes of their misery, and without proper guidance the situation may even get worse. The successful cases, such as the ones in this book, are not rare at all, quite the contrary; and I am surrounded by living examples of them. (One does not need to possess any special sophisticated traits in order to practise Vipassanā successfully). But we still have to remember that this is not always the case. With this in mind, let us move on to Shira's story, and see how it demonstrates Vipassanā as a practice of non-neglect.

Shira

Shira, a senior educator, describes how she moved away from denying suffering, shutting herself off from it and avoiding experiencing it,
to being able to notice negative feelings and to process them. Up to a
certain point in her life, Shira held a world view whereby there is no
suffering, no hardship, and no pain. This was underlined by the
unconscious injunction that negative feelings are forbidden. She grew
aware of this habitual way of conducting her mental life when she
began to systematically observe her bodily sensations through Vipassanā meditation. Since each mental action is accompanied by a physical sensation and because our habitual mental actions bind together
and manage the various planes of experience, the same pattern also
expressed itself on the level of sensation, taking the form—in this
particular case—of many "blank" regions on her body: areas in which,
even once she focused her attention, she was unable to pick up any
emergent sensations.

Slowly, Shira discovered that an automatic tendency to cast off any
difficult experience as soon as it was encountered was at work in her,
a habit she identified as a mode of dissociating from (unpleasant)
bodily sensations and, subsequently, from (negative) emotions. One
day, as she was attending a Vipassanā course, she experienced a very
unpleasant sensation in her chest. "It simply drove me crazy, that
sensation . . . I went to the teacher and told her 'I keep on observing
this sensation, I'm not reacting to it, and it doesn't pass' . . . I was
under the illusion that I was not reacting to the sensation, while in fact
all I was doing was to try to make it pass by means of the meditation.
The teacher answered: 'Why do you want it to pass?'"

At a later stage, Shira began to form a deeper understanding of
what was happening inside her. She found out that every morning,
without realising it (and unrelated to her meditation practice) she
would scan her entire body: whenever she found all body sensations to
be light and pleasant, she felt everything was "all right", but when she
registered any sensation on the spectrum of heaviness and tiredness,
which, in her mind, was unknowingly associated with depression, an
inner alarm was triggered in her, an alarm that prompted her to try
and "cheer herself up" in all kinds of ways so as to rid herself of this
sensation at any cost. She learned that her behaviour was related to her
mother's mental illness and with the fear (of whose existence until then

she had not at all been aware) that she might have inherited the same illness which could break out any moment. "That sensation in my chest wasn't driving me nuts for nothing. It was reeking of depression. But depression, after all, doesn't exist! One mustn't be miserable. I understood that that's where the denial of suffering came from, and I understood how all this was connected with mechanisms I carry inside me, of dissociation from certain sensations and feelings."

That part of her, at some point, stopped getting rid of those unpleasant experiences. Initially, the process involved a deterioration in her mental wellbeing: the sadness and anger from which, hitherto, she had been barred now became present in her life. Once, in addition, the eliminating reaction stopped being automatic, adaptive behaviours she had previously used to "cheer herself up" also went away. Some more time passed before she learned to regain equanimity when facing those feelings rather than to become passively immersed in them. Now, when they arise, she copes with them in a healthy manner, using the many mental resources she has at her disposal. Even so, when meditating, she notes how her mind still recoils from the blank regions, in an attempt to keep their existence "out of her sight" by quickly passing them in order not to notice, or by inventing non-existent sensations, convincing itself that it actually feels them. Anger and sadness appear openly in relation to various events in her life, sometimes after a short period of delay. When they eventually appear, she is aware of them and does not try so hard to get rid of them.

CHAPTER THREE

Perceiving reality through the experience of self

"It is the nature of our waking thought to establish order in material of that kind, to set up relations in it and to make it conform to our expectations of an intelligible whole. In fact, we go too far in that direction. . . . In our efforts at making an intelligible pattern of the sense-impressions that are offered to us, we often fall into the strangest errors or even falsify the truth about the material before us"

(Freud, 1900a, p. 499)

I have, so far, mentioned projection mainly in the context of the impulse to expel. Projection, however, does not only serve the mind as it tries to fend off what is unpleasant. It is a basic feature of thinking (Ornston, 1978) and takes a key role in how our reality perception is constituted.

Freud used the term projection to describe a number of distinct mental processes: what they have in common is that they are all acts of relocating mental contents to the external world (Bell, 2001). His many references to projection can be seen to include three categories: projection as a defensive activity, projection as a constitutive mental activity, and projection as a mode of thinking and feeling in everyday life (Ornston, 1978). In the first sense, as a defensive activity, it is an attempt to put up a shield against distressing internal excitation (Freud, 1920g) by creating the illusion that the source of distress is external and, therefore, according to this mental logic, easier to avoid (Freud, 1915e, 1917d). This aspect, as mentioned, was expanded and developed through the notion of "projective identification" and I shall return to it at length. As constitutive mental activity, projection origi-nates in the infant's tendency to orientate herself by defining herself in relation to the surroundings (Ornston, 1978), or the tendency of an infant or "primitive man" "to project his existence outwards into the world and to regard every event which he observes as the manifesta-tion of beings who at bottom are like himself" (Freud, 1927c, p. 22; Ornston, 1978, p. 121). Projection as a mode of thinking and feeling is a connection the mind makes between something external that is registered in the present and internal material stored in the memory which is perceived as being the same. Thus, present and past become tied together, perception and memory, conscious and the unconscious (Freud, 1912–1913). Here, I would like to focus on this third category.

Perception as a projective process, or the snake, the blackbird, and the wrong patient

The psychoanalytic concept of projection demonstrates the Buddhist notion that the human individual, normally, does not see reality as it is. What he sees and what reality presents him with, are not one and the same. The relationship between the subjective and the objective is marked by a gap caused by the nature of the perceptual process. Why this gap exists is something I now address, and I begin by looking at some of Freud's ideas.

Once the "pleasure-ego" determines whether an object is good or bad and, accordingly, whether it should be taken in or thrown out, the "reality-ego" tries to make its own appraisal. Like the pleasure-ego, it, too, is preoccupied by questions of inside and outside, but it has a different agenda: it tries to decide whether or not the encountered object is subjective or objective: that is to say, whether it only exists internally or has an external existence as well. We know that the real-ity principle is subject to the pleasure principle, and, therefore, this ostensibly rational and neutral determination is in the service of the same basic desire: it is not enough to know that something is potentially gratifying; it must be established whether it can actually be taken hold of and enjoyed (Freud, 1925h).

Another reason for the gap between the objective and subjective is that the mental function that comes to establish whether something is real only goes into action after the event. The mind can only examine what it has already registered: the images that emerged in it as it encountered reality. Since all these images are replications of sensory perceptions formerly stored in the memory, it actually examines a reproduced image rather than the object as it appears before it in external reality (Freud, 1925h). It processes, therefore, information that is no longer actually present. Rather than cognising, it *re*-cognises. Hence, "The first and immediate aim . . . of reality-testing is, not to *find* an object in real perception which corresponds to the one presented, but to *refind* such an object, to convince oneself that it is still there" (Freud, 1925h, pp. 237–238). Things get even more complicated because the internal image that the mind creates on perceiving something does not always faithfully reflect the objective features of that thing. It is very likely that certain details will have dropped, or different elements might have become blended together. The reality-testing process is supposed to pick up these distortions, yet, since it can only take place when the actual perceived object has already gone and turned into a thing of the past (Freud, 1925h), the entire process takes place on rather dubious and shaky grounds.

So, we do not actually perceive objective reality. We reproduce it, rather, and this reproduction is done by means of the only tools we have at our disposal: the tools of subjectivity. They function as a kind of filter through which we register the world, perceive and understand it, and they are saturated with mental materials that affect the process or "are projected onto it". Freud believed that

> *attention*, which "meets the sense-impressions half way, instead of awaiting their appearance"; *perception*, which "is not a purely passive process"; and *reality testing* are developed on the basis of the way one has learned to orient, define, and sort during infancy. (Ornston, 1978, p. 130)

Thus, rather than empty receptive functions, what we are dealing with here is functions charged in a way that affects their own actions and outputs. The mind's way of processing what it receives through the senses feeds on what already inhabits it in the first place: memories, thoughts, states of mind, feelings, wishes, and expectations. If, on a warm day, I find myself walking near an overgrown place, I will hear an inner voice resonating my parents' warnings, long ago when I was a child in the village: "The snakes wake in the spring and they're full of poison." Because of those warnings, actually, it is very unlikely I will ever set foot in such places. I will even be a little tense when walking only near them, with each stirring or shifting making me even more tense. In this simple example, the sensory impression registered by my consciousness will be a rustling sound or a slight movement in the undergrowth, but processes of memory (from my childhood), thought ("Careful!"), state of mind (tense expectation), and emotion (fear) will affect the way I perceive the sensory input, how I organise it inside me, and interpret it. To me, the slightest stirring in the grass or undergrowth, when the weather is heating up, is, before all else, a potential snake, and I must be on the lookout. Only then can I take another glance to discover a sweet blackbird that is looking for food.

This *a priori* impact of the mind's contents on what it perceives comes with an agenda: our psyche likes order and coherence. It likes to understand. It likes to know. It likes to feel that what it sees is familiar, clear, and, hence, under control. It dislikes being caught unprepared. To avoid feeling excessively surprised, shaky, or devoid of solid ground, it appeals to its projective characteristic to form, to restore to itself, or to impose an illusive sense of inner order and synthesis (Ornston, 1978; Wollheim, 1993). This provides the mind with the experience that clear logic governs all, and enables it to predict and expect. The advantage of the manner in which the mind anticipates and organises whatever it registers into conceptual categories by reference to past experience is that it allows us automatically to process large quantities of information, with no need to appeal to the costly resource of conscious processing. Still, it comes at a price: when the intellectual function that requires homogeneity and coherence of all mental materials fails to achieve this, it will not hesitate to make them up, even if this bears no relation to the truth (Freud, 1912–1913; Ornston, 1978). This is why, for instance, we often attribute wholly mistaken explanations to our own and others' behaviour (e.g., Forgas, 1998; Laird & Bresler, 1992; Shepperd et al., 2008).

When we say that our reality perception is a projective process, we mean that we see what we expect to see, or what we are used to see, or, at least, what we have already seen in the past. To be more precise, it means that we have an organising–reproducing function which, once it perceives something, will associate it with something internal and familiar which possesses similar features, and which it then pronounces to be the same. A lot of information becomes lost in the process; other information is distorted or simply is invented.

If, then, certain attributes of the object perceived right now do not correspond with the pre-existing internal object, we might not even take note of them. If other attributes of it closely resemble those of the internal object—while not being identical to it—they might be polished and moulded to improve the fit. If certain attributes in the external object turn out to be lacking when compared with the internal one, the projective process might cover up the hiatus by creating something out of nothing, so to speak. Certain Australian species, unaware that they should flee from humans, because the latter's physical attributes were missing from their existing concept of "predators", fell prey to massive hunting and became extinct (Harari, 2015). About half of the participants in a research study who were asked to follow how a group of players were throwing a ball, failed to note a person dressed up as a gorilla appearing in their field of vision as the game was going on (Chabris & Simons, 2009). And we all are familiar with the somewhat embarrassing situation when we just cannot seem to recognise someone when we meet him or her outside the usual context. While each of these lapses occurs for reasons of its own, what they share is that they all originate in the absence of a preconception or of an expectation, or as a result of preconceptions and expectations that are so unlike the reality we encounter that a great deal of information is lost in the process.

It follows, then, that an "excess" of preconceptions, too, might result in forms of blocking out, loss of detail, and falsification. If I am conditioned to look for snakes in the bushes, then I might take a blackbird for a snake. If I am used to being judged, someone in the room not smiling at me will be enough for me to feel she must think badly of me. This is also why a physician, who seeks to diagnose the physical condition of her patients, runs the risk of developing a tendency to observe diagnostic categories instead of whole, complex human beings. She might also fail to pick up a rarer, more complicated medical condition when it does not fit the immediately available familiar categories. A psychologist who is intent on diagnosing his patients' mental state might well end up observing diagnostic categories instead of whole, complex human beings. He might also not notice details that should have been very useful in the therapeutic process, only because they did not naturally match his familiar conceptual categories. This obviously is not inevitable and usually it seems not to occur in very extreme forms, but there is always a certain degree of bias, reduction, distortion, and blindness when one person observes another in the attempt to slot him or her into a category. When the professional demand is to do just that, this process becomes legitimised, receiving unequivocal support. In other contexts, too, such processes occur spontaneously, automatically, and unconsciously, as we always perceive reality through the lens of what already exists in our minds and of what we expect. This is why there are those in the mental health community who believe that, with the exception of purely medical–physical processes or acute psychiatric conditions, any attempt to categorise and diagnose should be avoided, or, at least, that one should know the diagnostic categories only in order to forget them. Bion, aware of the high price of a saturated and desiring mind, took this even further by striving to relinquish all the camouflaging effects of the memory's impressions, future expectations, and the need to organise and understand: "Every session attended by the psychoanalyst must have no history and no future" (Bion, 1988, p. 15), and "The psychoanalyst should aim at achieving a state of mind so that at every session he feels he has not seen the patient before. If he feels he has, he is treating the wrong patient" (Bion, 1988, p. 16).

The wrong patient is one whom the mind has already saturated with its knowledge and desires. This is not the actual person who is facing the therapist, changing from moment to moment.

Sometimes, we come across someone who, having finished reading an excellent book that has changed (however subtly) the perspective of hundreds of thousands of readers, will comment, "But there's nothing new in what she's saying there." Or someone who, on encountering a new clinical concept or a new psychotherapeutic approach, will immediately feel that it is exactly what he has been doing for years anyway. Or someone who, when we ask him how he is doing, will reply, "Everything's as usual, nothing new." To all these people on such occasions something tends to feel familiar, used, or known. This is because the (normal) projective or replicating function of thinking dominates the way they experience and perceive the world. This is what causes them to sweep the difference under the rug, or pass straight by the change and state: I have seen this. It is all familiar. Nothing new under the sun.

Yet, if this gifted writer really had not said anything new, or, at least, said it in a new way, how could she have left such an impression on so many people? And if the same idea, as well as the same clinical way of expressing it, were already available to this psychotherapist, then how come he did not develop them? And if today's reality is the self-same as that of tomorrow, then what exactly is the meaning of time passing?

This should not suggest, of course, that two people cannot think the same thought, have the same idea—one way or another—or create similar creations in similar ways. It also should not imply that those who never made their ideas or creations public did not conceive or generate them. And life, obviously, does not always announce loud and clear the changes it presents us with from day to day, hour to hour. What I am thinking of here, however, is a certain mental attitude or state of mind. It comes with a certain perceptual and intellectual mode, and produces a sense of familiarity that aborts the vitality of uniqueness, leaving behind a stale, used feeling. Even when it comes in the guise of a sharp eye gained by experience, this attitude makes us lose out on the direct encounter with the world. What seems to be open-eyed realism, it turns out, could often prove to be illusory, an illusion originating in the mind's tendency to bring together what it registers into a well-defined, familiar, and known whole.

Martin Buber wrote,

—What, then, do we experience of *Thou*?

—Just nothing. For we do not experience it.

—What, then, do we know of Thou?

—Just everything. For we know nothing isolated about it anymore. (2010, p. 11)

To encounter "Thou", who is present reality, the mind must have space that enables the fresh reception of whatever it touches. Such space will open up only when the mental functions that—under the influence of memory and desire—keep a tight hold on the familiar and already known by clamping down and equating what is freshly perceived with ready-made concepts, are suspended (at least briefly): "Every means is an obstacle. Only when every means has collapsed does the meeting come about" (Buber, 2010, p. 12). In these conditions, a person is in a state of mind that resembles the one Bion described, fortunate to meet the truth as such. Direct encounter with reality can only occur when the veils of prejudice, the need to understand and to define, and desire are lifted. It cannot occur when the replicating nature of projection is active in the mind. It cannot exist when the mind examines the components of reality, through the pleasure principle, as objects that must either gratify it or be pushed away. It cannot exist when mediated through pre-existing categories, when past conceptions and future expectations squash the present moment.

Residues of experience, crevices of reaction

Projection paints external reality in the hues of the inner world and leads one to approach the subjective as though it were objective. It creates a model of thinking based on familiarity, which attaches former impressions on to something perceived in the here and now. The preconception entails expectations and constructions, as well as a tendency to make whatever has been registered cohere into something that is whole, known, and well-defined. This results in a mind that is not free to register reality as it is.

In Buddhist terms, these processes come under the function of perception: *saññā*. *Saññā*'s role is to connect between former impressions stored in memory and the characteristics or features of a presently perceived object, and it does this in the same way as a blind man "sees" an elephant (VIS XIV: 130 in Nāṇamoli, 1991): without actually and directly seeing the object, it concludes it is facing an elephant—or winter, or fear—relying on a connection between the earlier impressions collected by the mind and certain qualities it identifies in the perceived object. *Saññā* does not act in isolation. It intertwines with all the other mental factors and, thus, with the accumulations of the *saṅkhāras* (the residues of past actions) and with ignorance. Ignorance, in the Buddhist sense, is the mental factor responsible for clouding perception to the real nature of things, just like a cataract will obscure visual perception (Bodhi, 1993). It is the obstruction that stands between the observing subject and the object of observation, preventing its clear and direct perception. In this sense, ignorance is not only an absence of knowledge, but also an excess of knowing: something that has to be removed in order to see better. If a superfluous preconception distorts perception, then projection, too, serves as an excess barrier to a world that is perceived other than it is. It is a world coloured by past experience, and the way it is perceived is affected by the mental materials that are projected on to it while being experienced through the above subjective "cataract". Thus, the entire world of perception emerges and is projected through the saññā (Johansson, 1979), an image resulting from subjective mental materials projected on to objective reality. Like the pleasure-ego, the saññā, too, sorts every object into either positive or negative (Hart, 1987), and like the reality-ego, it, too, re-cognises things with reference to skewed prior knowledge, rather than perceiving them directly. So, even apparently neutral basic actions such as perception and reality testing are, in fact, the outcome of a subjective position, marked by a division between inside and outside and by a pleasure-related agenda. Since they involve different, filtering mental functions, they are indirect: relying on deduction and construction, they are prone to be misleading.

Whatever impressions past experiences have left in us feeds into the way in which our perceptual function operates as it aims to transform a whole cluster of features into a coherent whole, and whatever we register now will form the basis for later perceptions. The key process in the formation of memory, it is both selective and active: it selects salient characteristics of the object, perceives them, or "creates" them as labels, based on characteristics and labels it has created in the past when encountering an object with similar characteristics. How some object is perceived in the present affects the mental reaction to it, and the mental reaction, in turn, will (especially if it is repeated) affect the way in which similar objects will be perceived in the future. The manner in which the present is perceived is informed by memory, where past perceptions have been welded to the mental reactions they evoked, and the desires that these reactions embody. All these build up into kammic residues or accumulations, the accumulations of saṅkhāras, the stocks of impressions left by past mental actions. These accumulations can be considered tendencies, not in the sense of being a potential that awaits realisation—they themselves and their outcomes are already very much actual and active—but by being like the riverbed that deepens the more water runs through it, thereby catching in its track future rains which will tend to flow to it and, in turn, further deepen the gorge.

This description squares with the current neuropsychological understanding of the learning process. In the course of what we call learning, experiences become imprinted as the neural firing they trigger forms a neural pathway that grows stronger the more these experiences are repeated. This neural pathway then becomes a default option, a tendency or habit on whose basis future experiences tend to be integrated. In both descriptions (the one in which mental actions carve their path in the rock and the one in which neural firing establishes a neural pathway), the degree to which the path becomes established is the result of many repetitions of similar experiences and reactions, or, alternatively, it might be the result of some few but particularly intense experiences and reactions that leave a profound impression, even if they are not repeated all that frequently. In this latter case, the "density" of firing, in neuropsychological terms, that is, the amount of synaptic firing per time unit, will be high, making for a powerful impact in a short time span.

According to Tomkins (1995), it is this density of neural firing that is responsible for the arousal of affect. Affect can be triggered by anything and it can be registered through any sensory gateway; from the moment it is activated, it will, in turn, trigger a next affect. In this approach, affective behavioural patterns function like implanted software which a person accesses from the very start of life. They interweave with one another and with the experiences that evoke them, forming complex patterns that involve high cognitive processes and factors such as associations and memory; they also involve many bodily systems, including the endocrinal and exocrinal systems, which secrete substances into the body (such as hormones) and out of it (such as sweat) (Nathanson, 1986).

Buddhist texts offer us the concept of *āsava*, which means taint, corruption, intoxicant, bias (Nyanatiloka, 1997), or, simply, toxin. It refers to sensual desire, desire of becoming, false views and ignorance, which the one who follows the Buddha's path aims to shed. One who reaches this goal is called *khīṇāsava*: he who has fully exhausted the *āsavas* and is now free of them. Examining this concept at the experiential level of sensations can clarify it in depth and concretely: in fact, it helps one to make sense of the processes that I have been describing above.

Goenka (1988) combines the literal meaning of the term—secretion or influx—with its other meanings to bring out its nature and what it means to be freed of it. These toxins, according to Goenka, function like secretions, much like what contemporary science calls hormones and neurotransmitters. When a stimulus makes contact with its appropriate sensory door, it is registered and perceived, leading to a bodily sensation. One might conceive of this sensation as something similar to what Tomkins considered raw affect, in the sense that it involves complex psycho-physical patterns which, in their turn, imply higher cognitive processes and factors such as associations and memory, on the one hand, and the endocrine and exocrine systems, on the other. These patterns, therefore, tie the residues of past experiences to what is perceived at present, and both of these to what the mind–matter secretes: hormones and neurotransmitters (from the material perspective) or *āsavas* (from the Buddhist perspective), which produce present sensational–affective experience.

Here is an example. An infant or child was left alone for stretches of time that were inappropriate for her level of maturation. Let us assume that when this happened, the baby's surroundings were typically silent, or dark, or simply marked by unresponsiveness while she was calling out for help. These sensory inputs, for the infant (or child), became associated with the harsh physical sensations aroused in these intervals and with the aversive reactions they evoked. This person, once grown up, will be supposed not to experience such intensely negative reactions in situations marked by silence, darkness, or lack of response, since she is now mature enough to deal with them. Yet, on encountering this kind of situation, she could well experience sensations and reactions similar to the ones she experienced in early childhood. Her *saññā* will identify the features of the present situation, associate them with the negatively experienced characteristics of the past situation, and interpret the event accordingly. Sensations no less severe than those in the past will arise as a result, and reactions of fear, anxiety, a wish to escape, and so on will ensue. This is how the affective pattern established in the past is activated by the associative relations and the memories triggered by the present stimulus. The same *āsava*, if you wish, whose action took root in her long ago, will start flowing in her psycho–physical system and set off an entire cluster of reactions: chemical, sensational, cognitive, and affective, creating an impact on her subjective experience and her whole perception of reality.

To return to Joel, it was presumably the silence and the temporary disconnection from everyone and everything he was tied to in his usual environment that caused the "secretions" involved in his anxiety—originating in separation anxiety—to start flowing in his system. His returns to the empty room during breaks, and his awareness, each time, of the time and distance separating him from his partner, from his home, and from all of his daily routines, caused him actual pain. Someone else might have experienced the very same conditions as a relief, as a reprieve, as something peaceful and pleasant. However, because Joel's body and mind had hosted certain difficult experiences relating to the absence of a holding, responsive presence, these very features of reality were a source of suffering for him. Of course, it was not merely the external conditions that triggered this reaction pattern, but also—and mainly—the Vipassanā technique that aims to bring such residues to the surface of the mind so that they may be analysed and dissolved. I shall come back to this later.

In spite of the gap between reality as it is and perceived reality, the mind confuses them. This mix-up between subjective and objective perspectives is manifested in the factor of mental reaction, the *saṅk-hāra*, and the residues it produces (Rhys Davids & Stede, 1921–1925). Like projection, the *saṅkhāra*, too, builds on past experience, on what it registers from a reality that was objective to begin with, but was internalised and distorted by a perceptual process already saturated with earlier reactions to a similar reality. The mind's reactions to similar experiences accumulate as they repeat themselves, forming mental residues that serve as the building blocks in the emergence of the individual. This individual, the fruit of his own mental actions and their residues, meets the world in the one possible way he can meet it: through the specific characteristics constituting his unique profile (DN 15). The individual's very contact with the world (internal and external) is determined by who he is: it occurs through the experience of the self and its filters.

Essential sense of continuity and the self as projection

The same projective model through which the mind perceives objects in the world also determines the way it perceives the self. So this means that to it, too, the mind applies a replicating mode of thinking based on familiarity; it pours what is ready to begin with into what, at this very moment, is being inscribed on it as it passes through the senses, and it fills in gaps when the need arises to create a well-defined and coherent whole. The need to perceive a defined and coherent whole is all the more potent and forceful where it concerns the self, to which we cling with all our might, but this does not alter the fact that here, too, we are dealing with a construct, not with reality. Just as the wrong patient is not identical with the real patient who sits in front of us, changing from moment to moment, the wrong self is not the same as the present self that keeps on changing. It is not that the self that was bears no relation to the present self: they entertain a very close relationship, but they are not identical since they do not possess solid and essential nuclei in the first place. They are a subjective experience, the outcome of mental processes tainted by distortion and fabrication.

As Freud saw it, because mental activity is based on a projective model, for the most part it is marked by a replicating mode of thinking concerning the relations between objects. This activity relies on the distinction between the various objects around, as well as between them and the self, and it prescribes an essential sense of continuity (Ornston, 1978). This continuity is related to the fact that all mental representations originate in perceptions and are repetitions of them (Freud, 1925h); this is why early experience tends to become ingrained. Rapaport (1944) argues that the psychoanalytic assumption of psychic continuity must rely on projection, since the physical world is discontinuous. The mechanism of projection, according to Kernberg (1987), is based on the ability to discern self-representations from object representations, and the self from objects external to it. This is combined with an ongoing sense of self that remains intact under clashing emotional conditions. As a result, in the (normal) situation "Self-awareness is now not only that of temporarily changing subjective experiences, but of a subjective self as something stable against which each subjective state is evaluated" (Kernberg, 1987, p. 800).

From a Buddhist perspective, the experience of being a separate and solid self is related, in addition, to certain characteristics of consciousness (i.e., *viññāṇa*), the third link in the chain of conditioned arising. It is consciousness that performs the act of distinguishing subject from object (Hart, 1987), and it serves as an "inner space" (Johansson, 1979, p. 58), thus producing a sense of separateness from the external world. Consciousness itself, too, is perceived as essential and continuous. However, when one examines the life story of the components of any specific moment of consciousness, it transpires that their simultaneity is fluid rather than static, and that, due to their transient nature, they meet as each is at a different stage of their "life". Some factors continue from the previous moment and then vanish, others appear in the present moment and disappear before the next, while yet others emerge in the present and continue into future moments.

> The fact that parts of other moments of consciousness may, as it were, spread over the present moment or extend beyond it makes for an intricate interlacing and a close organic continuity in the world of mental phenomena. There are no "empty spaces", no disconnected events in the universe of the mind, though the connection may often be very loose and remote. Even if a psychic event breaks in quite unexpectedly, it does not arise from nothingness but is related to a perhaps distant past, the gap being bridged by subconscious mental processes. (Thera, 1998[1949], pp. 95–96)

According to the Buddha's teaching, the basis of the experience of mental continuity is formed by the reality of conditioned arising and conditioned relations.[4] It is the energy inherent to these conditions (*paccayasatti*) that produces what is experienced as continuity or ongoingness (Thera, 1998[1949]), not an essential, continuous self. Consciousness presents itself as having a connective or continuous characteristic simply because each state of consciousness that emerges follows immediately upon the one preceding it (Thera, 1998[1949]). Each moment of consciousness arises, prevailing for some time in a relatively stable seeming manner before it passes away or dissolves. While it has individual traits, it lacks stability or self-identity. This movement between the various stages of existence of the moment of consciousness matches the changes occurring in the greater temporary composition called "personality" (Thera, 1998[1949]) or "individual".

The transition from the particulate reality of consciousness to a perception of a stable self requires the illusive bridging between things as they are and the invented object, a linking that the Buddha described as "an attempt to build a tall staircase leading to the highest floor of a palace upon which no person has ever set eyes and whose proportions no one knows" (Biderman, 1995, p. 80). Yet, we perceive our unified sense of self as point of departure, basic assumption, almost axiomatic, and one of our most fundamental intuitions (Biderman, 1995). Rather than five clusters of psycho–physical functions and a system of mutually conditional factors, what we perceive is something whole, essential, and separate which we experience as the self. Thus, mental activity that relies on the illusive filling of gaps or on projection produces an experience of self, and this self comes to be the point of reference through which the world is perceived and experienced.

The self as point of reference and the vicious circle of the "as-if reality"

It is through the connective feature of consciousness and perception's projective behaviour that a continuously flowing personal point of reference comes into being. This point of reference is from where we tend to see every phenomenon as such in its relation to our self.

> There thus runs through my thoughts a continuous current of "personal reference", of which I generally have no inkling, but which betrays itself by such instances of my forgetting names. It is as if I were obliged to compare everything I hear about other people with myself; as if my personal complexes were put on the alert whenever another person is brought to my notice. This cannot possibly be an individual peculiarity of my own: it must rather contain an indication of the way in which we understand "something other than ourself" in general. (Freud, 1901b, pp. 24–25)

The mind uses (external and internal) reality in order to again and again define the self and experience it as concrete, and it uses the experience of self to define and understand reality in relation to it. Our preferences, fears, and desires lead us expediently to assess and judge each factor in reality as either desirable or undesirable, wishing to preserve the self and to get rid of what is hard to experience. This same attitude characterises the act of splitting, which automatically divides the components of reality into good and bad, safe and dangerous, gratifying and painful. This division produces a dual image of the world whereby the components of reality are arranged in two camps around the centre of gravity—the perceived self—which serves as a constant point of reference.

If we take these basic human tendencies a little further to those cases when the mechanisms of splitting and projection are more dominant and far-reaching (in infancy and in certain mental conditions), we will see how they affect reality perception more radically. Klein, for instance, writes, "the child's earliest reality is wholly phantastic" (1930, p. 26). At least in part, then, the infant creates his reality by means of what can be seen as the projection of his inner world into the objects outside. So strong is the effect of this projection that the mother in fantasy, the product of projection, has a more powerful hold than the actual mother (Ogden, 1986). When the predominant mode of being relies substantially on splitting and projection—which is what happens in the paranoid–schizoid position—signifier and signified become emotionally equivalent (in a "symbolic equation", according to Segal (1957, 1998)). This entails a two-dimensional form of experience from which the presence of an interpreting subject, who mediates between the perception and his or her reaction to the perception, is almost entirely absent:

> In this mode, thoughts and feelings are not experienced as personal creations but as facts, things-in-themselves, that simply exist. Perception and interpretation are experienced as one and the same. The patient is trapped in the manifest since surface and depth are indistinguishable. (Ogden, 2004a, p. 21)

Those who observe things in this manner are caught in their own subjective viewpoint, unable to recognise it as subjective, and, thereby, unable to see through its mind-made character.

Mental activity characterised by splitting is "a state of mind in which there is 'no in-between.' A plane has two faces and two faces only; an observer can never see both sides at once" (Ogden, 1986, p. 62). As a result, it yields a narrow, partial, and distorted view of the world. Such a black and white mindset, typical of the paranoid–schizoid position, lacks the perception of complexity that evolves in the depressive position when the whole object is recognised. In Buddhist terms, what is missing here is the middle path, the wisdom of seeing the phenomenon in depth, recognising the entirety of all its attributes, its constantly changing nature, and its interrelations with surrounding phenomena. (This is not to say that achievement of the developed depressive position is tantamount to a world view based in the Buddhist middle path.) This is why someone in a splitting-based (or projective) state of mind will be in the grip of an extremely rocky experience:

> When a borderline patient [people with borderline personalities often deploy primitive defences based on splitting] feels angry at and disappointed by the therapist, he feels that he has now discovered the truth. The therapist is unreliable, and the patient should have known it all along. What had previously been seen by the patient as evidence for the therapist's trust-worthiness, now is seen to have been an act of deception, a mask, a cover-up for what has become apparent. The truth is now out, and the patient will not deceive himself or be caught off guard again. *History is instantaneously rewritten.* . . . The present is projected backward and forward, thus creating a static, eternal, non-reflective present. (Ogden, 1986, p. 62)

The mechanisms of splitting and projection produce an extreme experience of reality. While it is perceived as absolute truth, it changes each time according to the projections created in reaction to the given situation: things are, on the one hand, perceived as stable and solid essences; on the other hand, each and every perceptual event may trigger a reaction that will turn the object's perceived attributes upside down. (Remember the woman whose idealised lover instantly turned into the devil?) This perceptual shift will occur in the absence of reflexive ability, or, from a Buddhist perspective, without the presence of mindfulness, without understanding of the transience of things, and without the equanimity that this understanding affords.

This erroneous way of seeing things is a vicious circle: a person who projects her feelings, urges, and fantasies into another person will feel accordingly towards her. Since she internalises this person saturated with these negative projected mental contents, she is likely to interpret neutral or well-intentioned behaviours as if they were critical or aggressive, react with anxiety or anger, and then expect the next negative reaction from outside (Joseph, 2001). A simple illustration involving a normative degree of projection can be found in all of us: much more often than we would like to think, we create a virtual world whose characteristics are the result of a thoroughly incomplete act of association between internal representations and external reality. Once we create it, we experience it and conduct ourselves accordingly. If a person is accustomed to live with a sense of being liked, then the world will appear inviting and secure to him.

He will obviously conduct himself in a sociable, smooth manner, which will evoke positive responses from his surroundings, and these, in turn, will confirm his perception and support it. If, however, a person is used to feeling rejected, the world will appear threatening and unpleasant. He is likely to act timidly, insecurely, or in a variety of compensatory ways—all of which might trigger negative reactions from his environment. And these reactions will, time and again, confirm him in his original feeling of being unwanted.

This vicious circle will be further perpetuated if it involves forms of projective identification that unconsciously affect external reality itself. Brodey (1965) says that when projection joins manipulation of reality so as to make reality validate the projection, elements out there in the world that do not support the projection are simply not perceived. If this mechanism dominates an interpersonal system, such as a family, where people learn from, and are influenced by, each other, then information will pass among them only to the extent that it may shape and manoeuvre them to support the projection. This process directly impairs reality testing.

> What is perceived as reality is an *as-if* reality, a projection of inner expectation. The senses are trained to validate; the intense searching for what is expected dominates and forces validation. It is difficult not to validate an unquestionable conclusion. Each validation makes the conclusion even less questionable. The restricted reality perceived is experienced as though it were the total world. A special kind of learning is needed to hold this restricted world intact. The narcissistic person learns to manipulate reality to conform with his projection. His experiments are designed to make prior conclusions inevitable. (Brodey, 1965, p. 167)

The way the world is perceived, in this case, is not informed by direct input from external objects. It produces a closed circuit of internal representations that interrelate and refer to each other, bearing no connection to things as they are.

> To the extent that the external world is blanketed in a shroud of transference projections, the individual is unable to learn from experience. The present is merely a re-enactment of the past using external objects as props for the re-creation of a timeless internal drama. (Ogden, 2004a, p. 85)[5]

Psychoanalytic thought focuses on the perceptual distortions caused by splitting, projection, and projective identification in infancy and in pathological cases. But it also claims that the forms of psychological organisation that evolve in infancy continue to constitute the groundwork of perception of both internal and external worlds, and of adult modes of coping with it. These same mechanisms, then, accompany us throughout life, along the entire spectrum stretching between normal and pathological, and in all types of relationships.

Mark

A simple and ordinary case of splitting could be observed in Mark, vice-president in charge of finances in a large company. From as long as he remembered himself, Mark had been rigid and critical with himself and with others, and he tended to see things through an internal lens that divided reality into "right" and "wrong". It had always been his role in the family to be the judge when his parents quarrelled, to tell his brothers what was right, to warn against mistakes, and ensure that anything that had to be shared would be distributed equally. For him, the world was black and white, and people were either righteous or utterly misguided.

This perspective was marked by a combination of self-righteousness and anger, along with argumentativeness and rationalisation. He tended to be ever ready with neat explanations of what was happening to him and between himself and his surroundings, and to "sell himself"—this is how he called it—theories about himself and his life that presented him in a "noble" light. When, for instance, a worker came late into the office, he would feel a surge of anger and he would shower her with rebukes backed up with lofty notions of justice and morality. As Mark himself formulated it very well in retrospect, "I was born being right. When I was angry it was not simple anger. It was holy outrage." It was obvious how each encounter with an event of this type "put on alert", as Freud formulated it, Mark's personal complexes. First, the event would serve to support his sense of identity and then it would be examined through the same self that was his point of reference in defining reality.

In Mark's case, the *saṅkhāra* as a complex, like the gully in the rock, consisted of seeing extremes, of "holy outrage", and of the rationalisation that kept the split world view and anger as precious possessions of his self-identity. (Of course, like any other person, it was not the only complex he was carrying around.) The *saññā* that was fed by this complex perceived and interpreted every relevant incident in terms of the "right/wrong" categorisation, evoking in Mark pleasant and unpleasant sensations accordingly. Extraneous incidents perceived as wrong came with unpleasant sensations, and explanations that took care to present the world as orderly and understood and himself as ethical and right were presumably attended by pleasant sensations. As a current mental reaction (like the water and sediment running in the gully at present), the *saṅkhāra* was reflected in yearning for the calm yielded by a coherent world view and a positive self image, and in the negative reaction to the sensations triggered by what was labelled as "wrong". This reaction was also projected outward to the person or situation that represented this category at that particular point in time.

When he began practising Vipassanā and grew aware of his bodily sensations and his reactions to them, something in Mark's way of looking at the world and at himself started to shift. Mental processes grew more transparent, and he became more conscious of his own characteristic chain of perceptions–sensations–reactions. He noticed, for instance, that the unpleasant sensations linked with anger would arise in him even before the actual situations on to which he was used to pin his anger occurred. Once he became aware of this, both the act of projecting the anger on to others, as well as the sense of self-worth that was associated with it, lost their meaning.

He explains, "In the very first years [of practice] I felt as though I had an additional sense, a sense that leads me to find out what really gets me going, below the surface. Often, what I found out was very unpleasant. All those lists of explanations I had, they just became void of meaning . . . The orderly and just world in which I lived shattered. Once I saw how I was endlessly reacting out of proportion to unimportant events or hurling my rage at someone else while being covered head to toes in good reasons myself—how could I go on taking myself seriously when the next situation presented itself? My whole perspective about what's important and what isn't had changed. From having very clear ideas about everything and total confidence in my abilities, I arrived at a very different place. I became less 'right' but also less angry."

Gradually, over the years, Mark's way of seeing extremes was replaced by a complex viewpoint: the tendency to expel by projection dissolved as splitting subsided, as he established an insight about the internal origins of his anger, and as his internal climate grew more mellow. His rationalisations became unnecessary and ridiculous as the "sense" of reflexivity became stronger. Thoughts and feelings, in this way, came to be experienced as personal creations, rather than facts. Perception and interpretation came to be seen as distinct. Now that he had the ability to differentiate between surface and depth, Mark was no longer trapped in the level of the explicit.

CHAPTER FOUR

Karma and the nature of boundaries between minds

*The law of karma and the actual influence
of a fantastic mental action*

Projection, like *saṅkhāra*, is a construct. It affects the perception of reality by projecting past residues on to what is perceived in the present moment and, by filling gaps, it leads one to perceive what is fluid as something solid, labelling a cluster of factors as an essential unified object. In its interpersonal manifestation, projection is involved in the distribution and reinforcement of disagreeable mental contents, with subjects using it to rid themselves of these materials by turning them on to others. They, then, have to deal with the pain entailed by the encounter between these disagreeable contents and their own specific subjective substructure, between these contents and their own constructs and habitual mental formations. So, projection constitutes the veil through which we see the world, perceive and experience it, or, if you wish, our virtual reality. It creates a perception of reality and also contributes to the creation of that reality.

Projection is a form of externalisation: mental–internal materials, that is, are expelled from the self's perceived boundaries. This is done in the fantasy—from an unconscious belief that it can be done—and, in a certain sense, also in actuality, when the same mental materials gain real influence over the (human) object into which they are projected, by means of certain aspects of the mechanism. Either way, projection, whether its "actual" aspect or its "fantastic" one, has real effects in the world. First, I briefly consider psychoanalytic thinking about this characteristic of projection, and then I discuss it from a Buddhist perspective.

The real influence of projective identification is a charged issue (Bell, 2001). Klein thought of projective identification as the infant's or the patient's fantasy rather than as a real act during which mental materials are put into the body or mind of the mother or analyst (Spillius, 1992). The outcomes of projection, for her, are still in the province of the subject (Bell, 2001). Yet, the illustrations she used and her choice of words when she wrote "into" (the mother, the object) suggest that the interpersonal aspect was implicit in her thinking about projective identification from the very beginning (Ogden, 1986). Her writings testify to her awareness of the real effects of splitting and projection:

> It is in phantasy that the infant splits the object and the self, but the effect of this phantasy is a very real one, because it leads to feelings and relations (and later on thought processes) being in fact cut off from one another. (Klein, 1946, p. 101)

Let us consider, for instance, a person who creates a split in his mind between sexual desire and affection, friendship, and respect. He will, as a consequence, make sure to have relationships that are based on sex, or, alternatively, relationships in which there is no sexual desire, not because his mind is free of desire, but because it is directed elsewhere. In the case of such a person, splitting (of both himself as well as his partners and the relationships within the range of his possibilities) may take place in fantasy but it has real consequences in the world. On the one hand, neither he, nor the women with whom he engages, are "pure desire" or "just friendship and respect", and one cannot really control or satisfy the deeper strata of the psyche in this way—that is why it is a fantasy. On the other hand, however, as long as he hankers after both friendship and sexual fulfilment while splitting prevails, his intimate relationships will remain unsatisfying, torn, and incomplete, and are very likely to be attended by a sense of not living his life to the full.

Now let us consider someone else, an old man who lives alone and is thinking of letting a small apartment that is attached to his own house. He has mixed feelings about this venture: his heart aches when he imagines a stranger moving into the unit where his beloved son lived when he was young. At the same time, he is lonely, the house is too quiet and large, and it seems to him that a little company, if it works well, would not do him any harm. What decides him, eventually, is financial considerations, and he gets the place into shape for a young couple. In his attempt to cope with his unresolved doubts, he makes an unconscious split: he labels the woman as pleasant and warm, and her presence makes him happy; he is pleased to welcome her and takes any opportunity to invite her for a coffee. As for the man, he gets the other side of the split: the frustration, bitterness, and sadness about his loneliness, about how far away his children are, and the fact that he has to seek the company of strangers and let them part of his house to keep himself financially afloat. As a result, the older man perceives the younger man as invasive, rude, and ungrateful in a manner that bears no relation to the latter's conduct or personality. Neither the young woman nor the young man actually fit the absolute fantastic categories into which they have been put. The old man's own emotional quandary also stands no chance of being solved by means of this splitting. Thus, all this has actual effects on their lives. He invites the couple for a meal and then makes exaggerated demands of them concerning the rental. He tells them things about his personal life and then takes offence at trivialities or causes trouble in their apartment. The woman feels his friendliness as suffocating, the man senses his hostility, and the atmosphere is generally uncomfortable.

It is clear, even from these simple examples, that the influence of the acts of splitting and projection is not limited to the mental–internal: the distortion they create in the reality perception of the one in whose mind they occur affects his behaviour and, hence, leaves its impact on those who surround him. Conceptions of projective identification, however, have developed in more interesting and complex directions, taking this dynamic much further. Bion claimed that, in addition to the projective identification being a fantasy, it also involves an actual interpersonal manipulation (Ogden, 1979): it is an aggressive insertion of self-parts, mental materials, or experiences, *into* the object of projection, resulting from a need for the latter to transform them into something digestible. This is, for instance, how he describes it:

> When the patient strove to rid himself of fears of death which were felt to be too powerful for his personality to contain he split off his fears and put them into me, the idea apparently being that if they were allowed to repose there long enough they would undergo modification by my psyche and could then be safely reintrojected. . . . Consequently he strove to force them into me with increased desperation and violence. (Bion, 1959, p. 312)

What does this notion of putting feelings or self-aspects into another person really mean? It means that the object of the projection is affected, activated, or dominated by something unconscious originating in the projecting subject; it is like the girl (or baby) in the poem who screams her intolerable experiences of destruction into her mother and, thereby, causes the latter to feel them. It is like the man who causes his wife to feel, in his stead, the contempt and humiliation he carries inside, the unprocessed result of his relations with his father. It is like the woman who, again and again, creates impasses in couplehood in order to make her partner give up on her and abandon her, as did her parents when she was a child.

Racker, too, refers to "bi-personal processes" (1968, p. 66). He offers many illustrations of how the patient "implants" in the analyst split off good or bad feelings from within him, thus pushing the analyst to play a role in his—the patient's—unconscious fantasy. A patient who cannot abide excessive guilt, for instance, might evoke guilt and anxiety in the psychoanalyst. A patient with masochistic tendencies might unconsciously induce irony and mockery in the analyst (Racker, 1968), thus reproducing the early object relations she internalised. In any case, "the patient's behaviour, though based on fantasies of the past, becomes a reality, which in its turn creates problems and conflicts that in one of their aspects, are equally real" (Racker, 1968, p. 54).

Ogden (1979) considers projective identification as a process with a distinctly interpersonal aspect, which depends on the existence of an interaction between the one who projects and the one who receives the projection. According to him an actual influence—or, at least, an attempt to have such influence—is at issue in projective identification:

on the other's emotional state and self-representation. It is an act of externalisation in the wider sense of the word: that is, it involves a movement of the fantasy of projection from the intrapersonal domain of thoughts, feelings, and psychological representations to the interpersonal domain and into the other's world. Projective identification includes mental action in which the projecting side brings to bear real pressure on the other party so that the latter will have to experience and conduct him- or herself in accordance with the projecting person's unconscious fantasy. Behind this pressure is an unconscious and inexplicit threat regarding the consequences of non-compliance with the projective identification. A father or mother, thus, might put pressure on their children to behave and to feel in a way that agrees with their own pathology, the veiled threat being that if they refuse to act accordingly, they will become non-existent to the parent. "'If you are not what I need you to be, you don't exist for me", or, in other language, "I can only see in you what I put there, and so if I don't see that in you, I see nothing'" (Ogden, 1979, p. 360). Ogden naturally does not reject the existence of a fantastic intrapersonal component in projective identification, but he argues that the interpersonal quality of the event is not a derivative of the unconscious fantasy: rather, the fantasy and the interpersonal act constitute two facets of one psychological event (Ogden, 1994a).

Grotstein (1995), unlike Ogden, considers projective identification itself as an intrapersonal event. For it to register as interpersonal, it must elicit a counter-introjective reaction and/or a counter-projective one in the object of projection. From this perspective, the one who projects always does so on to the representation of an object (i.e., it occurs, still, inside the self); for there to be communication driven by projective identification, the receiving party must become a consciously, unconsciously, or subconsciously reactive and intentional subject. Grotstein, therefore, considers projective identification as a dynamic composed of an intrapersonal process in one subject that elicits an intrapersonal process in another subject.

So, there appear to be a number of approaches to the issue: in one of them the influence on the object of projection is inextricable part of the mechanism, so there is no projective identification in the absence of interpersonal influence. In a different approach, influence on the object does not come under the mechanism's definition: it is a reaction to it. Yet another definition includes both possibilities, while a distinction is made between situations in which projective identification induces a relevant emotional reaction (corresponding to the projector's experience or complementary to it) in the object, and situations in which it does not (Bell, 2001). One way or another, it is currently assumed that patients could conduct themselves in ways that cause the therapist to feel in their place what they cannot contain or cannot express (Spillius, 1992). This, as said, is the case not only for the relations between therapist and patient, and not only for their origin in the relations between mother and infant. Its reflection can be observed in any other kind of relationship. Even though each situation in which projective identification is at work will be *sui generis* depending on its specific contents, it will always be marked by unconscious aggressive behaviour in which one person tries to insert mental elements into another person to pressure the latter into feeling, thinking, or acting in certain ways which, had this person not become involved in this dynamic, she would not have come up with. This dynamic is also characterised by a certain furtive air:

> The analyst feels he is being manipulated so as to be playing a part, no matter how difficult to recognize, in somebody's [sic] else's phantasy – or he would do if it were not for what in recollection I can only call a temporary loss of insight, a sense of experiencing strong feelings and at the same time a belief that their existence is quite adequately justified by the objective situation without recourse to recondite explanation of their causation. (Bion, 1952, cited in Spillius, 1992, p. 69)

When, in the best case, the object of projection becomes aware of what is happening, it will feel as though he "catches himself" in the middle of some murky intrapersonal and interpersonal behaviour, manages to shake off the fog of illusion, and lets go of the positions in which he got himself stuck.

What are the relations between a fantastic or intrapersonal act (i.e., what we normally conceive as internal) and an actual or interpersonal act (usually perceived as external)? And what can this discussion possibly contribute with regard to Buddhism's ethical perspective? We usually think of external negative actions—whether physical or verbal ones—as carrying real weight and consequences. Internal negative actions—in thought, in feeling, or in fantasy—we usually condone. But, in Buddhist thinking, it is the internal or mental act that takes the foreground, in the sense that it is what determines the meaning and consequences of any verbal or physical act (e.g., AN 6.63; AN 7.49; Hart, 1987). Buddhism's guiding principle in this matter is encapsulated in the law of *kamma* (*karma*), which pre-existed the Buddha's teaching but underwent important change. The revolutionary (subversive, one might add) change of mindset which the Buddha offered in this regard consisted of the internalisation, and, thereby, the ethicisation, of the law of *kamma* (Biderman, 1995). From this point of view, individuals are fully responsible for their own actions—not just for the external expressions of their internal world in the form of words and physical actions, but also for every mental act that arises and takes place within them. If a person, until then, could be awash with anger, hate, or vengefulness, yet still carry out certain rituals or religious behaviours to perfection and expect a good outcome, now she was told (if she was willing to listen) that what was inside her mind determined her fate. People, in this approach, must become fundamentally and profoundly ethical, and they can expect that whatever they do, whether it is internal or external, will have real ramifications, both immediate and in the near and more remote future.

> Mind precedes all phenomena, mind matters most, mind is the source.
> If you speak or act with an impure mind,
> Suffering will follow you
> As the wheel of a bullock cart follows behind the bullock.
>
> Mind precedes all phenomena, mind matters most, mind is the source.
> If you speak or act with a pure mind,
> Happiness will follow you
> As a shadow that never departs.
> (Dhp 1–2, translated from the Pāli by William Hart)

Hence, will and intention, desire and hate, preference and compliance, splitting and projection are all considered actions in the full sense of the word. They have concrete implications even, and indeed, with a vengeance, when they are unconscious. Furthermore, a person cannot escape these consequences even, and indeed, with a vengeance, when he tries to throw them out and on to another.

So, someone who has split off feelings of shame and cannot experience them himself might notice certain characteristics in another person that will cause him to insult the latter, who then experiences shame in his stead. Another person, who feels trapped and suffocated in her life, might express to whoever is with her—the therapist in the clinic or, perhaps, a potential partner on a first date—that she is uncomfortable with the open window, with the light that is blinding her, or with the position of the chair, and gradually cause the window to be closed, the curtain to be drawn, and to move up very near the other person who will, in his turn, come to feel trapped and suffocated. Yet another person might sit wearing a furious expression in the boardroom, the therapy group, or at the family dining table, thereby distributing his anger to the people around him, pushing them to feel anger towards him, or, alternatively, to shrink defensively. In spite of their differences, all these situations feature a certain mental act: shame, feeling suffocated, fury, which, having become associated with another, more primitive mental act (the urge to expel what is unpleasant) has been extended into the human environment (concretely affecting it, that is) through verbal and bodily behaviours. Where, in these cases, runs the dividing line between physical and mental action? Does a look full of lust or envy count as a physical act? I definitely believe it does: in fact, I think that the mental quality shining forth from a person's gaze is an excellent example of how mental acts dictate the nature of external behaviour and its effects. Still, whether or not we establish the exact location of the division between the physical and the mental, however important, makes no difference to another, more fundamental determination according to which fantastic acts, too, have actual effects in the world or, according to the Buddha's teachings, that it is the fruit of mental action that we reap.

When an unintegrated mental reaction comes to be expressed in actuality, this is called "enactment". If projection is enactment, then what does it enact? It enacts pain inadequately endured and, hence, actively (though unconsciously) evacuated, or, alternatively, it leaks, of its own accord, into the human environment, which, either way, absorbs it and is affected by it. I shall return to these two (hard to distinguish) modes of transferring pain to the interpersonal sphere (active evacuation or passive percolation), but for now I would like to address the fact that such evacuation and percolation can occur because the boundaries between one mind and another are by no means solid, as phenomena such as projective identification illustrate.

Boundary-based thinking

A liminal conceptual model permeates psychoanalysis and its derivative approaches. It is easily picked up in many major ideas and
concepts: in repression, which separates conscious from unconscious;
in the protective shield that prevents the uncontrolled invasion of
the external world; in the dynamic field formed by the duality of the
instincts, and where occurs the battle between the conflicts that
threaten the integrity of the ego, on one hand, and the defences that
act against them for the ego's protection, on the other, as well as in the
notion of the setting as a container for the therapeutic process (Abadi,
2003). The boundaries thus defined are not only spatial in nature, but
temporal as well: the psychosexual stages of development Freud
formulated represent an effort to draw such boundaries, as well as his
notions of fixation, regression, memory, and repetition compulsion
(Abadi, 2003). Two of Freud's main ideas about the therapeutic objective, moreover, "to make what is unconscious . . . conscious" (Freud,
1916–1917, p. 114), and "where id was, there ego shall be" (Freud,
1933a, p. 80), are liminal in nature (Abadi, 2003). The first, argues
Abadi, is articulated from the explorer's point of view, while the
second refracts a colonialist mindset that aims to take control over the
illogical–chaotic to replace it with organised logic (Abadi, 2003). The
boundaries between one mind and another are perceived through the
lens of the paradigm of the border, and the phenomena associated
with projection and projective identification rely on it. The very same
phenomena, however, seem to undermine the liminal approach and
force it to dialectically engage with another form of thinking.

Freud (1920g) designated the perception–consciousness system
("the system Pcpt.–Cs." p. 24) as what marks the boundary between
subject and world. He assumed the existence of a "protective shield",
a kind of "dead" or inorganic layer that prevents most external stimuli from penetrating the system in an uncontrolled manner—that is,
in their original intensity—and overwhelming it (1920g, p. 29).The
projective mechanism behaves as though unwanted excitation of
internal origin is streaming in from outside. What is expelled in the
act of projection, in the Kleinian sense, is fantastically expelled outside
this metaphoric layer. In Bion's and others' terms, too, what is expelled
goes outside this layer, though this time concretely. In the case of
projective identification, on the other side of this layer there is another

subject (or are other subjects) who has his or her (their) own protective shield, which the projected materials manage to penetrate and affect to varying extents.

How does a person decide where her feelings come from, and what is the status of such a decision? In this context, Nathanson (1986) describes a mechanism he calls "the empathic wall". This mechanism, according to him, forms the basis of both normal and pathological defensive actions, yielding a distinction between self and other and locating the source of experienced affect, whether it is external or internal. The feelings of others in the subject's vicinity affect him, "infect" him, and—in a different version—transform into his own. It is the empathic wall that protects him from being totally overwhelmed by others' feelings, which, in the absence of such a wall, would constantly be converting into his own. When the mother extends intense and unwanted feelings, the empathic wall allows the child to stay emotionally connected with her while simultaneously separate from the rejected feeling. In this manner, he remains himself, and the negative feelings from the outside remain external: they are not associated with his self. But the young subject extends this function to use it also for negative affective experiences that arise from within:

> Here, then, is a mechanism which allows the individual to sample his own affective state and determine its source, a mechanism valuable for an organism whose perceptual and communicative apparatus are not developed adequately to allow symbolic communication. If such a mechanism can allow the child to wall off external affect, to feel that this affective state comes from outside the self and rightly should remain outside the self, then that mechanism is capable of being recruited for further use when unpleasant affect derives from inner conflict. The child can wall off the feeling, even to the extent that the feeling is viewed as an intrusion from the outside, the result of affective broadcast. Denial utilizes the affect-blocking portion of the empathic wall, while projection makes use of its ability to perform a "vector analysis"—to determine from which direction a particular affect originated. (Nathanson, 1986, p. 178)

This description, which chimes with Freud's conceptualisation of defensive projection, suggests the fundamental need (i.e., the self's survival largely depends on it) to separate inside from outside, self and non-self, and to determine from which direction each input arrives and to whom it belongs. This relates first and foremost to the young, immature, and evolving minds of the infant and child. But these functions that come to separate inside from outside remain active in us: to a certain point in a healthy and appropriate manner; beyond it, as central participants in the basic illusion that sustains our continued existence, in a split, dualistic, and selfish mode of being.

There is no air in this room, or whose mental material is this, anyway?

Let us consider, for instance, a group whose members get together for a certain purpose—therapeutic or educational. Let us also assume that one of its members, at some stage, starts to experience anxiety or anger. A number of potential scenarios are possible. In the first, the person will experience a growing sense of discomfort, something inside him will shift into a projective mindset and he will (unconsciously) choose to locate its source outside himself. If this is the case, then he is likely to put the responsibility for his unhappy feelings on various external factors: he might blame the therapist or teacher or the subject matter he presents, attack one of the other group members because of something he or she said or did, or even treat concrete features of time or physical space as evil or having destructive power. Statements such as "You're not really holding the group very well," or "How would you even know, you have no children yourself," or "There's no air in this room" all are types of conduct inspired by a logic that externalises, locates things elsewhere or outside, expels and projects. In the second case, the person will assume (not necessarily consciously) that the discomfort originates inside. He will turn his attention inward, he will choose to explore or not to explore the mental materials he experienced, with the help of others or alone; in any case, he will not look for external reasons, or dispose of his pain to others located outside himself. Although this is the better scenario, the question arises, to what extent is the person in the second example also aware of the reciprocal relations between himself and his surroundings and of their impact, every smallest segment of time, on the situation which he calls "his own" or "himself"?

Let us assume a therapist is working with a group of this kind when tension starts building up. She begins to feel unease slowly wrapping itself around her; a lump forms in her throat, and her heart pounds. She is afraid of being attacked. Noticing how the group members are steadily becoming immersed in themselves, she assumes, on the basis of what has been happening so far, that most of them probably feel different versions of this experience, compatible or complementary, different versions that come with the specific, typical reactions they evoke in each individual. She might, at this point, simply ask who feels his heartbeat has been accelerating in the past few minutes. She can ask who has a sense of pressure in his throat. She might perhaps ask who feels fear. Realising that the increased heart rate, the tightness in the throat, and the fear—all ostensibly personal, private sensations and feelings—are, after all, not all that private, could unsettle the illusion of separateness. It might also offer a "vector analysis" slightly unlike the one each of the participants' minds produced when taking stock of the situation by itself. Consequently, the veil of illusion that enveloped each participant, isolated and alone in their difficult feelings, is lifted a little. This is just one, hypothetical but typical, illustration: I have often been present in such situations. Like drops of dew on a huge spider's web, or like the tiny flutter of butterflies' wings, contributing to the build-up of a tornado, we are all subject to the laws of chaos. Dynamic non-linear systems within dynamic non-linear systems are what we are, interdependent and sensitive to conditions, influenced by the tiniest and largest changes alike. Self and non-self, inside and outside, close and far, immediate or delayed, past, present, and future: none of these is truly separate. Singular in our specific traits but inseparable, we are mutually dependent, sustained by the same sensory–emotional climate which we jointly produce, prompting one another, connected.

So, the truth abides in a third domain: neither in the one in which responsibility is projected outward nor where it is restored inside while leaving the subject locked in a closed causal system that ignores the close reciprocities between it and its surroundings.

Therefore, let us, at this point, draw a line between two factors: the causal relationship that is characterised by interdependence, and the degree of responsibility for suffering or absence-of-suffering which it generates. External reality exists, is there, and affects us in infinite ways—coarsely and subtly, explicitly and implicitly. Nevertheless, suffering is the exclusive creation of the mind's own actions. The conditions of our lives (whether they are the foods or medicines we do or do not consume, the space that surrounds us and everything it contains, human and non-human, concrete and abstract, material or mental), in accordance with their specific features, these all produce sensations in us. However, a sensation, pleasant or not, does not in and of itself carry (mental) pain or joy. Pain or suffering only arise when the mind reacts to the unpleasant by hating and to the pleasant (absent or present) by craving. Suffering is the creation of desire and hate, and happiness is the creation of their absence.

Obviously, the therapist does not always manage to hold the group adequately; not always does every group member produce the hoped-for empathy and understanding, and not always is there enough air in the room. Still, this does not alter the fact that the suffering people experience in reaction to these resides inside themselves, and that it is their responsibility alone to cope with it. One person might experience the room as nice and warm and protective while another might feel suffocated. One participant might experience the way that the thera-pist encourages the group to dwell in the space of not-knowing as the latter's failure to hold, while another might sense that the same thing affords expansion and an opportunity to grow. On the other hand, someone who is in a damaging environment—such as a destructive relationship in which he finds himself put down or dismissed or manoeuvred into immoral behaviours—should not limit his coping with this situation to the level of introspection alone. Introspection and an investigation of his mental actions will also yield a clearer insight into the inner sources of his pain, but, equally, the exploration of the mutualities between the mental and the physical and the internal and the external will show him the damage caused by maintaining a rela-tionship of a negative nature. He will see how he and his partner are entangled, and how the mental contents of the one encounter those of the other, stirring up unhealthy reactions. In certain cases, he will find how taking a distance from the other makes him feel better and restores him to himself, and in others how this distance allows him, at least, to start trying to pave a different, new way for himself.

Crossing the boundary

I return now to considering projective identification as a phenomenon that illustrates how permeable the boundaries between one mind and another are, and how much people are subject to the interdependence of conditioned arising. Addressing projective identification implies touching a by no means simple issue that frequently tortures we humans: recognition of dependency and the wish to avoid it, the yearning for it and the dread of losing oneself in it. Here we tread the metaphoric line between self and other, slipping away from it, erasing and reconstituting it, at times in a different location, at times marking a self that has transformed into an other in the process. Let us see how this happens.

In Freud's notion of defensive projection, merging between self and other occurs on the level of internal representations: the other is perceived as possessing features of the projecting subject. This blending between self and other deepens in Klein's development of the notion of projective identification, exposing the fluidity of their discreteness. Nathanson's (1986) description of the infant struggling to keep close affective relations with a primary figure while dissociating from problematic broadcasts issuing from that figure renders the tension between separation and union, a major characteristic of projective identification.

For Sandler (1993), relief through getting rid of something projected is attained only if the person is aware—to some extent, at least—that what was projected actually belongs to her. All varieties of defensive projection, he suggests, show a constant oscillation between momentary states of fusion marked by a primary confusion of boundaries and states when an arbitrating function comes into action, creating a distinction between self and other. This motion allows the subject to instantly feel that what she projected is hers, then immediately to experience the soothing knowledge that it is not. This arbitrating, "boundary-setting function" (Sandler, 1993, p. 1102) will usually switch on forcefully, rapidly, and unconsciously, and it announces, "No, that isn't me, that's the other." Often, too, it is suspended, leading to a blurring of boundaries between representations of self and other, and to their temporary fusion. So there is in the psyche a continuous, unconscious fluctuation in the degree to which these boundaries are set and in their intensity, as well as an elasticity of boundaries which allows for phenomena such as projective identification (as well as others, which are beyond the scope of this discussion), where mental materials pass from one person to another. The boundaries between self and not-self (and between self-representations and object representations), therefore, must not be seen as carved in stone. They are not fixed entities that stay in place once they come into being (Sandler, 1993).

In projective identification, states of merging between self and others arise where self parts and mental functions are "deposited" with an other (Shaw, 2014). In this way, a patient can, for instance, deposit her despair with a therapist so that she herself can feel hope, at least for a while (Yarom, 2010), or she could, alternatively, deposit confusion or a sense of being stupid in order to feel clear-minded, knowing, or clever. The opposite is equally true: someone might leave his sense of hope with another and remain in despair, or empty his ability to think into him and be left without it. In such cases, the experiences of one person pass into another: they become his own and he experiences them in the first person. His experience, however, is not precisely identical: it is filtered through his own particular body–mind system, which naturally leaves the imprint of its own specific features. This is how psychoanalysis understands it (Ogden, 1979; Wender, 1993), and a similar insight can be gleaned from a Buddhist perspective.

According to the latter, every encounter with the world is an encounter with a specific mind-and-matter phenomenon: it receives interpretation depending on past experiences of this individual phenomenon, leaves an impression informed by its past accumulated *saṅkhāras* (or stocks of mental reactions), and produces experiences on the basis of all these, which, in their turn, lead to new reactions. In this view, experiential input received by means of what psychoanalysis calls projective identification is also regarded as occurring within the domain of the individual's mental–material system. It has no more external status than the sound that on its way in encounters the apparatus that processes it. Thus, the duality between inside and outside is lifted, leaving the distinction between them a purely functional one. Anything that is an "object"—whether it is a sight, a smell or a thought—is called "external" in Buddhist terms, and whatever registers it is called "internal". This approach, therefore, implies the absence of distinct, independent, essential entities, while recognising the existence of specific, conditioned phenomena. It implies the absence of essential boundaries between inside and outside and between self and non-self, while acknowledging the existence of functional interfaces.

Psychoanalytic ambivalence regarding boundaries

For Buddhism, the very need to make the distinction between the one who is me and the one who is not, between what is mine and what is not, testifies to a certain blindness regarding the nature of reality. From this perspective, it is not merely that the boundaries between self and other are not fixed, but, on the deeper level, the entities these boundaries pretend to keep separate are not fixed, either, and they have no independent essence. While psychoanalytic discourse engages with boundaries profoundly and extensively, it is, however, much less conclusive (Pelled, 2005). Inherently occupied with questions of inside and outside, the concepts of projection and projective identification are closely related to the concept of the boundary. The psychoanalytic literature, however, suggests that they perforate that boundary, cross it, erase it, deny it, and reinstate it over and over. These concepts serve psychoanalytic thinking, on the one hand, to question the existence of the boundary and, on the other, reach out and hold on to it. This field of study, then, maintains a constant, ambivalent, and complex relationship with the issue of the boundary.

Obviously, psychoanalytic thinking about how the boundary between self and other is achieved relies on different assumptions than Buddhism's not-self and conditioned arising. Psychoanalysis's main position on the need to constitute interpsychic boundaries and a distinction between self and non-self is a dialectic one that tries to accommodate a variety of mental phenomena, some extremely pathological ones along with normal, everyday ones. It is grounded on the assumed basic need for a sense of separate self alongside recognition of dependence on, and relationality to, the other. According to this view, the normal, non-psychotic perception of reality is supported by the ability to distinguish self from object and internal space from external space. In contrast, the inability to tolerate awareness of the separation between self and object signposts a lapse into psychotic mind states. Following Klein, Bion, and others, Shaw (2014) describes how perceptual differentiation between self and object develops at the beginning of life in ways involving projective identification, projection, introjection, and containment. The infant projects her fears of death into the mother, the experienced hatred and envy for the absent breast. If the mother is able to bear these projections, then the infant's frustration is managed and taken care of, allowing her to evolve an awareness of the object as separate from herself and of its being what manages and takes care of her frustration. The containing mind of the mother produces a three-dimensional experience in the infant, which involves the perception of an internal space—the mother's mind—that can hold the infant's experience. Experiencing this three-dimensional space produces the experience of an own inner space in the infant.

The repeated experience of this process leads to the formation of a perception of self as distinct from object, and, thus, the foundation of the ability to separate, contrast, categorise, and name aspects of both the inner and the outer world. When the internalisation of a mind capable of containing the infant's projections is not possible, distortions in the infant's perception of internal and external space are likely to occur, as well as a sense of fusion with the object into which parts of the self were projected. The confusion of boundaries between self and other is characteristic of serious dysfunction, while a non-psychotic reality perception is characterised by the distinction between inside and outside and between self and object (Shaw, 2014). Hence, when projective identification is deployed as a communicative function and it meets with an appropriate response, it leads to a healthy development of boundaries between self and other and a proper perception of reality. Should this process derail, then projective identification becomes pathological and serves to evacuate and erase all awareness of boundaries between self and other (Shaw, 2014). From this a view emerges according to which proper reality perception commands differentiation between self and non-self, while the absence of inner space, as opposed to external space, and fusion with the other are seen as negative, pathological, or regressive states. At the same time, however, mechanisms such as Sandler's "boundary-setting function" and Nathanson's "empathic wall" are expected to be flexible enough to allow healthy persons to make contact with their fellow beings through empathy:

> It is my feeling that mature empathy can occur only in a person with a healthy empathic wall mechanism, who is in addition capable of relaxing this ego function in order to merge briefly with the affective broadcast of the other. (Nathanson, 1986, p. 176)

It is, therefore, all the more important for the therapist, when at work, to be able to relax automatic separating mechanisms in the service of the therapeutic process, which requires the utmost receptivity.

> In the analytic situation, of course, it is vital that we allow ourselves to regress in a controlled way, to relax the anti-regressive function, to permit what Ernst Kris called "regression in the service of the ego" (Kris, 1952), in order to allow ourselves to listen and to respond sensitively to the unconscious communications of our patients. (Sandler, 1993, p. 1104)

The ability to allow, in a controlled way, states of non-differentiation between representations of self and other is necessary if one wants to be open to connection and communication, including the connection and communication occurring through the materials the patient transfers to the therapist by means of projective identification. This ability, however, hinges on the prior establishment of boundaries between self and other (Sandler, 1993). On the other hand, this very same early establishment of boundaries depends on the exchange of mental materials with the mother through functional projective identification: that is, it, itself, relies on the permeability of the interpsychic boundaries.

One important conceptual clarification is in order here: the Buddhist notion of *anattā* (not-self) according to which phenomena have no independent and essential self-core, does not refer to the loss of boundaries that we find, for instance, in massive projective identification, a condition psychoanalysis defines as regressive and pathological and one of the characteristic features of psychotic thinking and personality disorders. The psychotic person becomes undifferentiated from a homogenous world when painful reality penetrates in a manner he cannot endure (Bion, 1962a; Shaw, 2014). He dwells, then, in great suffering and confusion, from both of which the Buddha's teaching aims to offer liberation. The absence of self, as Western psychoanalysis construes it, is entirely unlike Buddhist *anattā* (Epstein, 1988a).

One way of looking at this difference and proposing a possible answer to the question of how the disintegration of the self, which Buddhism envisions could be a healthy objective, is the following. The self in its psychological sense, according to Epstein (1988a) can be divided into a representative aspect and a functional one. The first, representative, aspect renders the process by which representations of self and world are constructed from a multitude of mental images and structures, and it is responsible for the sense of a solid self. This sense is entailed by a continuous sensory–affective experience, and it is rooted in an idea or in abstraction, and, hence, as we have seen, in projection. The functional aspect, by contrast, refers to the self's role in adjustment, growth, and the maintenance of psychological equilibrium. This is a synthetic function similar, which acts to integrate a variety of sometimes clashing impressions, assimilating the many and frequently changing products of the mind without rejection and, thus, promoting a coherent and stable experience.

Epstein argues that the functions of the ego associated with the first aspect—linked to internal representations and to the narcissistic illusion of a perfect and independent self—come undone through Vipassanā meditation, while the functions related to the second aspect—those involving the subject's ability to directly process what her or his senses register and to assimilate it without rejection—grow stronger. Obviously, there is a connection between the disintegration of the one and the build-up of the other. It is only on the basis of a firm functional aspect that the illusory parts of the representative function can be healthily dissolved (Epstein, 1988a), and, along with them, the tendency to project and to perceive a distorted reality through the lens of the past.

CHAPTER FIVE

One mind constituting another: the network paradigm and non-dualistic thought

"To be cured is to have the integrity and mastery of one's personality restored; and to cure is to integrate the patient's psyche by integrating one's own, re-establishing the equation non-ego (you) = ego. To understand is to overcome the division into two, and to identify oneself is, in this aspect, to restore an already pre-existing identity. To understand, to unite with another, and hence also to love, prove to be basically one and the same"

(Racker, 1968, p. 174)

A conceptual model based on boundaries is limited and limiting by definition:

From the paradigm of the frontier we can only think in terms of division and confrontation between two irreconcilable spaces or times: outside or inside, before or after. This hypothesis implicitly carries the notion of a being having fixed frontiers and an identity which was consummated in infancy—a being condemned by his/her past to an irrevocable destiny. (Abadi, 2003, p. 225)

Indeed, when one considers the nature of projective identification, it transpires that psychoanalysis developed, alongside the boundary paradigm, a notion of boundaries as relative, elastic, and permeable.[6] If the boundaries between one mind and another are not concrete and are constantly reinstated, if an individual can experience shared or partly overlapping feelings and sensations with a whole group of people, and if the experiences of one person and his self-parts can be projected into, and deposited with, another person, then clearly an essential distinction between subject and object (or between one subject and another) does not really exist, and the minds of people are interdependent. Such a view of things is underwritten by a "network" paradigm, a mature form of non-dualistic thought. This is a conceptual model based neither on splitting and illusions of separation nor on fusion and a denial of the specific properties of various phenomena and the complex relations between them at any given moment. This perspective recognises that the truth passes through a "third territory" in which creator and creation, no longer seen as two contrasting factors, are revealed as two aspects of an ongoing process of change. It implies the realisation that all phenomena—material and mental alike—exist in reality in a non-autonomous, non-essential, and non-isolated way.

The network view is unmistakably implied by Buddhist thought: one of its later variants actually uses the image of the net to render reality's infinitely mutually conditioned relations of becoming. Here, the image is one of a net hung with precious stones, covering the palace of the god Indra. Each of these gems reflects the others that mirror themselves in it: "If we touch one, we will affect all others. If we look at one, we will see all the others" (Raz, 2006, p. 40). I would like to qualify this by adding that the notion of the net suits the perception of reality I am trying to describe only to the extent that it refers to something multi-dimensional, dense, and infinitely extending. Every point in it is an intersection of certain factors of the past, the present, and the future, each related differently to this point and affecting it differently. Yet, such a point is neither essential nor stable. This network thinking, unsurprisingly, is reflected in quantum physics, something to which I shall return shortly. For now, let us see how it can also be taken up experientially through interpersonal phenomena associated with projection and projective identification.

Projective identification, countertransference, and the interpersonal web

The experience of projective identification situates those who partake in it—projector and receiver alike—in a web of interdependency. The perspective of the network, which recognises reality as conditionally arising, a reality in which the self is not a sealed nuclear entity, offers an alternative to the perspective whereby the self constitutes an almost entirely fixed and absolute point of reference, an invisible prism through which reality is perceived and experienced.

The most patent illustration of how projective identification operates as a means whereby one mind constitutes another is the mother–infant dyad. Klein (1946) has described how the subject projects his feelings and thoughts on (or in) to his loved and hated objects, then to introject reality mixed with the distortions it has undergone by his projections (Waska, 2013). These dialectical descriptions are mainly pertinent to the way in which inner and outer perception come into being through processes of projection and introjection, and how these processes take part in the construction of the self. Later elaborations of Klein's ideas, however, centre on distinctly interpersonal processes. As said, in Bion's model the mother serves as a container for the mental materials her infant projects into her. This container, rather than being an empty vessel or a passive thing, is an active site in which a process occurs whose nature and quality crucially affect the infant's development. To the extent that the mother is able to allow the infant's projected materials to enter her, to "contain" and to adequately process them by means of her reverie, they return to the infant in a more digestible form, having been transformed inside her. When this process is repeated again and again, the infant does not internalise only the materials the mother transformed, but also the containing and metabolising function itself, gaining a healthy ability to absorb and process reality. However, if the mother, on the other hand, is unable to adequately perform this process, or if the infant's projections are persistent and excessive, then these metabolising functions will not properly form in the infant and will not be available for a healthy intake of reality. If the mother denies the right of the infant's projections to enter her, the infant is bound to internalise an obstructive object or negative container that will subvert his ability to perceive or think (Bion, 1959, 1962a; Grotstein, 1995).

This implies that the infant's experience invades the mother and that her ability to experience and process it returns into the infant, constituting his world and circumscribing his abilities. Whatever is in the infant's psyche becomes part of the mother and *vice versa*, so that their minds interdepend and are conditioned by one another, in terms of contents as well as of functions and processes.

According to Bion, "If the infant feels it is dying it can arouse fears that it is dying in the mother" (1962a, p. 308): that is to say, the infant's fear of dying passes to the mother and becomes a fear of her own, a fear of the infant's death. He further writes,

> A well-balanced mother can accept these and respond therapeutically: that is to say in a manner that makes the infant feel it is receiving its frightened personality back again, but in a form that it can tolerate— the fears are manageable by the infant personality. (Bion, 1962a, p. 308)

If, then, the exchange of mental materials unfolds adequately, the infant's mental materials (experiences or self-parts) will be restored after having been transformed within the mother in a way that now allows the infant to hold them (the very things that previously needed to be projected). These are functional relations between mother and infant who are attuned to one another (Bion, 1962a) and what they produce is healthy and builds competence.

If however, "the mother cannot tolerate these projections the infant is reduced to continue projective identification carried out with increasing force and frequency. . . . Reintrojection is affected with similar force and frequency" (Bion, 1962a, p. 308). In such a case, the infant's sense of dying remains devoid of meaning and, rather than internalising a now tolerable fear of death, he internalises a "nameless dread" (Bion, 1962a, p. 309). Here, what comes into being is ill and leads to illness. Whether ill or healthy, anyhow, the process relying on projective identification illustrates an exchange whereby one mind instigates events occurring in another and has a formative effect on the traits and abilities the latter develops. The infant's and mother's mental lives intertwine, and the mental reality of the one deeply affects the other. This is why for Winnicott, "There is no such thing as an infant" (1960, p. 587): that is to say, no infant exists in isolation from his or her mother.

In the relations between therapist and patient, various aspects of early relations are recreated and resurrected by means of the transference–countertransference dynamics. These dynamics arise on the basis of projective identification or of other projective behaviours of the mind. Transference (something to which I return at length in Chapter Seven) is a condition whereby a person projects formerly imprinted emotional and relational patterns on to present people or situations. In the therapeutic situation, transference is directed at the therapist and is examined with reference to her countertransference: her assorted reactions to the patient, including those to what the patient projects or transfers (in) to her. Freud, having formulated the notion of countertransference, believed it to include the therapist's own blind spots and warned against the possible pitfalls (Berman, 2009). Defining it as the outcome of the patient's influence on the analyst's unconscious feelings, Freud (1910d) expected the analyst to identify his own countertransference and to overcome it. Ever since, there have been those who consider the therapist's countertransference reactions as reflective of her own pathological and unprocessed parts, and those who define countertransference as the sum total of the therapist's reactions to the patient. The latter make a distinction between the countertransference originating from the therapist's pathology and that which is the result of her mature empathic parts (Grotstein, 1995; Kernberg, 1987; Ogden, 1979). Either way, there is general agreement about the important role of countertransference in the analytic process (Grotstein, 1995; Racker, 1968; Sandler, 1993) and also that addressing it is demanding and laborious.

The therapist's countertransference reactions hold important information and valuable opportunities, alongside hazards and traps. What determines which of these will come to the fore is the nature of the reactions, their origins, and mainly the therapist's awareness of them and his ability to cope with them in a healthy manner. One could think, for instance, of a female patient who projects on to her female therapist a whole system of perceptions and feelings that recreate her early relations with her mother. Let us assume that this woman was raised by a mother who was immersed in herself, showing limited, conditional interest in her child. As a result, the woman developed, early in life, behaviours that were meant to stir her mother's interest, as well as a very strong sensitivity to the degree of interest and attention her mother showed. Whenever, in addition, she failed to arouse her mother's sincere attention, she would temporarily suspend any effort to make contact, withdraw, and turn a cold shoulder. These were the early patterns the patient was now reproducing in her encounter with the therapist. Now, too, with the therapist, she felt she was not interesting enough or somehow unsatisfying, and now, too, she was constantly checking her attention and emotional involvement. With the therapist, too, she acted in ways meant to draw her interest, and with her, too, she would withdraw and maintain a distance whenever something inside her registered that the therapist was not entirely there, that she might prefer to be elsewhere, or would rather do something that would touch her more deeply. So much for the transference.

The therapist, from her side, alternately felt the patient as too strenuous, trying hard to fill spaces and to come up with the goods, as it were, and then as closed down, treating her in a chill and indifferent way. Being subject to the interpersonal field sustained by the patient, related experiences and reactions were likely to arise in her. This was her countertransference, whose character obviously bore the stamp of her personality, her reality perception, and her own formative experiences. She could have, for instance, felt oppressed or impatient in the face of the patient's efforts to generate interest, or she could have found herself activated by them, showing the latter again and again that she was with her. She might have tumbled deep, along with her patient, into the latter's anxiety or joined her effort to seal each breathing space. She could have found herself annoyed at her patient's frequent withdrawals or hurt by them, or she might have worried she was doing something wrong. She could have been overcome by this dispiriting routine, with effort giving way to withdrawal, giving way, in its turn, to effort again, and lose hope that a significant process and relationship between them would ever materialise. She could, however, manage to become conscious of her own feelings and, along with it, of the interpersonal field that was the context of their emergence; then she would be able to let things be for a while, study them, and gain experiential knowledge concerning the patient's world, a kind of knowledge she would not have been able to access without all these feelings and reactions. In this manner, she would manage to perceive her patient's efforts to produce interest as sincere attempts at making contact, and identify the withdrawals as her attempts to protect herself from pain, as well as, perhaps, a way of arousing in her, by means of projective identification, the same rejection, injury, anxiety, and anger that the patient herself felt whenever her mother's attention failed. She would sense—in her own body and mind—the patient's pain in reaction to the merest hint of a loss of interest and the creeping despair whenever it seemed that she would never again have true contact. In this manner, even when she felt compelled by the patient to feel, sense, think, or play out some role, the therapist, once she was aware, could benefit from it.

The countertransference has a two-dimensional function that is entailed by the therapist's two-dimensional role. Being in the position of both experiencing these unconscious processes and interpreting them, the countertransference can help him in their perception, or, rather, distort or prevent it (Racker, 1968). From the other side of the interpersonal space, the therapist's experiences, reactions, and inter-pretations contribute to those of the patient. This is how the ways they perceive one another, the ways they experience and respond to one another, interlace; this is how the road they may take jointly emerges in a mutually conditioned manner.

> . . . the countertransference affects his [the analyst's] manner and his behaviour which in turn influence the image the analysand forms of him. Through the analyst's interpretations, the form he gives them, his voice, through every attitude he adopts towards the patient, the latter perceives (consciously or unconsciously) the psychological state he happens to be in—not to speak of the debatable question of telepathic perception. Thus the countertransference, by affecting the analyst's understanding and behaviour, influences the patient and especially his transference, that is to say, the process on which the transforma-tion of his personality and object relations so largely depend. (Racker, 1968, p.105)

The dynamics between transference and countertransference forges a profound connection between the unconscious of two people (Racker, 1968), embroidering the "total environment in which both patient and analyst pursue a 'life' together" (Bollas, 1987, p. 202). So, just as no infant exists in isolation from its mother, though they are "separate physical and psychological entities" (Ogden, 1994a, p. 4), similarly, "there is no such thing as an analysand apart from the relationship with the analyst, and no such thing as an analyst apart from the relationship with the analysand" (Ogden, 1994a, p. 4). The mother–infant and therapist–patient units exist in dynamic tension with their separateness (Ogden, 1994a). The inner state of the one yields the outer sphere of the other; the experience of the one generates the experience of the other; the interpretation of the one produces the interpretation of the other. This interpretation does not have to be psychoanalytic and neither does it even have to relate to therapist–patient relations. Anyone in an interpersonal situation is bound to serve as an object of projection; everyone experiences the interpersonal field, with or without projection, and, whether consciously or not, everyone is the interpreter of his or her own experiences. This is the interpersonal web that emerges between one person's broadcast and the other's perception and sensation, between attention and reaction, between the one who projects and the object of the projection, and between transference and countertransference. And if this is how things are, then, in Freud's theory, this perspective actually was "where this paradigm has been implicit from the beginning, in harmony or discordant with the paradigm of the frontier" (Abadi, 2003, p. 226.).

If we revert to projective identification as a specific instance of the way one mind constitutes another, we find that it is a type of metaphorical conduit through which mental materials pass from one mind to another. We find that someone might unconsciously plant a variety of feelings, such as anger, anxiety, guilt, rejection, vengefulness, and hate, in another person, thoughts or states of mind (Racker, 1968), and even bodily sensations (Yarom, 2010). Moreover, through this, a person can affect the actual conduct of the projection's object by pushing the latter to play into the defensive process currently active (Joseph, 1975). How can a person "plant" feelings, thoughts, and sensations in another person? What is the nature of this channel through which mental materials pass between subjects? The reciprocal relations denoted by the phenomenon we call "projective identification" are so complex they might, on occasion, seem shrouded in mystery, remaining not understood, or understood, but only in theory and in the abstract. Let us explore a few possible ways of understanding these relations.

Actions of mind, actions of speech, actions of body

How exactly a patient does succeed in imposing a phantasy and its corresponding affect upon his analyst in order to deny it in himself is a most interesting problem. .... A peculiarity of communications of this kind is that, at first sight, they do not seem as if they had been made by the patient at all. The analyst experiences the affect as being his own response to something. The effort involved is in differentiating the patient's contribution from his own. (Money-Kyrle, 1956, p. 366; also in Spillius, 1992, p. 69)

In explanations of projective identification, a distinction is usually made between the fantastic and the interpersonal aspects. The assumption is that the depositing or planting of mental materials occurs in the fantasy, while the actual influence on the object of projection (the person into whom the materials are projected) is achieved through a variety of behaviours by means of a multitude of interactions. The fantastic aspect relates, one might say, to "internal" actions, actions of the mind, while the interpersonal or actual aspect refers to those actions that find their way out through speech and the body.

Let us imagine a situation in which a woman starts going out with a man. He seems gifted, he is nice to look at and intelligent, but whenever she meets with him, she starts feeling very agitated after some time. To begin with, she does not understand what is troubling her, and she finds it hard to put a finger on what this particular discomfort is all about. But as the experience repeats itself each time they meet, and she feels how the tension begins to spill beyond their actual meetings, seeping into her mind, her feelings gradually become clear to her. When she is with him, she notices, she feels silenced, and this feeling grows more and more intense, until she feels as though her mouth is covered and her hands are tied. She notices how, in his presence, she becomes superfluous, and eventually it is as though she transforms into a thing. What is happening there? What was the fantasy and what was it that helped, at least in a sense, to realise it? There is a legion of possibilities, of course, in the absence of further detail, but let us think of a specific case.

Let us assume that the man's unconscious fantasy was to plant these experiences in the woman in order to make it easier to control her, as he would do with other people in his life. And let us also assume that this need for control was related to his profound fear, whenever the possibility arose, of a real connection with a real person, exposing him to what was not in his control and what he thus experienced as dangerous. On a different level, this man's unconscious behaviour came in response to a more primary state in which he himself was subject to a projection of this kind: here, he had been deprived of his human identity, having been turned into an object by his mother, who was incapable of acting otherwise. One might say that he projected a self-part into his partner in order nevertheless to maintain contact with that part, and so that he might directly communicate to her his unprocessed, exiled, and split off experience.

So much for the fantasy. On what we might call "the actual" level, this man could have achieved his influence on the woman by means of a variety of interpersonal patterns which are, in fact, the verbal and bodily expressions of his mental actions. He might, for instance, again and again have dismissed things she said. He might have invented clever and implicit means of forbidding her to act in certain ways. He might have presented her with conditions requiring that she efface her own identity, or else he would discontinue the relationship. All this would contrive to convey—without his being conscious of doing so— a message to the effect that he was not really interested in who or what she was, none of her personality or characteristics, other than the fact of her being there, as his object, his partner.

The intersubjective space and the "subjugating third"

It is by making the distinction between the fantastic aspect of the act of projection and its real aspect, that the influence it achieves through acts of speech and behaviour can be explained. Another way of looking at this process defines an "intersubjective space" between the one who projects and the one who receives the projection: it is by virtue of this space that real—as opposed to fantastic—influence comes about. Moore (1995) argues that once Freud introduced the concept of the unconscious, he showed that the subject is not tantamount to, or resides in, his consciousness. Thus, Freud removed the subject from its fixed anthropocentric position. Projective identification further adds to this shift: however primitive, it is one of the major ways in which the subject is cast toward others and into the space between it and them (Moore, 1995).

When one conceives of the subject as identical with the brain or consciousness and, therefore, as enclosed in something solid such as the skull, it is hard to understand how a phenomenon like projective identification, which often appears as a kind of invasion of the mind, might operate.

> Such encapsulated minds appear isolated from other subjects and thus we become hard pressed to understand how projective and introjective identification could move from inside one skull to another. This becomes especially problematic as one tries to picture parts of the subject being transported into another person. However, when the subject is decentered (no longer equated with mind or consciousness), then, projective and introjective identification becomes more plausible. (Moore, 1995, p. 126)[7]

This viewpoint allows us to understand the subject as being in a dialectic relationship with an intersubjective dimension, the space between subjects. And if, indeed, there is such a space into which both subjects project, the one subject's projections do not directly penetrate the other's mind and the mystery of the process is somewhat relieved. In this approach, if one of the subjects projects something into the intersubjective space which partly overlaps with the other's projection, the result is intensified projection. If one, for instance, feels slightly worried and projects this or only denies it in part or weakly, the worry will reach the intersubjective space anyhow. If the other is simultaneously projecting intensely into the same space, this might attach itself to the slight or only partially denied worry, which will be amplified as a result, and evolve, for example, into a panic. On this scenario, the projection of one person did not directly enter the other. It only did so indirectly through the change it effected in the part-overlapping material projected into the intersubjective space (Moore, 1995).

The idea of intersubjectivity and the existence of projective and introjective identification suggest that a fixed subject position is an impossibility and that there is no stable boundary between one subject and another: rather, they entertain mutually formative dialectic relations (Moore, 1995). The solution this approach offers to an explanation of the phenomenon of communication between people's minds relies on the space between subjects, which is to say, on a third element between them.

Benjamin (2004) designates this third space as one in which there occurs a dialectics between recognition of the other as a separate and distinct feeling subject like oneself, and the recognition that it is possible to be empathic with, and stay connected to, him or her. For Benjamin, the "third" is what one must surrender to, and thirdness is the intersubjective mental space that allows this surrender or is entailed by it. This surrender (rather than submission) enables a person to *be with* someone, and this, says Benjamin, requires a third, a principle or process that mediates between self and other. This involves "a certain letting go of the self, and thus also implies the ability to take in the other's point of view or reality" (Benjamin, 2004, p. 8). "The co-created third has the transitional quality of being both invented and discovered. To the question of 'Who created this pattern, you or I?' the paradoxical answer is 'Both and neither'" (Benjamin, 2004, p. 18). This can be put in different terms relating to an easing of the boundaries between self and other and to the ability to take in the other's projections. Ogden (1994b) uses the notion of the "subjugating third" in order to analyse this: it offers yet another perspective on the way the intersubjective space functions in the mutual becoming of two subjects. For him, projective identification produces a mutual subjugation which itself subverts the separate subjective experience of the participants in the process.[8]

> The interpersonal facet of projective identification involves a transformation of the subjectivity of the "recipient" in such a way that the separate "I-ness" of the other-as-object is (for a time and to a degree) subverted: "You [the 'recipient' of the projective identification] are me [the projector] to the extent that I need to make use of you for the purpose of experiencing through you what I cannot experience myself. You are not me to the extent that I need to disown an aspect of myself and in fantasy hide myself (disguised as not-me) in you." The recipient of the projective identification becomes a participant in the negation of himself as a separate subject, thus making "psychological room" in himself to be (in unconscious fantasy) occupied (taken over) by the projector. (Ogden, 1994b, pp. 99–100)

Thus, projective identification is an interpersonal psychological event in which two subjects unconsciously deny themselves in order to create a new subjectivity, or a different experience of "I-ness" which they could not have achieved alone, without the other.

> In one sense, we participate in projective identification (often despite our most strenuous conscious efforts to avoid doing so) in order to

create ourselves in and through the other-who-is-not-fully-other; at the same time, we unconsciously allow ourselves to serve as the vehicle through which the other (who is not fully other) creates himself as subject through us. In different ways, each of the individuals entering into a projective identification experiences both aspects (both forms of negating and being negated) in this intersubjective event. It does not suffice to simply say that in projective identification one finds oneself playing a role in someone else's unconscious fantasy (Bion 1959). More fully stated, one finds oneself unconsciously both playing a role in and serving as author of someone else's unconscious fantasy. (Ogden, 1994b, p. 103)

Whoever participates in the process both yields his or her selfhood to be constituted by the other and participates in the formation of the other's selfhood. Projective identification, when seen from this angle, is a channel whereby a person unconsciously eliminates part of her separate individuality in order to transcend its boundaries. This goes for both parties.

The recipient of the projective identification is engaged in a negation (subversion) of his own individuality in part for the unconscious purpose of disrupting the closures underlying the coherence/stagnation of the self. Projective identification offers the recipient the possibility of creating a new form of experience that is other-to-himself, and thereby creates conditions for the alteration of who he had been to that point and who he had experienced himself to be. The recipient is not simply identifying with an other (the projector); he is becoming an other and experiencing (what is becoming) himself through the subjectivity of a newly created other/third/self. (Ogden, 1994b, p. 102)

The one who participates in projective identification subjugates himself—unconsciously—in order to be extricated from himself. This kind of release depends, however, on both sides recognising, after a temporary confusion of boundaries, the individuality of the other (Ogden, 1994b). Due to the centrality of the negation of the separate self and the institution of a new experience based on interdependence with another person, the process Ogden describes brings to mind the Buddhist notions of "not-self" and "conditioned arising". Yet, this negation of the self (subverting it) is not identical to the Buddhist not-self; the release Ogden describes is by no means a release from subjective experience: rather, it is an expansion of the psyche relying on the exchange of mental materials with one-who-is-not-me and the subsequent formation of a new dialectic subjectivity. I shall explain.

To begin with, the process of projective identification—as is mentioned often—is unconscious and it involves confusion (of boundaries) and denial:

> ... projective identification is a process by which the subjectivity of both projector and recipient are being negated in different ways: the projector is disavowing an aspect of himself that he imagines to be evacuated into the recipient while the recipient is participating in a negation of himself by surrendering to (making room for) the disavowed aspect of the subjectivity of the projector. (Ogden 1994b, p. 100)

It is an action, therefore, which relies on delusion and confusion, lacking the clear vision that results from realising the self-less nature of reality. The negation of self, here, is associated with evasion, expulsion, and fantasy, making it a negation in the nihilist sense of the word: a denial of what exists. Release from subjugation, in this event, involves restoring what has been rid of in fantasy and the suspended individuality. Here, an inverse symmetry seems to obtain: Buddhism holds that subjugation is related to the illusion of self and that liberation involves becoming aware of this illusion and recognising the transient, conditioned, and self-less nature of things. In Ogden's descriptions, however, subjugation is related to the negation of individuality while liberation comes with its recognition and subsequent reinstatement. The picture is more complicated, however. The Buddhist notions of not-self and conditioned arising do not actually negate the existence of individual phenomena. Such a negation would carry the flaw of denial and nihilism, as, in some sense, happens in the unconscious process of projective identification. The freedom of extrication Ogden describes is, therefore, only a kind of half-way extrication. It does, at least, attain a renewed awareness of the individual features of phenomena (or, in this case, subjects), and it achieves the abolition of the denial of certain components of reality (here, the split off parts expelled into the object of projection). If, moreover, the process is dealt with successfully, it results in "disrupting the closures underlying the coherence/stagnation of the self", and in psychological growth and expansion:

In projective identification, analyst and analysand are each limited and enriched; each is stifled and vitalized. The new intersubjective entity that is created, the subjugating analytic third, becomes a vehicle through which thoughts might be thought, feelings might be felt, sensations might be experienced, which to that point had existed only as potential experiences for each of the individuals participating in this psychological–interpersonal process. In order for psychological growth to occur, there must be a superseding of the subjugating third and the establishment of a new and more generative dialectic of oneness and twoness, similarity and difference, individual subjectivity and intersubjectivity. (Ogden, 1994b, pp. 101–102)

Where the experience of projective identification, therefore, is well handled, it leads to the dissolving of a fixated self-cohesion and to a more elastic movement along the power line between subjective separateness and interconnectedness. This achievement is not identical (and obviously does not strive to be identical) to recognition of the principle of conditioned arising as it appears in the Pāli Canon. The insight underlying the conscious work with projective identification, as the psychoanalytic literature describes it, does not abandon the self *qua* point of reference and neither does it quite let go of dualism and the model of the boundary: rather, it oscillates between the latter and the network paradigm. Where it negates the self, projective identification nihilistically relies on blindness, and if this negation of the self is to bring about growth and release, the self must be reinstated (which, as said, involves a lesser degree of illusion than its negation). The experience of projective identification has the potential to expand the psyche and extricate it from confinement, but it simultaneously suffocates and limits. It leads to an awareness of co-dependency, but returns to subjectivity as an elementary, essential experience.

While the intersubjective conceptualisation envisions a non-dualist model of experience and offers profound insights regarding the growth potential of understanding non-separation, it reaches for the "third" as a mediator between I and you. This mediating third, I believe, testifies to a difficulty in digesting the ideas concerning interdependent becoming in the deeper sense, concerning the existence of a two-way movement of experience and the absence of duality between I and you, and it reflects the complex manoeuvres required to settle this difficulty. It seems an additional support, or scaffold, is needed to cross the gap between the fundamental essentialist assumption and the clinical reality which presents us, again and again, with the fact that this assumption is unfounded; the gap between our most basic intuition of having a separate existence, and the tendency to perceive subject as split from object (or other subject) and the awareness of the interdependency between one mind and another. Perhaps the third, or the intersubjective space, or the dialectic process between recognition of separateness and openness to mutual influence, is exactly this: a scaffold.

Now I would like to propose an additional layer to our understanding of projective identification as a way of passing mental materials from one mind to another. This layer springs from a sensational–particulate understanding, achieved by means of Vipassanā meditation.

The classic level, the quantum level, and the (un-)proud owner of shame

Every material entity is defined by certain characteristics entailed by its components: molecules made up from atoms, which are constituted by sub-atomic particles, which are in turn constituted by elementary particles—currently the most basic ones known to science. We find it easy, on an everyday level, to distinguish between "flowing" materials (fluids, gases) and "solid" materials. The former move and spread in space while the physics according to which solids behave is different, leaving an impression that they are static or fixed. This is why it is intuitively clear to us how the smell produced by the factory across the road reaches our nostrils, or that the heat of the fire in the sitting room warms us even when we are in the next room and even when we do not actually see it. It is, in contrast, really hard for us to imagine how interaction is possible with a wall or a chair in the next room, though they are exactly at the same distance from us (unless they are subject to a process whereby they pass into another physical state which in turn will carry smell or heat). This difference is not a mistaken perception: it occurs at a certain level of reality, the one that classical physics addresses. There is, however, a deeper, more fundamental, level of physical reality, and this is what quantum physics, among other things, looks at.

Taken from this perspective, the whole material world is composed of phenomena that obey the same basic natural laws, part of which are already understood by science, while other parts we might never unravel. According to these laws, all material particles are treated as wave packets describing physical phenomena that change in time and space. These wave packets may be more or less situated in space (that is, they are bound to appear to us as more or less static or might not even be visible at all), depending on their constituent particles and on the conditions. These conditions are the surrounding environment, which itself is made up of particles of certain properties and which might be arranged in some fashion. It is the interaction between these wave packets and the relevant conditions that will define the range of their effective interaction (how far their influence extends and remains significant), for instance, the dimensions of a small box as we apprehend it with our eyes and hands. In spite of particles' (effective) confinement in space, which is related to the spatial decay of their constitutive waves beyond the region in which they are defined, fundamentally their presence extends infinitely, and simply fades over distance. This allows us to imagine various interactions among all material particles in the universe, even when they are very far apart, and even when these interactions are not felt in our physical world (Einstein et al., 1935; Schrödinger, 1935, 1950).[9]

This physical quantum theory I would like to apply to mental phenomena as well. Every mental phenomenon is characterised by certain features entailed by its components, combinations of elements made up by more subtle elements, which, in turn, are composed of basic mental "particles", the most basic that any human, according to Pāli Canon Buddhism, has ever managed to experience. The mental aspect of the self, which we imagine as continuous, stable, and relatively solid, appears at a deeper level as a quantum phenomenon in its own right. It, too, with all its thoughts, feelings, memories, expectations, sensations, and reactive habits, whether conscious or not, making up a "personality", all this is nothing but a phenomenon that can be broken down into its components: mental particles which constantly arise and fade away, conditioned by one another and subject to change. Its presence, too, whether "solid" or "fluid", extends infinitely (though gradually fading), and its particles interact with all other particles in the universe. So, it is only reasonable to assume that the influence of the self's particles does not remain limited to its perceptible boundaries but, to some extent, touches and affects its surroundings. This is why the surroundings of a depressed person will be characterised by some of this person's particles, will be in some significant interaction with them, and whoever happens to be there will be affected, consciously or unconsciously. The surroundings of an angry person will either carry particles of her or be in significant interaction with them, and whoever happens to be there will be affected, consciously or unconsciously. Similarly, the surroundings of someone who is happy, loving, or calm, will either carry particles of her or be in significant interaction with them, and whoever happens to be there will be affected, whether or not they are aware of this. From this perspective, the illusion of separateness is wholly unfounded. Indeed, that illusion dissolves in the particulate process of analysis that Vipassanā meditation offers, as it transforms the experience of conditioned arising into a straightforward and accessible experiential infrastructure. Anna, a Vipassana student puts it like this: "When I take a peep inside and check what's really there, what I see is an infinity of mind and body particles in constant motion, emerging and vanishing, each, as it were, bumping into other nearby particles and setting them in motion . . ." What Anna experiences inside herself is quantum logic and it affects her entire perception of reality, inner as well as outer.

She continues, "It's on the level of my sensations and it's always there. Something in the solidity of the structure of my self keeps dissolving steadily, gradually, in a very unmysterious way. The construct of the self is definitely present, and I feel how tightly I hold on to it and the complex ways in which it shapes my experience. But I can see it for what it is: a construct through which I see myself and the world, not an absolute truth."

A long way away from Ogden's description of the borderline mode, in which one is stuck in one's own subjective point of view, unable to perceive it as such, Anna's subjective perspective became transparent to her, losing its status of absolute truth and allowing her to look deep into the nature of her inner reality. Recognition of the particulate and ephemeral nature of the self, which, according to Vipassanā, can be achieved by means of systematic investigation of bodily sensations, draws attention to the following aspect of reality: the self, like all other surrounding phenomena—mental or physical— is nothing but a vibrating accumulation or mass (even if it is not formally accurate to refer to the mental as a "mass"). In this manner, realisation of the inconstant nature of phenomena forms a gateway to realisation of the conditioned nature of things, devoid as they are of an essential self-core. If I am nothing but a vibrating mass of particles and if you are nothing but a vibrating mass of particles, and if both the wall and the air between us are nothing but a vibrating mass of particles, then obviously the boundaries between us are not fixed, and we are, one way or another, dependent on one another, exchanging particles (of mind and of body), "flowing", or oscillating, in space, our influence on each other extending into infinity.

"Just as I see multitude of particles inside me," Anna continues, "all in collision and setting each other into motion, I also see how my particles encounter those of the people around me, how they are set into motion and influenced by them, and how my particles collide with those of others, set them into motion and affect them in return."

Yet, this should not imply that the phenomenon called "Anna" is identical to the phenomenon "Mark" and to that of "wall". Neither does it suggest that "Anna" and "Mark" can fuse or that "Mark" can pass through the "wall". For the "classic" level still exists and holds. The perceived boundaries between inner and outer environment, therefore, are largely illusory, or only conventional, but not to an extent that denies the very existence of individual phenomena, and not to an extent that denies the more relative level of reality where there appear to obtain—even if only superficially—rather different laws.

Returning to the issue of how mental materials pass from one person to another and the direct influence of mind on mind, we must acknowledge that not all mental material that passes in the way described above is projective identification. What I described just now refers to a law that relates to all types of influence between minds (and bodies), not only to those cases that the psychoanalytic literature calls projective identification. For a mental action to qualify as projective identification, it must evince one of the following (unconscious) intentions: the fantasy of planting something in the other with the aim either to control them or to destroy them from inside, the wish to evacuate an intolerable experience or to expel an unacceptable self-part, or the urge to stir in the other the same unprocessed experience for the purpose of communicating it to them and so that they may digest it for us. However, the very recognition of the self as a vibrating particulate phenomenon makes this "mysterious" influence achieved by means of projective identification into something more palpable and present.

In projective identification, the evacuation (in fantasy) of mental materials into the other is an active process: something in the projecting subject's mind wishes to expel these materials and takes action. In those cases that cannot be properly called projection or projective identification, does the influence of a person's mental materials on the people around him occur of its own accord? Is the subject from whom such influence emanates a passive participant? Should we think of it as a kind of diffusion or seeping, like that of fluid materials, or as an influence like that of the oscillations one observes in apparently solid materials, so that the person in question plays no role whatsoever? I believe the answer is that mental materials in these cases impact their environment by their mere existence, like particles of matter. But the way the materials are constituted inside the subject is very much an active process, and someone is responsible for it. Thus, it is not only the unconscious wish to expel mental material into an object for a certain purpose, which constitute as projection, enactment, or an externalisation, but the very emergence of this mental material too is an enactment, an externalisation, and it is actually expressed: actual in the sense that it itself is a non-neutral mental act, with consequences in the world, and an accountable owner.

If, let us say, at some point or another, I harbour a sense of shame, something of its qualities will diffuse into the interpersonal space in which I take part. I have no control over this. The encounter between the residues of my own past actions and the components of the present moment has, one way or another, generated this sense of shame and now it is here. Being the owner of the shame, I am responsible for it, and, right now, for the mental action I generate or fail to generate in response to its unpleasantness. If my mental structure, at this particular moment, is unable to bear the unpleasantness, it will try to expel it and rid itself of it, turning me, as a result, into the (unproud) owner of the act of projection. If, however, my mental structure can contain the shame, then the associated pain will remain, more or less (though never entirely) limited within my mind–body "boundaries". Still, because the boundaries staking out my mind–body are permeable, relative, tentative, and illusory at the deepest level, something will always seep out (if we follow the model of "flowing" materials) or, alternatively, will affect my surroundings through oscillations and infinite extension (if we follow the quantum model). In this case, it will at least not be accompanied by projection's *kammic* charge, which I discuss shortly. But if I manage, in addition, to maintain a true equilibrium *vis à vis* this shame (i.e., to be in no way distressed by its unpleasantness), then my own pain, too, will begin to dissolve so that, at this particular moment, no more pain will leak out or otherwise affect those around me.

Acknowledging the particulate nature of the self, its non-essentiality, and the fluidity of the boundaries between it and the so-called "external" world, might be a threatening experience. The experience of being the object of projective identification might also be felt as threatening—though in a different way—to the unified, well-defined, and seemingly protected sense of self: one finds oneself invaded by mental materials "from the outside", materials which are, as said, by no means pleasant. If suddenly I find myself overwhelmed by a sense of suffocation or crushing pressure that appears out of nowhere, what, here, is internal and what external? What, if anything, envelops me and protects me with a boundary? Who am I, or what am I not, in other words, and is there anywhere safe against such invasions? The need for a solid, well-defined sense of self is a basic need. But I think that this, precisely, is what Epstein was thinking of when he said that the reinforcement of the functional aspects of the self—those that promote equilibrium, integration, and a synthesis based on the non-rejection of contradictory impressions—is a necessary condition for the healthy disintegration of representation-building aspects, which one clings to as an illusory remedy against anxiety. Anna, who has the ability to empty her self-experience of an absolute personal meaning while not experiencing rupture and who can slowly dissolve her self without going to pieces, can also naturally and undramatically experience the chaotic complexity of her very existence and its conditioned becoming with the people around her without feeling threatened.

* * *

If we acknowledge the permeability and relativity of intermental boundaries, and if we recognise the exchange of mental materials between one mind and another and the manner in which each constitutes the other, we find ourselves in a fluid, web-like reality. The components of this reality affect one another in complex and particular ways and they always arise conditionally. The realisation that we constitute one another leads to a number of insights: that the harmful influence of negative mental materials in one person's mind can spread to others, that one does not really get rid of undesirable materials by expelling them into an other, and that hurting the other by projecting negative materials also hurts the one who projects. A person might find himself invaded by another's mental materials, temporarily lose his sense of solid selfhood, and be impelled to act in various ways. What happens here, however, is not an exact duplication of experience from one subject to another, or the transfer of mental material as such from one empty and passive human vessel to another. The recipient of the projection, whether it is a mother, an infant, a therapist, patient, partner, peer, or anyone else, takes in the transferred material as he or she does with any other component of reality, according to the law described by the chain of conditioned arising. He or she perceives and experiences it through the subjective apparatus, self-screen, interpretation, and pushing-away-or-preferring reaction that are specific to her or him. This is how the experience arising in them becomes "theirs": not just in the sense that it was passed on from another person and now they, too, feel it, but also by its encounter with their personal mental substructure and interaction with its specific traits. Although the principle of conditioned arising suggests the absence of separation between subjects in the way they generate mental materials, it does not cancel out the subject's part in what results. While the feeling, the sensation, the state of mind or behaviour that has passed to the one who received the projection indeed arose in him as a result of the other's projections, now they are his and so he becomes responsible for them; they turn into his own mental action, into his own *saṅkhāra* and *kamma*.

CHAPTER SIX

Projection as mental action that induces suffering

Sometimes I forget completely
what companionship is.
Unconscious and insane, I spill sad
energy everywhere. My story
gets told in various ways: a romance,
a dirty joke, a war, a vacancy.

Divide up my forgetfulness to any number,
it will go around.
These dark suggestions that I follow,
are they part of some plan?
Friends, be careful. Don't come near me
out of curiosity, or sympathy.

(Rumi, 1995, p. 47)

When a person does not contain his emergent experience, when he is unable to be aware and even-minded about it, he will express it in action. A therapist might observe a note of sarcasm in her own voice when answering a patient who was acting aggressively, or she might find that she is recoiling in her chair. Struck by a revolting thought in the presence of the person facing her, she might flinch, or she might frown when feeling critical or disapproving. In the best case, these mental–vocal–bodily actions receive the therapist's microscopic attention as she feels professionally and personally obliged to do so. In everyday life, however, such expressions pass across our faces unnoticed, and even when we are aware of them we often do not feel obliged to stop them, or, at least, to keep them to a minimum. In all these instances—and even more so where it concerns projective identification—two minds are playing catch with their mental contents: each in turn identifies the input coming from the other side, "catches"—or perceives—it, and reacts. One person's projections, sensations, and reactions constitute the projections, sensations, and reactions of the other; the two are tied together, mutually conditioned. This way of understanding the interpersonal process, or, alternatively, construing it according to the quantum model, both illustrate how a mental action can actually influence the other person, thus supporting the point of internalising the law of *kamma*: that is, perceiving the internal (mental) action as a factor that carries real results in the world. They also illustrate how one cannot escape the painful consequences of one's unhealthy mental actions, even (or, the more so) when they are unconscious, and also (or, the more so) when one tries to get rid of them by expelling them into another. By reference to these two aspects, this chapter describes the act of projective identification as *akusala kamma,* a mental action that inflicts suffering on both sides involved.

The "kammic" charge of projection

The law of *kamma* relates to actions of the body, speech, and mind, but its internalisation entails that all of these are fundamentally marked by *saṅkhāra*—the mind's action or volition. Similarly, in the case of projective identification, the transfer of mental materials is achieved by means of a plurality of interactions along various channels of communication through acts of speech or body, verbally or non-verbally (Kernberg, 1987). All of these, however, are nothing but enactments of mental actions and intentions, their evolving outwards, indications of their presence and intensification.

According to Meltzer (1983), just as words pass information from one mind to another, so, too, language can serve as a tool for projective identification to transfer states of mind from one person to another. A certain choice of words will pass mental materials, as well as the tone, pace, volume, and style in which they are conveyed. As long as it is charged with the unconscious intention to expel, evacuate, control, manipulate, or effect communication by means of the transferral of experiences the one who projects cannot himself bear, almost any act can serve as a means for projective identification. Any action can fulfil this function, even, as happens in the following case described by Ogden, through the body odour a person develops.

> Robert developed an intense bodily odor that silently accompanied him and that lingered for hours following his departures from my office. He would lie back in the soft chair in my consulting room with his greasy hair on the hard, padded back of the chair. The aspect of the transference–countertransference interaction that I was most aware of at the time was the way in which I felt invaded by this patient. When he left my office, I could not feel that I had a respite from him. I felt as if he had managed, in a literary way, to get inside of me—to get under my skin—by means of his odor that was saturating my furniture (with which I had become closely identified). I eventually understood these feelings as my response to (unconscious participation in) a projective identification in which the patient was engendering in me his own feelings of being painfully and unwillingly infiltrated by his internal object mother. (2004a, p. 57)

Projective identification is a mental action with a "*kammic* charge"; it is, in other words, reactive and, hence, generative, a constitutive part of the process of becoming. Projective identification is based on the wish to be rid of what is insufferable, or on greed for the object, expressed in a wish to control it from within. It is often based on the rejection of difficult mental materials and the wish to expel them, accompanied by envy, hatred, and destructiveness directed toward the object of the projection (Klein, 1946), and in extreme circumstances, toward reality as a whole (Bion, 1959). It is rooted in ignorance, confusion, and illusion because it relates to a false perception of reality, and because it has a blinding quality that tempts those who engage it into involuntary participation in a reality suffused with pain.

> The unconscious intersubjective "alliance" involved in projective identification may have qualities that feel to the participants like

something akin to a kidnapping, blackmailing, seduction, a mesmer-
ization, being swept along by the irresistible frightening lure of an
unfolding horror story . . . (Ogden, 1994b, p. 105)

It is grounded, then, in what Buddhism conceives of as the three
roots of suffering: craving or greed, aversion or hatred, and ignorance
or delusion. Its *kammic* charge is, therefore, "akusala"—negative or
harmful. Being *akusala kamma*, projective identification is an act
entailed by ignorance and suffering which, in its turn, brings about
ignorance and suffering to both parties involved.

The suffering experienced by the object of projection

Materials passed on through projective identification are connected to
suffering. In Ogden's illustration, above, what got under his skin was
the experience of being "painfully and unwillingly infiltrated", and
we have already encountered Bion's description of how the infant
projects her death fears into her mother. The projection of disgust,
destruction, guilt, anger, and objectification were already mentioned
earlier. Benjamin (2004), for instance, describes how feelings of shame
and being "bad" invade the object of projection by means of projective identification; and Feldman (1992) describes the projection of
resentful submission or angry recrimination and blame. Such distressing contents threaten the mind and body of the one into whom they
are projected, especially when that person is, like the therapist, in a
state of containing openness and empathy (Abadi, 2003). They
threaten his mind by invading it and leaving their traces and they
threaten his body by possibly affecting it and sparking off unpleasant
physical reactions and sensations, as well as—in very extreme pathological cases, when transference of murderous rage finds expression
in an actual deed—leading to aggressive behaviour (Grand et al.,
2009). Projection, then, carries a painful charge: it is the result of the
projecting person's suffering and injects suffering into the recipient of
the projection.

The nature of this charge depends both on the particular contents
projected and on the motive of projection. Clearly, the projection of a
reasonable degree of anxiety, guilt, or sense of injustice, due to an
unconscious wish to connect to the person into whom they are

projected, the unconscious yearning to be known and familiar to her, or the wish to arouse her empathy is relatively harmless compared to the massive projection of murderous rage or feelings of suffocation or paralysis, guided by the violent attempt to invade the object and control her from inside or destroy her. The more extreme the trans-ferred contents, the more dramatic their effects. The more "malignant" the motive for the projection, the more pain, potentially, it will carry. Whoever uses projective identification, in any case, causes suffering to the receiver of their projection.

> Herein, I believe, lies a great misunderstanding in the concept of "normal countertransference." Both theoretically and ideally the analyst is supposed to be mature enough, and well analyzed enough, to be able to "handle" all of the patient's projections. The concept of trial identification (whether counterprojective or introjective) seems to cover this idea. Yet I believe, if therapists were really honest, they would admit to experiencing suffering from virtually every instance of symbolic or actual assaults by their patients, including practically all instances of negative transference, disrespect, intrusion, manic defenses, etc. (Grotstein, 1995, p. 483)

Mental pain passes from one person to another in the transference (Grotstein, 1995, p. 485), even where the object successfully copes—in psychoanalytic terms—with the transferred negative materials. Grotstein (1995) argues that the transference, as an event, reproduces the mythic structures of exorcism and crucifixion. For projective iden-tification to work, there is a similar need for human sacrifice. In projective identification, and especially where it features as part of transference–countertransference dynamics, the subject chooses an external object who will absorb his frustration and dissatisfaction. This role is fulfilled by the mother and by the therapist: they take into them-selves the infant's and the patient's pain which actually passes into them through projective identification. In doing so, the former sacrifice themselves for the latter, they suffer for them, taking away their pain for them in much the same way as does the shaman or the healer. For the infant, the expectation that the mother will function not only to feed him, but also to remove pains and secretions, as did the placenta and the umbilicus when he was in her womb (Grotstein, 1995), is a proper and necessary part of his development. However, because projective identification may occur throughout life and as part of all kinds of relations, the responsibility of the adult person for the materials produced and passed on by his mind is another question.

The suffering of the projector, and the role of the object in fuelling or interrupting it

The projector hurts her object of the projection in some way or another, but projective identification is associated with suffering for the one who projects as well. Klein and her followers point out that the very (unconscious) effort to exert control over the object of the projection to get him to behave in accordance with the projector's fantasy requires a great investment of psychic energy and is a huge strain. The process depletes and impoverishes the projector until the projected parts are successfully returned to him (Ogden, 1979). Someone who projects her ability to love or to understand stays without them until they are restored and reintegrated into her mind and someone who projects her envy and anger stays bereft of the ability to process and include them in her personality which, instead, becomes riddled with gaps, splits, and disconnections coming between her and the ability to be fully in touch with reality.

The Buddhist perspective centres its attention on the suffering of the one who generates the mental action. According to Buddhism, any act that harms another person harms the one who carries it out. If one strives (consciously or unconsciously) to harm another person, one must produce a negative mental reaction stemming from the three unskilful roots (i.e., delusion, greed, and hatred), and these destroy the very mind that produces them (Iti 50). One aspect in the internalisation of the law of *kamma* is its ethicisation: the mental action has actual consequences, and the person in whom it arises is held fully accountable for it. The act of projection involves an (unconscious) attempt to remove an internal danger by relocating it, in fantasy, outside the self, as if it were somebody else's (Ogden, 1986); thus, it entails an attempt to dodge responsibility for a mental content by attributing it to an external source or by expelling it into another. Projection is done on the unconscious assumption that the attribution of the unwanted (representation) or the evacuation of the unwanted (mental component) into an external object will alleviate suffering. This, however, is not the case.

Useful as this mechanism may seem in allowing the individual to disavow some portion of the meaning of an event or a percept in order to reduce the associated painful affect (Weisman and Hackett, 1961), it alters rather than solves the problem. As Waelder (1951) said, even if projection shifts the focus from self to other, "the denied instinct remains in the limelight; he who projected his aggressiveness onto others has his mind occupied with aggressiveness, albeit somebody else's" (p. 174). The noxious affect is still being experienced, but it is attributed to the other. (Nathanson, 1986, p. 178)

As it is understood that the boundaries between one mind and another are not solid and that the minds of different people mutually depend through relations of conditioned becoming, it is natural to assume that, unlike the fantasy underlying splitting and projection, it is not possible to get rid of unwanted mental components by casting them outside the perceived boundaries of the self. The psychoanalytic literature, in fact, also suggests this. Any attempt to discard a difficult feeling or a conflict by placing it, through projective identification, with someone else alters the problem but does not solve it. The projector stays in close touch with what he wished to remove; he is preoccupied with it and affected by it (Nathanson, 1986, p. 178). If something was projected into another person, who now, as a result, is induced to act in a certain way, then the projector, having unconsciously attempted to avoid dealing with a distressful feeling, now finds he has to deal with an externalised version of that feeling. Someone who projects outward his destructive and hateful feelings will take back in a persecutory world; a person who projects confusion, frustration, inanity, indifference, or contempt will re-absorb the image of an other with these properties and be hurt by them. To the extent that his projections are part objects hailing from his earliest relations, he will tend to experience the suffering associated with the reproduction of a painful past reality.

Here, the influence of the object of projection on how things evolve is highly significant. The notion of projective identification and the container–contained model have served as the basis of in-depth discussion of the role of the object of projection and of the outcomes of the latter's reactions to what has been projected into him. The therapist, or anybody else on the receiving end of projection, rather than an empty receptacle, is a dynamic field situated between listening and interpretation (Wender, 1993), between sensory input and evoked reaction: "Between listening and interpretation lies the analyst and the man, his cultural–historical circumstances, his own neurosis, his countertransference, the phenomenon of the 'overlapping worlds': all that set in a unique dynamic field . . ." (Wender, 1993, p. 1137).[10] The material that is transferred to the therapist is charged and, hence, it takes an effort to deal with his experiences as they meet with his own psychological apparatus, his past experience, his repressed unconscious, his personal conflicts, fears, and difficulties (Ogden, 1979). When the specific psychological apparatus of the object of projection does not allow him to properly cope with the projected materials, he himself will deploy non-integrative mechanisms such as denial, splitting, projection, projective identification, or enactment. These mechanisms take one of two ways of rendering the failure to process the projected materials: by avoiding conscious experience of the transferred experiences, or by acting out these experiences or the defences formed against them. This failure in coping with projection has harmful implications: now, when the projector reinternalises the projections, they are already augmented with the fears belonging to the object of projection and with his impaired ability to cope with them, thus further increasing the projector's pain (Ogden, 1979). This is why the therapist, who is expected to function as a "professional" or "skilled" object in terms of receiving his patients' projections, must profoundly investigate his own complexities.

> We have noticed that no psycho-analyst goes further than his own complexes and internal resistances permit; and we consequently require that he shall begin his activity with a self-analysis and continually carry it deeper while he is making his observations on his patients. Anyone who fails to produce results in a self-analysis of this kind may at once give up any idea of being able to treat patients by analysis. (Freud, 1910d, p. 145)

Yet, no matter how professional and skilled, the therapist will still face many occasions when he loses his mental bearings and gets stuck in the quicksand of the situation. Then he will experience a variety of reactions which either leak into the interpersonal sphere or, if he manages to keep them relatively confined to himself, will nevertheless be felt to be suffocating, or paralysing, or in any other way making it hard for him to extricate himself from the situation and get a grip on the events, of which he is likely to become aware only after the fact

(Waska, 2013). On such occasions, the therapist (reacting to the patient's projections) is immersed in his own ignorance and suffering, which lead to enactments reproducing the patient's painful realities, further fuelling his projections and suffering. Thus, having absorbed the projector's pain, the object of projection either transforms this pain or is himself transformed by it (Grotstein, 1995). He, therefore, either manages to "neutralise" the activating influence of the pain by means of the awareness he successfully directs at what is happening to him and by means of his reverie, which transforms it, or, failing to do so, he plays into the hands of projection and finds himself acting and feeling other to himself. (This failure does not have to last. He can later recover and use the insight gained by the experience in service of the therapeutic process.)

Working with projective identification and countertransference means consciously engaging with the interpersonal sphere as within a web that is spun while it is being investigated. This is the paradoxical mode of being of the person who is determined to see reality from the margins of the blind spots that mark her field of vision, to know it through the ability to know, which lies at the edge of her unknowing. If the mind, perforated by blind spots of ignorance, is the only instrument by which it can investigate itself, then every single interpersonal moment holds the tendency to perpetuate the cycle of projection and suffering as well as the opportunity to break it. This is how Racker puts it,

> Now the decisive moments arrive. The analyst, subdued by the patient's resistance, may begin to feel anxious over the possibility of failure and feel angry with the patient. When this occurs in the analyst, the patient feels it coming, for his own "aggressiveness" and other reactions have provoked it; consequently he fears the analyst's anger. If the analyst, threatened by failure, or, to put it more precisely, threatened by his own superego or by his own archaic objects which have found an "agent provocateur" in the patient, acts under the influence of these internal objects and of his paranoid and depressive anxieties, the patient again finds himself confronting a reality like that of his real or fantasied childhood experiences and like that of his inner world; and so the vicious circle continues and may even be re-enforced. But if the analyst grasps the importance of this situation, if, through his own anxiety or anger, he comprehends what is happening in the analysand, and if he overcomes, thanks to the new insight, his negative feelings

and interprets what has happened in the analysand, being now in this new positive countertransference situation, then he may have made a breach—be it large or small—in the vicious circle . . . (1968, pp. 141–142)

Where the therapist is unaware of his own charged countertransference reactions, he might, by re-exposing the patient to an archaic object, cause him to stay locked in a cruel vicious circle (Racker, 1968). If he deploys the difficult feelings the countertransference aroused in him in a conscious and non-reactive way, then he is in command of a powerful tool for interrupting the vicious circle. Following the logic of an eye for an eye, Racker argues, every positive transference is answered by positive countertransference and every negative transference is answered by negative countertransference, and conscious awareness of this process is a necessary condition if one wants to avoid drowning in one's own countertransference. The therapist should also develop awareness of his own, ongoing countertransference reactions because they are instructive about the patient's experiences. Thus, he can place himself in a position that allows him to make effective use of his countertransference reactions instead of being controlled by them (Racker, 1968). According to Vipassanā, what this involves is a person's awareness of the sensations she experiences in her encounter with reality and of the mental reactions this brings in its wake. It is only natural that the positive feelings and ideas expressed for a person (holding, as we all do, a firm grip on her sense of self) trigger "positive" (and by this I mean, in this context, pleasant) sensations in her, and that the negative feelings and ideas yield "negative" (i.e., unpleasant) sensations. In the absence of awareness of such occurrences, or in the case of failure to understand their conditioned arising, the result is craving or aversion, perpetuation of the cycle of suffering, and "immersion" in saṃsāra. The person who functions as an object of projection is at a crossroads: either she identifies her mental reactions to the transferred material or she acts out on them. What will determine the path taken is her tendency to anxiety, her defence mechanisms, and, more than anything, the predominance of her tendency to repeat as opposed to her ability to bring things into conscious awareness (Racker, 1968).

The practice of Vipassanā casts light on this crossroads, drawing full attention to it. This can be formulated as follows in Buddhist terminology. At any given moment, two paths unfold before man: either he is aware and clearly comprehends the true nature of the sensations arising in him, his interpretation of the event, and of his reactions to these sensations and interpretation, if there are any, or he is unaware of these phenomena or their true nature, and remains blind ("blackmailed" or "immersed" or "mesmerised"), deluded in other words, leading him to react in an unbalanced manner by generating yet further craving and aversion. Which path a person will take is determined by the old aggregates of *saṅkhāra*s he or she carries. It is they that dictate whether the person will tend to repeat—create new *saṅkhāras*—or be able to become aware and to develop equanimity, lack of preference, and lack of reaction. For Buddhism, this constitutes the crossroads between the continued feeding of the chain of becoming and suffering and its reversal. While non-knowing and repetition perpetuate the cycle of suffering, it is broken by awareness and equanimity. (I discuss these factors and the manner in which they break the circle of suffering in Chapter Eight.)

The pitfalls in using the notion of projective identification

Safran (1999) warns that using the notions of projective identification and containment could form a subtle barrier protecting the therapist against the full and immediate experience of troublesome feelings. The very fact of looking at things through these concepts, which form a ready-made frame for understanding the experience, is bound to generate a distancing perspective: "In the moment that I think of myself as 'containing my patient's projective identification', I distance myself from my lived experience" (p. 7). For the party on the receiving end of the projection, another risk of interpreting a certain action as projective identification is that of avoiding responsibility: if something that has been deposited with me comes from outside, then it is not mine and, therefore, I carry no responsibility for it. Ogden (1979), discussing the nature of the interpersonal influence deriving from projective identification, restores full responsibility to the object of projection for the way he copes with the projected material: "In fact, the 'influence' is real, but it is not the imagined absolute control by means of transplanted aspects of the self inhabiting the object; rather, it is an external pressure exerted by means of interpersonal interaction". He continues,

... The recipient's feelings may be close to those of the projector, but those feelings are not transplanted feelings. The recipient is the author of his own feelings albeit feelings elicited under a very specific kind of pressure from the projector. The elicited feelings are the product of a different personality system with different strengths and weaknesses. This fact opens the door to the possibility that the projected feelings (more accurately, the congruent set of feelings elicited in the recipient) will be handled differently from the manner in which the projector has been able to handle them. A different set of defenses and other psychological processes may be employed by the recipient so that the feelings are "processed", "metabolized" (Langs, 1976), "contained" (Bion, 1959a) or managed differently. (Ogden, 1979, p. 360)

There is a gap between the projector's fantastic wish to "plant" parts of him or herself in the object of the projection, and the actual influence of the process of projective identification on the one who receives the projection. Although influence occurs in actuality, it does not exactly coincide with the realisation of the projector's fantasy. According to Ogden, the actual influence is the outcome of the inter-personal interaction. While the experiences that arise in the object of projection are induced by the pressure for them to be experienced, and while they do resemble those of the projector, they arise within a different person (Ogden, 1979). This can also be considered from the point of view of quantum theory, in which matter's capability for motion in space, for flowing or "seeping", is not a necessary condition for its capacity to influence its surroundings. It affects these surroundings by virtue of its very being, and its influence takes different forms because it possesses certain qualities. What this implies is that the one who receives the projection is not a passive object, shorn of responsibility, who is under the influence of magical powers stemming from the outside. Rather, she is the owner of her reactions: her own traits matter in determining "the effective range of interaction" that the "wave packets" (the projected materials) will have in their surroundings (i.e., her mind). Her abilities will decide whether she succeeds in undergoing a "trial identification" instead of total identification with the material projected into her: that is, whether she is able to be tentatively involved with it, but, at the same time, manages to transcend it, or whether she is crushed by it (Grotstein, 1995), subsequently reacting with projective counter-identification[11] (Grinberg, 1962). Her ability to contain and to process whatever arose in her as a result of projective identification will determine whether she will either add another link to the cycle of blind reactivity or contribute to undo it.

These observations are in tune with the view that the materials transferred to the object of the projection become "his own", and, thereby, enter the domain of his responsibility. From a Buddhist perspective, it does not (essentially) matter whether what triggered a certain experience originates in the weather, food, the look of another person, or his words. The sensory input differs, obviously, but the way in which it is dealt with is the same. When one happens to be somewhere where it is either too hot or too cold, one will have to (mentally) cope with the resulting unpleasant sensations and either one succeeds or one fails. When eats spoilt or bitter food, one has to deal with the unpleasant sensations this entails—successfully or not. Similarly, when one finds oneself the object of another person's projections, one will have to manage the unpleasant sensations brought about— successfully or not. "Success", here, implies a non-reactive way of coping which does not pass on the suffering, which does not involve enactments and does not involve generating suffering in the one who received the projection. "Failure" would be an unbalanced reaction, *akusala kamma* or *saṅkhāra*—that is to say, a reaction reflecting the fact that the object of projection failed to transform the pain and instead underwent transformation himself.

Additional issues: the projection of "good" elements and the unconscious nature of projection

Although Klein mainly referred to the aggressive side of projective identification, we have seen that, from the outset, she noted that good parts of the self, too, get projected into the object and deposited with him or her. This is due to the projector's unconscious fantasy that they will be safe there from her own destructive impulses. So, even if certain theoreticians (such as Kernberg) adopted the view that only aggressive, unwanted, and unappreciated parts are disposed of by projective identification, others include in their definition the projection of "good", wanted, or valued materials or contents as well (Lotz, 1991; Sandler et al., 1989). The question, then, is, does the transfer of "good" materials by means of projective identification differ in terms of its *kammic* charge from the projection of "bad" materials? The answer is that since each and every action has certain outcomes in accordance with its specific attributes, each action has its own particular *kammic* charge. But, essentially, whether projected material is a "good" or a "bad" part/content does not determine whether the projection itself is *akusala* or *kusala*, harmful or beneficial. Where the projected materials are advantageous, the act still causes suffering to the receiver of projection as well as the projector. So, when the patient, for instance, projects into the therapist the little hope he has for the therapy to succeed in order to defend it, in fantasy, against the inner forces he (unconsciously) feels are threatening to destroy it, then the therapist will feel hope in his stead, while he, the patient, will have lost the ability to experience it. Perhaps the therapist will have, as it were, an agreeable feeling: "hope". However, this hope is a burden. It is an external imposition and she is now likely to feel impelled to come to the rescue of the patient or take unrealistic responsibility for him. She will now, moreover, have to interact with a patient who is entirely devoid of hope—something that entails suffering in its own right. For the projector (the patient in this case), too, the act is marked by suffering. Having deposited his hope with another, he is left with his despair; a self-part has left a void in him that will remain empty until it is restored. The fact that projective identification is *saṅkhāra*— a reactive mental activity involving aversion and craving—places it in the chain of conditioned arising, which indicates that it naturally brings about suffering. From a Buddhist point of view, then, projective identification, even when the transferred contents are "desirable" or "good", is never free of a negative charge.

As said, not merely the interpersonal aspect of projection, but also its intrapersonal, fantastic aspect, has actual consequences. *Saṅkhāra* is *kamma*, whether it is perceived as interpersonal or as existing in the "external" world, or whether it appears to be only internal. By extension, not only an "internal" action has actual outcomes, but so does an unconscious one. In fact, the outcome of unconscious actions is graver and more significant. Freud (1920g) assumes that all excitatory processes leave fixed traces that form the basis of memory. These traces have nothing to do with conscious activity; actually, when the process engraving them in the mind does not enter conscious awareness at all, they are the stronger and more persistent. The same logic obtains for the *saṅkhāras* whose residues reflect the traces of past experience (affecting both present and future): they have powerful influence when they remain outside conscious awareness, and when they are investigated in its light, their power wanes (given that this awareness is accompanied by non-reactivity). A charged mental action that remains unconscious will tend to hold sway over the subject that hosts it. If he is unwittingly anxious or angry, he is bound to project this anxiety and anger on to various elements of the situation or other people. If he is aware of the anxiety and anger, chances are that he might take responsibility for them rather than allow them to impel him. This is the case for every situation and every feeling: "However much he loves his patients", says Winnicott, "he cannot avoid hating them, and fearing them, and the better he knows this the less will hate and fear be the motive determining what he does to his patients" (1949, p. 69). Whether or not he can avoid hating or fearing them, Buddhism and psychoanalysis do *not* agree about this. Yet, I believe we can definitely say that they see eye to eye about the latter part of Winnicott's statement.

To emphasise this point, here is another observation. The Western literature errs, according to Nyanatiloka (1997), where it considers *saṅkhāra* a subconscious tendency or an unconscious force. As a link in the chain of conditioned arising, *saṅkhāra* is a wholly conscious and active *kammic* volition, rather than a latent tendency and, as one of the five aggregates (consciousness, perception, sensation, reaction, and materiality), only some of the factors *saṅkhāra* includes are subconscious, and they, too, are not mere tendencies. It must be noted, however, that considering *saṅkhāras* as an intentional and conscious action does not suggest that it is an intentional and conscious action in the psychoanalytic sense. Moment by moment, day and night, *saṅkhāras* are generated in a process that usually remains outside conscious awareness (unless this generative process is interrupted and reversed, as I shall demonstrate in the final chapter); yet, they are not "repressed" in the psychoanalytic sense of that word, since they are actually always accessible to conscious examination, as long as they receive the proper attention. *Saṅkhāra* is an automatic reaction; it does not happen intentionally. It is affected by reactions which, having been repeated in the past, now inform present actions. Still, it is an intentionally directed action, in so far as it includes a predisposed, non-neutral internal movement of the kind that strives to get rid of the unpleasant and maintain the pleasant, and it is a tendency in so far as it is like a riverbed through which water flows along the same track that earlier water has carved out. It is, however, not "a mere tendency" in the sense that it has, as said, real consequences in the here and now.

*   *   *

Projection, as we have seen, is based on a false perception of reality and, via various channels, it creates suffering for both parties involved. This process, however, much like the one described by the chain of conditioned arising, is neither linear nor one-directional. This is why it is not just that a false perception of reality entails suffering; suffering itself, too, leads to false reality perception. Suffering and grief affect the mind negatively. Where they occur, it becomes troubled and confused: "Sorrow, pain, grief and despair are inseparable from ignorance, and lamentation is the norm for the deluded being. For that reason, when sorrow is fully manifest, so also is ignorance fully manifest" (Payutto, 1995, p. 47; VIS 576).

Ignorance arises with the rise of suffering (Payutto, 1995; VIS 577), and prevails as long as suffering prevails (Payutto, 1995; VIS 529). In the case of projection, projective identification, and the transference–countertransference dynamic, the transferred suffering brings along confusion, "temporary loss of insight" (Bion, 1961, p. 149; Spillius, 1992, p. 69), the experience of being seduced and mesmerised (Ogden, 1994b), and the risk of getting caught in a cruel vicious circle (Racker, 1968). Thus, the suffering that passes through these actions breeds deception or non-knowing, which, in their turn, cause more pain. In Buddhist theory, the vicious circle between suffering and non-knowing is expressed by the notion of *saṃsāra*, whose cyclic, self-perpetuating nature is explained by the chain of conditioned arising. The next chapter, referring to the notions of "transference" and *saṃsāra*, discusses the close interrelations between the absence of conscious awareness and the reproduction of suffering.

CHAPTER SEVEN

Transference and *saṃsāra*

"It is precisely psychoanalysis that, in the ambit of scientific thought, subverts the radical split between the subject and its object of observation, by introducing the concepts of transference and countertransference. That is how psychoanalysis revealed the historical and unconscious determinants in the individual's disposition to knowing—inaugurating a revolutionary theory of knowledge in which the outer edge is given by the blind spots present in the observer"

(Abadi, 2003, p. 224)

Nothing remains static in the world of mental activity. If the reactive mental action behaves like water and sediment carving a gorge in the rock, then the more they flow through the gorge, the deeper it gets, and the deeper it gets, the more water and sediment tend to flow through this particular gorge. The mental function *saṅkhāra* refers, as mentioned, to the water and sediment as well as to the gorge, to the fabricator and the fabricated, the forming element and the element being formed, to the reaction generating a habit, and to the habit generating a reaction. Doidge speaks of "the plastic paradox", according to which the neuroplastic qualities of the brain are responsible both for its flexibility and its rigidity. On the one hand, they allow it to change according to the conditions it encounters, and to adapt itself to them; on the other hand, they lead to fixations when these adaptive behaviours repeat themselves and become habits (Doidge, 2008). These two points of view explain why, in terms of the nature and quality of the mental action, as long as we do not reverse harmful mental habits, not only do we not "develop" or "grow", but we contribute to the relentless slide down the slope of our own personal suffering. Fixation is not stagnation; it is a generating–reproducing process. What lies between generation and reproduction? One possibility for exploring this dialectic can be found in the dialogue between the psychoanalytical concept of *transference* and the Buddhist concept of *saṃsāra*.

That same old pain: transference as a reproductive saṃsāric *activity*

In transference, the patient unconsciously attributes feelings, qualities, and ideas originating in his or her earlier relationships to the therapist (Ogden, 1979). In a sense, transference brings the past back to life along with the feelings, defences, and object relations that used to characterise it (Klein, 1952). Freud explains it as follows:

> What are transferences? They are new editions or facsimiles of the impulses and phantasies which are aroused and made conscious during the progress of the analysis; but they have this peculiarity, which is characteristic for their species, that they replace some earlier person by the person of the physician. To put it another way: a whole series of psychological experiences are revived, not as belonging to the past, but as applying to the person of the physician at the present moment. (Freud, 1905e, p. 116)

Some of these transferences, he says, replicate the original situation in every way except for the therapist, who serves as a surrogate. In others, the repetition is expressed in more sophisticated forms: their content is sublimated, and they are likely to become conscious by using a feature of the therapist or the situation as an anchor they can cling to in order to create those "revised editions" (Freud, 1905e, p. 116).

Under the influence of their inherent dispositions and early experiences, every individual develops a particular way of conducting
mental life, which can be identified as organised according to specific
stereotyped patterns. These patterns come alive, are repeated, and re-
imprinted time and again, as much as the circumstances of life allow,
and they are directed at figures and situations in the present (Freud,
1912b). From a Buddhist point of view, the perceptual function, *saññā*,
whose role it is to attach a mark to the object so that it can be recognised again in the future (VIS XIV: 130), plays a central part in creating those stereotyped patterns according to which a person perceives
and handles reality. The other central player in forming these patterns
and reproducing them is the *saṅkhāra*. As mentioned earlier, in one of
its senses, *saṅkhāra* is a tendency or an impression: it is an accumulation of residues produced by past mental actions, which now directs
present and future actions, or, in other words, the particular way in
which a person's mental life is conducted. Since *saññā* is fuelled by the
subject's blind spots and existing stocks of *saṅkhāra*s, it cannot operate
in a clean or lucid manner. Therefore, the mark it attaches to the object
(in this case, a person or a situation) is affected by its "inherent dispositions and early experiences". "Early", in this context, refers not only
to infancy or childhood, but, rather, to any time in the past: moments
that have just gone by, previous years, and even the more distant past
of previous lives that Buddhist perspective assumes.

According to Freud, when reality fails to fully satisfy a person's
need for love, he or she is bound to approach every new person they
meet with a mental state of anticipation. In transference, this state of
anticipation joins the mind's tendency to resort to prototypes it perceives outside, attach itself to pre-existing internal stereotyped patterns, and bring the two together. Thus, the subject's mental energy is
transferred to the therapist, and invested in him or her (Freud, 1912b).
Through the operation of *saññā* and *saṅkhāra*, the mind introduces the
therapist "into one of the psychical 'series' which the patient has
already formed" (Freud, 1912b, p. 100), and, as in every projective
activity, it connects the past with the present, the conscious with the
unconscious, and the pre-existing with what is currently being experienced.

The concept of projective identification expanded our understanding of the nature of transference and the process by which it occurs
(Joseph, 1985). Joseph points out that the substitution taking place in

transference—the substitution of a figure from the past with that of the therapist—can be seen as an aspect of projective identification as defined by Klein. According to this, parts of the self and internalised object-parts are projected (in fantasy) into the therapist, who then becomes identified with them (Joseph, 2001).

> If we go further and enquire what is it that is being projected, we can observe that sometimes it is more a part of the ego, for example it may be the patient's capacity to think is projected into the analyst, and the patient becomes passive and pseudo-stupid; or it may be the sense of guilt which is felt as unbearably persecuting by the patient who then tries unconsciously to rid himself of it by making the analyst feel at fault and guilty . . . (pp. 182–183)

In other cases, transference might manifest as the repetition of the "total situation" (Joseph, 1985) or an entire relationship, in which case the patient tries to manipulate the analyst into playing a role that belongs to his past, but still holds great significance for him in the present in terms of his inner world and his unconscious expectations from the external world (Joseph, 2001).

For example, let us imagine a man who, as a result of his early relationships, came to experience himself as unbearable; perhaps because he was a particularly temperamental baby, who was restless or difficult to soothe, or perhaps because his parents had a poor ability for bearing. Let us consider further the possibility that this man goes on with his life, conducting it in the particular way he acquired from this experience, which involves the (unconscious) urge to repeatedly re-create the experience of being unbearable in the world. So, he might, through projective identification, induce his therapist, friend, or wife to feel that he is "too much"; probably by repetitive, dramatic, or tedious behaviours, until they are exhausted and compelled to abandon him, physically or emotionally, just as his mother or father did early in his life. The position of the therapist comes with a built-in responsibility to be aware of this possibility and resist the urge to succumb to it; that is, to participate in the re-creation of abandonment and, thus, fuel the painful repetition of the patient's past. Others, however, are not as obligated to this kind of careful therapeutic demeanour, and often might choose (and perhaps rightfully so) not to remain in close contact with someone who makes them feel this way. Ultimately, the one responsible for the outcome of this "transference", although it happens unconsciously, is the one from whom it emerges. He is the one whose mental actions generate it, and he is the one who will not be able to escape the suffering it re-creates. He is the one who will continue to encounter the same old painful patterns everywhere he turns, as long as he does not extricate himself from the urge to replicate them through transference.

It is clear, then, that along with the entire situation, including all the experiences and mental processes involved, transference replicates suffering. Freud saw this, of course, and described how

> Patients repeat all of these unwanted situations and painful emotions in the transference and revive them with the greatest ingenuity. They seek to bring about the interruption of the treatment while it is still incomplete; they contrive once more to feel themselves scorned, to oblige the physician to speak severely to them and treat them coldly; they discover appropriate objects for their jealousy; instead of the passionately desired baby of their childhood, they produce a plan or a promise of some grand present—which turns out as a rule to be no less unreal. (1920g, p. 21)

Why, asked Freud (who, up until then, used to think in terms of the pleasure principle and the reality principle subject to it), does such systematic and persistent repetition of painful patterns occur in a creature dominated by the search for pleasure and the avoidance of unpleasure?

Freud identified this fundamental problem manifest in the phenomenon of transference, and in other forms of systematic and persistent repetition of unwanted painful experiences, such as the post-trauma tendency to vividly and compulsively relive the traumatic event time and time again through nightmares and flashbacks. In the face of this reality, he went on to re-examine the predominance of the pleasure principle. As a result, he developed the idea of "repetition compulsion", which he defined as an uncontrollable process, in which one intentionally (albeit unconsciously) puts oneself in distressing circumstances replicating certain experiences from the past, without remembering the prototype they are re-creating and without understanding the connection between them (Lazar & Erlich, 1996).

Freud argued that under this compulsive tendency, one tends to repeat unhealthy patterns, which lead to the same miserable results, time and again. He considered, for example, someone whose *protégés*, though very different from each other, all end up deserting him in anger, leaving him to experience the bitterness of ingratitude, or someone whose friendships all end up with the friend betraying him. Or the person who, time after time, promotes someone to a senior position, only to replace him with another after a short time. Or yet another, whose romantic relationships all go through the same phases and all reach the same conclusion (Freud, 1920g). None of these situations caused those experiencing them pleasure in the past, and it would be reasonable to assume that if they were to reappear in the form of memories, they would cause considerably less pain than when they reappear as live re-creations. Nevertheless, they happen again and again, as if under compulsion, as if this was predestined to be, sentenced by some higher power. It is even more curious, according to Freud, when this painfully accurate repetition does not seem connected to the subject's active behaviour:

> This "perpetual recurrence of the same thing" causes us no astonishment when it relates to active behaviour on the part of the person concerned and when we can discern in him an essential character-trait which always remains the same and which is compelled to find expression in a repetition of the same experiences. We are much more impressed by cases where the subject appears to have a passive experience, over which he has no influence, but in which he meets with a repetition of the same fatality. There is the case, for instance, of the woman who married three successive husbands each of whom fell ill soon afterwards and had to be nursed by her on their death-beds. (Freud, 1920g, p. 22)

The feasibility of these cases could be explained by the law of *kamma* (*karma*) and the chain of conditioned arising. According to these, as mentioned earlier, it is not only external acts (physical or verbal) which have consequences, but, rather, first and foremost, mental actions, whose cumulative effect serves as the central force both in the formation of what is referred to as the subject—his personality, traits, and the way he encounters reality—and in the unfolding of his life's circumstances. Therefore, even the reality of the woman who found herself nursing three different husbands on their deathbeds is a product of some form of "active behaviour" from the near or distant past, even if it was "only" mental behaviour, even if it was never conscious, and even if we are unable to track down its specific details.

Repetition, production, and preservation

Freud (1920g) examined the forces behind the re-creation of painful experiences, and tried to find the instinctive roots of the repetition compulsion. He asked: how is being instinctual related to the compulsion to repeat? In his answer, he came to far-reaching conclusions regarding the very nature of instinct and of life:

> At this point we cannot escape a suspicion that we may have come upon the track of a universal attribute of instincts and perhaps of organic life in general which has not hitherto been clearly recognized or at least not explicitly stressed. *It seems, then, that an instinct is an urge inherent in organic life to restore an earlier state of things* which the living entity has been obliged to abandon under the pressure of external disturbing forces; that is, it is a kind of organic elasticity, or, to put it another way, the expression of the inertia inherent in organic life.
>
> This view of instincts strikes us as strange because we have become used to see in them a factor impelling towards change and development, whereas we are now asked to recognize in them the precise contrary – an expression of the *conservative* nature of living substance. (Freud, 1920g, p. 36)

Every modification forced on the course of the organism's life is received by the preservation instincts and "stored up for further repetition" (Freud, 1920g, p. 38). Therefore, even though these instincts seem like forces striving for change and progress, all they are truly after is to return to the oldest, most initial state of things, a state more ancient than existence itself—death (Freud, 1920g). If that is so, Freud concluded, then "The aim of all life is death" (Freud, 1920g, p. 38), and the theoretical importance of the instincts of self-preservation, self-assertion, and mastery suddenly seem far more inferior. In this light, they appear as instinct components whose sole function is to "assure that the organism shall follow its own path to death, and to ward off any possible ways of returning to inorganic existence other than those which are immanent in the organism itself" (Freud, 1920g, p. 39). If this is the case, then these life keepers (the self-preservation instincts) are none other than death's submissive slaves.

We find ourselves faced with a paradoxical situation in which a living being fights with the greatest intensity against those events (namely, dangers) that could have helped him attain his goal faster by some shortcut or other. Sexual instincts, from Freud's perspective, are the only ones that do not constantly strive to return everything to the way it supposedly was; none the less, their actions merely delay those of the death instinct, which aspires to drive the organism as quickly as possible toward death (Freud, 1920g). This death is not a general death: the forces Freud described operate within individuals in order to lead them along the specific path designated for them, towards the specific death designated for them, and towards it alone.

In his prominent essay *Beyond the Pleasure Principle*, Freud draws a dualistic distinction between life instincts and death instincts. Far from being simplistic (he never is), he is determined to examine this duality thoroughly; he presents it, doubts it, subverts it, and then validates it once again. He describes a complexity which is not fully resolved: the ego instincts are the preservation instincts, which operate under the reality principle and direct the individual towards behaviours that will (one hopes) not expose him to dangers stemming from a clash between his desires and the circumstances he lives in; on the other hand, they are defined as instincts that strive for conservation, for repetition and not renewal, and, in fact, serve death. As opposed to them, the sexual instincts strive for gratification in ways which, had they been allowed to be expressed and acted upon in an uncontrolled manner, would endanger the individual, and, thus, bring him closer to his death; none the less, they are defined as life instincts, which aim towards the new and delay the movement of the death instincts toward the inorganic end (Freud, 1920g). In the light of all this, it would be reasonable to ask: what creates life and what brings about death? Are preservation and repetition life or death? Does being driven by sexual instincts—which are described here as the only ones not trying to restore things to the way they used to be— really reflect progress toward the new? Are they themselves not compelled and, therefore, repetitive, too? Are sexual instincts not reproduction instincts, namely, instincts to *"re-produce"*?

Buddhist thought puts things in a different light, thus offering some interesting answers to these questions. The Buddhist texts distinguish between three different kinds of "thirst" or desire: the desire for sensual pleasure or attractive sensual objects (*kāma-taṇhā*); the desire for becoming, for life, for specific modes of existence, or for self-identity (*bhava-taṇhā*); and the desire to cease or not to be, which is the craving to escape hated or unwanted objects and situations and be rid of them (*vibhava-taṇhā*). The latter form of thirst is connected to states of despair, self-hate, and self-pity on one hand, and to resentment, anger, and aggression on the other (Payutto, 1995). As expected, some have compared Freud's life instinct to the desire to become, and his death instinct to the desire to cease being (Payutto, 1995). However, according to the Buddhist point of view, the seeming polarity of the concepts is ultimately not very significant on a deeper level. It is true that each of these forces is connected to different mental actions, which lead to different results, but, above and beyond all that, thirst is thirst: a tendentious mental reaction constituting a life-creating force, and, therefore, a force driving the continuous becoming of the individual in *saṃsāra*, and in the inherent misery of it.

Buddhist conceptualisation offers an outlook which settles, if one could say such a thing, the unresolved complexity Freud was dealing with: it suggests that those same "life giving" or "creating" forces—namely, the mental reaction (*saṅkhāra*), craving (*taṇhā*), clinging (*upādāna*), and becoming (*bhava*)—are indeed the forces that lead to the repetitious re-production of harmful habits associated with suffering. According to this approach, the urge to preserve and the urge to interfere with preservation serve the same objective: as long as they stem from blindness, they repeatedly lead the individual through the same old patterns—like those described and discussed by Freud—in a never-ending *saṃsāric* cycle. Therefore, "preservation" and "production" do not contradict each other, since Buddhist preservation is not static preservation such as death, such as the restoration of an "inorganic" state or an "earlier state of things". It is the preservation of a pattern, the perpetuation of a cyclic (or spiral) movement, the elements of which are constantly changing, constantly creating and being created.

Repetition compulsion in motion: burning, inertia, and the misconstrued "nirvana principle"

Freud postulates that the objective of the forces of preservation and control is to see to it that nothing diverts the organism from its unique and particular path toward death. This corresponds with certain aspects of the law of *kamma* and conditioned arising. According to the law of *kamma*, the actions generated by an individual create her individuality with its unique characteristics, and these, in turn, stipulate the manner in which the person continues to perceive the world and react to it—or, in other words, influence her future actions. The actions—*kamma* and *saṅkhāra*—accumulate, or, in Freud's words, are "stored up for further repetition". The more they repeat themselves, the more they mark out the particular path that person follows, determine the course of her life, and lead her to her own specific death. What is *saṃsāra* if not a process sustained by the forces of repetition and habit, by the mental action's tendency to reinforce itself and perpetuate the painful results of the gorge it deepens every time it re-creates itself? What is *saṃsāra* if not the compulsion leading a living being towards its own specific death, again and again and again?

However, thinking about this process in terms of inertia, as Freud suggests, seems too passive in relation to the forces that maintain the cycle of *saṃsāra* as described in the Pāli Canon: the forces of action, urge, will, desire, thirst, and becoming, which are also depicted as "burning" (SN 5.7). Freud calls the inertia principle the "Nirvana Principle" (1920g, p. 56), defining it as mental life's dominant tendency to strive to reduce internal tension, keep it constant, or remove it altogether; a tendency manifested in the pleasure principle, which simultaneously indicates the existence of the death instinct (Freud, 1920g, p. 56). This definition seems far from the original and correct definition of *nibbāna* (Sanskrit: *nirvāṇa*), which, even though it refers to a state which can be defined in negative terms (cessation, extinguishment, i.e., literally, putting out fire by depriving it of what usually feeds it), nevertheless, this extinguishing is of every fire, this cessation is of every desire, including the desire to cease.

> Then he neither mentally creates nor wills continuity and becoming (*bhava*) or annihilation (*vibhava*). As he does not construct or does not cling to anything in the world; as he does not cling, he is not anxious; as he is not anxious, he is completely calmed within (fully blown out within *paccattaṃ yeva parinibbāyati*). And he knows: "Finished is birth, lived is pure life, what should be done is done, nothing more is left to be done". (Rahula, 1974, p. 39)

Thus, in *nibbāna*, all internal tension is removed, or, more precisely, suffering (*dukkha*) can no longer arise, since its direct cause—the burning of thirst—has been eliminated. However, the cessation in *nibbāna* is not a return to an earlier state of things, neither is it the "cessation" expressed in the notion of death, which, according to Buddhism, is but another link in the chain of conditioned arising and is not final at all; rather, it describes a different state: one which does not belong to the sphere of life and death. Even the term *nirodha* (destruction, cessation, annihilation) which serves as a synonym of *nibbāna*, and which is considered a stronger expression when referring to the active destruction of the causes for becoming (Rhys Davids & Stede, 1921–1925), does not indicate the cessation of something that already exists. Instead, it indicates the non-appearance of something due to the elimination of its cause (Payutto, 1995), and, therefore, is not in keeping with Freud's description in regard to the reduction, conservation, or removal of internal tension. Hence, Freud's inertia principle is situated between the pleasure principle and the death instinct, between the craving for pleasantness inherent to the reduction of tension, and the craving to return to an inorganic state, and, therefore, is closer in its field of reference to the desire to be and the desire not to be than it is to *nibbāna*.

If the model of inertial movement does not accurately describe the nature of *samsāric* movement, how can one better characterise it? Lazar and Erlich (1996) name three spatial behaviours, through which the human mind produces repetition: linear, circular, and spiral. Of these three, the linear alternative is obviously irrelevant: *samsāric* movement is a complex chaotic movement, and is, therefore, not in line with a world in which events are directed toward any particular purpose. Instead, it suggests an exceedingly dynamic reality (Biderman, 1995), consisting of countless unstable particles, constantly moving and shifting, appearing and disappearing, affecting and conditioning each other through multiple reciprocal relations. Out of the three spatial models, then, only the second and the third can be rightfully attributed to *samsāra*. *Samsāric* motion is circular in the sense that, from moment to moment and from life to life, the twelve links (of the chain of conditioned arising) and the five aggregates (four mental and one material) comprising the so-called individual are endlessly re-created: whatever arises out of ignorance or the absence of awareness leads to suffering, which, in turn, feeds an additional delusion; whatever comes into being and is born goes through illness and/or old age, and then death, which is immediately followed by an additional coming into being and birth; whatever touches consciousness is taken in, recognised, experienced, and evokes a reaction which gives rise to the consciousness of the next moment. But the word "circle" indicates a return to the same point every time a certain route is completed, which, in a sense, is inaccurate in this context. The mental and physical functions do indeed repeat themselves in the process of becoming and passing away, from moment to moment and from life to life; however, it is impossible to say that the consciousness of this moment is the consciousness of the previous moment, and certainly not that of a previous life (Biderman, 1995). The same applies to the other functions constituting the subject: it is true that they all feed on the past and come into being on the same "*kammatic* continuum", but, since they are ephemeral and conditioned, they are not identical to themselves. These functions are definitely returning or repeating, but not to the same point, and not of the same thing; therefore, their return or repetition could be more spiral in nature, and this, too, not in an orderly, predictable, and purposeful manner. The *saṃsāric* fabric is a highly dynamic, transient, quantic fabric. Its motion is cyclic and replicating, but it can never really go back to the exact same point. It is infinite, but at the same time can be interrupted and transcended.

The long reach of saṃsāra *and intergenerational transmission*

The dynamics Freud describes, in which the organism's inner forces compel it to repeat, re-create, and replicate situations that generate suffering, and to be pushed, as a default, towards its own specific death, can be seen as a version or a case of *saṃsāra*. However, Freud's *saṃsāra* is limited to a single lifetime and, therefore, its repetition is limited as well. In this sense, it is perhaps comforting: at least there is an inevitable end to suffering. From a Buddhist point of view, this is a nihilistic outlook—one that denies the results of actions, or, in this case, limits them to a period of one lifetime. According to the Buddha's teachings, a person's responsibility for his actions does not end after the few decades of his present existence, and, as long as the chain of conditioned arising in which he is captive has not been broken, he will continue to be held accountable for his actions—good or bad, those rooted in ignorance, craving, and hate, and those not rooted in ignorance, craving, and hate—even when he is no longer the individual he is today.

In this context, it is interesting to introduce the phenomenon of intergenerational transmission, in which certain patterns of conducting mental life and the suffering accompanying them are transferred from one generation to the next. As mentioned, the minds of the parent and the child are inseparably connected. They are dependent on each other, condition one another, and grow out of each other. This being the case, the impressions left by past experiences in the parents' minds, along with the manner in which they navigate their experience of reality, and the way they conduct themselves in the world (especially in the world of interpersonal relationships), will inevitably be significant factors in the constitution of their children's external and mental reality (see for example: Barratt, 2016; Berger, 2014; Lassmann, 2013; Shabad, 1993). Each of us carries within him or herself the lasting impressions left by positive nourishing experiences, but also those left by deprivation, hardship, and, in certain cases, trauma. When a mother or a father are unaware of painful experiences they underwent earlier in life, or of the effect these had on their minds, whether relatively minor and subtle, or profound and all-embracing, one can only assume that some of the resulting complexes will be transferred, one way or another, to their children. An example from the more subtle end could be that of a woman whose mother's behaviour always led her to believe that she did not have enough time for her. That woman grew up experiencing reality through a sense of stress and urgency, and, therefore, might communicate a similar message to her children through her words, her deeds, and her very way of being. An example from the more pathological end of the spectrum can be found in a man who was physically or verbally abused as a child by his father, and has now become an abusive father himself. Either way, "The fathers [and mothers] have eaten sour grapes, and the children's teeth are set on edge" (Jeremiah 31: 29); and the determining factor in how much they will be set on edge, or how much the suffering re-creates itself over the generations, will be the degree to which the parent is aware of the impressions left in her by those difficult past experiences, or the degree in which the feelings associated with those impression are accessible to her consciousness and are not repressed (Fraiberg et al., 1975).

But awareness of feelings and of those past events that evoked them is often not enough if those individuals, who have now become parents, truly want to break the chain of suffering they themselves were subject to and not pass it on to their children. In order to achieve this, according to Vipassanā meditation, it is also necessary for them to become aware of the physical sensations that arise when those past impressions imprinted in them meet the specific characteristics of current reality, and for them to develop the ability to stand firm in the face of these sensations, not to act on them, but to see them for what they are, without rejecting or inciting them. Shira, the woman whom I mentioned at the beginning of the book, and who went through a process in which she stopped unconsciously pushing away unpleasant sensations and feelings, was capable, upon becoming a mother, of allowing her children to fully express their negative feelings without trying to deny them, silence them, or shut them out. Even though such expressions on their part evoked sensations that were very unpleasant for her, she was able to cope with them. She did this by observing her physical sensations, understanding their transient nature, and cultivating equanimity toward them, which gradually started replacing the urge to unconsciously and automatically get rid of them. Unlike her former self, her children are allowed to feel sadness and anger without fear, and, therefore, when these feelings come up in them, they are able to experience them consciously. In this sense, the process Shira went through enabled her to start breaking the chain of intergenerational suffering, not only for herself, but for her children as well.

Although very different, intergenerational transmission, operating within the Western psychoanalytical frame of thought, and not according to the multi-period paradigm of conditioned arising, provides another model indicating the continuation of suffering created by one's blindness, beyond one's lifetime as one particular individual. The suffering described in the case of intergenerational transmission does not occur on the same personal "*kammatic* continuum", but, rather, skips from one individual to another; however, this model also stretches one's responsibility for one's mental actions, both conscious and unconscious, beyond the span of one's own individual life, since the results of these actions do not have an obvious end when this specific life is over. The end of suffering must be attained; it is not to be passively awaited.

Transference as an arena for the struggle between awareness and ignorance

According to Freud (1914g), transference is inseparably intertwined with resistance to remembering, succumbing to forgetting, and the compulsion to repeat, and serves all three of them. It plays an important and complex role in the analytical process: it is the arena in which the struggle between the impulse to remember and the resistance to it takes place—the struggle to make the unconscious conscious. Every time an unconscious complex is about to be exposed, it is partially pushed forward into consciousness through transference, and then immediately pushed out again by persistent defences. The further the process goes, the more the patient repeatedly realises that the distortions her mind creates in the pathogenic material—distortions by means of transference—are unable to provide real protection against its exposure, and, paradoxically, consistently continues to create these distortions (Freud, 1912b). The patient re-creates her unconscious urges and acts them out in order to avoid "remembering" them (Racker, 1968): She must ". . . *repeat* the repressed material as a contemporary experience instead of, as the physician would prefer to see, remembering it as something belonging to the past" (Freud, 1920g, p. 18).

These repetitions or "reproductions" of painful patterns from the past, which reappear "with such unwished-for exactitude" (Freud, 1920g, p. 18), are acted out in the realm of transference; that is, they manifest themselves in the patient's attitude towards the therapist, and, thus, turn the neuroses into "transference neuroses" (Freud, 1920g, p. 18), whereby complexes imprinted in the past become complexes expressed toward the therapist in the present. The struggle between the ability to understand and the impulse to act takes place, according to Freud, almost exclusively in the field of transference, and "It is on that field that the victory must be won—the victory whose expression is the permanent cure of the neurosis" (1912b, p. 108).

The transference to the figure of the therapist is only a part of the whole picture, in which repetition, used as resistance to remembering, is expressed by displacing the forgotten past into the situation in its totality and into other relationships the patient is maintaining at the time (Freud, 1914g). The original definition of the term "transference" refers to the analytical situation, but it is clear that it is a much wider phenomenon, which occurs throughout life and affects all relationships (Klein, 1952).

Let us imagine a baby who, nearly every time he nursed, was interrupted and stopped by his mother before being fully satisfied. Let us assume that, as a result of her impatience and poor ability to devote herself to him which brought about these rash interruptions in nursing, she also developed a habit of suddenly pushing him away when he was snuggling up to her or looking for warmth and contact later on in his childhood. Due to her own personal complexes, this mother was unable to adjust herself to her child's pace and needs. So, the repeating experience created for him was one in which any nourishment, love, and satisfaction are always abruptly and prematurely withdrawn. Now, let us also assume that as this child grows up, the same basic experience that was so deeply imprinted in him is re-created; that in every interaction he has with others and with the world, a situation comes up for him in which, in some way or another, someone or something interrupts him abruptly or leaves him "prematurely". He is studying for an examination, and is suddenly overcome by a splitting headache that forces him to stop studying, and, as a result, he ends up with a mediocre grade on a test that he otherwise could have succeeded in. When spending time with friends and family, he becomes tedious or annoying after a while, so they tend to interrupt him or rush off before he gets the chance to complete his ideas or feel satisfied in some other way. At work, he always seems to get caught up in some kind of interpersonal turmoil, or otherwise unintentionally sabotages the task he is in charge of, and, as a result, is dismissed or loses his status just when he is about to start enjoying the fruits of his labour, which were well deserved up until then. He hurries to end romantic relationships that seem good and promising, or he becomes unbearable at some point, and his partner leaves him herself.

This person is creating new editions of the story of his past misery. He is driven to re-create them uncontrollably and unconsciously, in keeping with the nature of the repetition compulsion. The *saññā*, or the projective function of his mind, recognises each of these cases as "a potentially nourishing and satisfying event", and this recognition gives rise to the same relational emotional pattern that is normally generated in such cases. He projects an early prototype of a situation on to current reality, and, through projective identification, induces those around him to take part in his "timeless internal drama" (Ogden, 2004a, p. 85). In this way, he influences external reality, causing it to take on certain qualities that are reminiscent of those past situations, qualities to which his *saññā* clings in order to re-validate the belief that "Yes, there really isn't any satisfaction (in the world/for me), and anything good will always be interrupted, taken away from me, or will leave me prematurely." Since his world, to use Ogden's words, is "blanketed in a shroud of transference projections" (2004a, p. 85), he cannot access new experiences or digest the ones he does have in relationships which are basically more healthy and nourishing, and which, under different circumstances, could have offered him that which he so longs for. In other words, he cannot learn from experience. He re-creates instead of remembering, and re-experiences instead of being aware. He finds himself caught up in a vicious circle, a closed circuit, unknowingly going round and round, enslaved in a *saṃsāric* prison in which ignorance and the residues of past mental reactions repeatedly feed the way he encounters the world, perceives and interprets it, reacts to it, and creates his own continuous becoming in that same prison.

It is almost unnecessary to say that in using the expression "a closed circuit" I in no way imply that the misery that person experiences remains confined and limited to himself; his relatives, colleagues, and spouse are all likely to suffer from the dynamic he creates, in which nearly every time a real accomplishment or contentment seems to be within reach, some discouraging and undermining forces interfere, cut short the positive momentum, and prevent its fulfilment.

* * *

The connection between remembering and transference is complex. On the one hand, an inverse correlation exists between remembering the original past experience and re-creating it through transference; therefore, according to Freud, the analyst must strive "to keep this transference neurosis within the narrowest limits: to force as much as possible into the channel of memory and to allow as little as possible to emerge as repetition" (Freud, 1920g, pp. 18–19). On the other hand, the very repetition that is carried out through transference embodies the potential of remembrance, and the connection between the original experience and the current one allows the unconscious to become conscious. Hence, the therapist cannot spare the patient this repetition on which the success of the therapy is dependent:

> He must get him to re-experience some portion of his forgotten life, but must see to it, on the other hand, that the patient retains some

degree of aloofness, which will enable him, in spite of everything, to recognize that what appears to be reality is in fact only a reflection of a forgotten past. (Freud, 1920g, p. 19)

According to Klein (1952), in order to access the past, one inevitably needs to pass through its later expressions: "In fact it is not possible to find access to earliest emotions and object-relations except by examining their vicissitudes in the light of later developments" (p. 437). When the therapeutic process opens up routes to the patient's unconscious, the impulse to transfer her early experiences, feelings, and object-relations to her therapist is kindled. In addition, since she finds herself facing the same conflicts and anxieties, which have been reactivated in her, she turns to the same mechanisms and defences she would have used in the past. This is how the past is revived in her: "The total situation" as well as all the elements composing it (Klein, 1952, p. 437). These "new editions" of infantile complexes, processes, impulses, and feelings, which present themselves by means of transference, are the ones, according to Racker (1968), that reintroduce into consciousness what memory cannot re-create. Through these current expressions, one can touch the past, with its real and fantastic aspects, all woven together in the patient's mind. Only by an in-depth analysis of the transference situation—both positive and negative—can the past, as it lives and breathes in the subject's mind, be revealed (Klein, 1952).

In the context of the struggle between the impulse to repeat and the ability to understand, the expression "to remember" is identical to the expression "to make conscious" (Racker, 1968), whereas to "repeat", to "transfer", and to "enact" are used to indicate not only the resistance to bringing into awareness something from the past, still operating and painful in the present, but also the situations which bring about the opportunities for it to emerge and enter conscious awareness. Therefore,

> If a female patient desires to have sexual relations with the analyst, she repeats this desire not "to not recollect" her sexual desire towards the father (since it is the same), but she repeats it instead of "remembering", for example, certain aspects of her situation as "the excluded third." (Racker, 1968, p. 51)

What we have here, then, is an unconscious mental activity, which carves an alternative route to the path leading to awareness; a route in which one unconsciously chooses to project one's formerly imprinted patterns on to present reality, thus creating a relived (internal–external) reality, instead of seeing one's internal reality for what it is.

The field of potential reversal

Transference is the field of the present where the past and its sorrows are revived and re-created; precisely for that reason, it holds the opportunity to touch what was created in the past, since it has now become present—the only true portal into the past. It is interesting to consider, at this point, two of the Buddha's "four noble truths", which deal, respectively, with the existence of suffering, its cause, the possibility of eradicating it, and the way to do so. According to the second noble truth, the cause of suffering is craving, which emerges, arises, and prospers anywhere in the (mental and material) world, where the subject encounters anything pleasurable. Therefore, according to the third noble truth, the eradication of suffering is dependent on the eradication of craving, and the field in which this eradication is possible is the same one in which it arises: that is, anywhere in the (mental and material) world where the subject encounters anything pleasurable (DN 22).

If the eradication of craving and suffering can only take place in the same field in which they arise and prosper, then it is impossible to face them and uproot them in any other place but the place where they are reawakened, rise to the surface, and are experienced as present. Just as the reactions of craving (and of aversion) were originally evoked at the meeting point between the subjective apparatus and its respective sense objects (where these reactions established themselves and became habits), so, too, the opportunity to uproot them exists only in similar circumstances, when those very same reactions arise and come alive. Just as in the transference situation, these circumstances are also characteristics of external reality, which, upon meeting the subjective apparatus, set themselves into its formerly imprinted prototypical patterns (*saññā*), so that they are reproduced in the present as habitual reactions (*saṅkhāra*)—compounds of processes, impulses, feelings, and physical reactions. They then re-create experiences, similar to those encountered in the past, such as that of being "the excluded third" in Racker's example, or that of being prematurely detached from everything good, which I described earlier.

The explanation provided by Goenka for the process of uprooting misery-generating patterns within their field of appearance focuses on the concept of *saṅkhāra*, and in directly experiencing the physical sensations evoked as those *saṅkhāra*s resurface. The *saṅkhāra* plays a dual role: in the chain of conditioned arising, it is the second link, the immediate prerequisite for the appearance of consciousness, and, of the four mental processes (which, along with the material aggregate, constitute the five aggregates an individual is made up of), it appears after sensation. (Although it is important to stress that this is not a linear process, and that complex relations simultaneously exist between all functions.) In this latter form, it appears again in the twelve-link chain of conditioned arising, as a reaction of craving or aversion (*taṇhā*), following the seventh link—sensation. This craving and aversion (desire and hate, coveting and rejecting) develops into clinging, which, in turn, leads to a new round of mental and physical activity. Hence, this process is an infinite, self-sustaining, circular (or, rather, spiral-like) process: each *saṅkhāra* starts off a chain of actions that lead to additional *saṅkhāra*s, which, in turn, lead to new chains of actions (Hart, 1987). This is what it means to be rolling in *saṃsāra*, the process of becoming, bound with suffering, depicted by the model of conditioned arising and the second noble truth. How can this process be reversed? The answer lies in the awakening of past residues in the present, and in the subject's mental attitude towards them.

As previously mentioned (see Chapter Two), every encounter with an object in reality gives rise to a sensation. This sensation can be the result of two material factors—food and the physical environment—and of two mental factors: a mental reaction occurring in the present, and past mental reactions, which are affecting the mind in the present moment. The body requires material food in order to sustain itself, yet it will continue to live without food, until such time as it has exhausted the stockpiles stored in its cells. So, too, the consciousness: it has a constant need for mental food (much more so than the body) in order to keep flowing, but will continue to flow for a while even if this sustenance comes to an end, until such time as it has exhausted all mental reserves it has accumulated in the past. This mental food is the *saṅkhāra*s—the mental reactions (Hart, 1987). These, on the one hand, are automatically created every moment and accumulated, on the other hand, in what can be referred to as a repository of influential past residues. (This is why *saṅkhāra* is considered to be a productive element, and the immediate condition sustaining *viññ-āṇa*).

What Vipassanā meditation as taught by Goenka offers is a process in which certain conditions are created that invite *saṅkhāras* accumulated in the past to resurface in the present, where they manifest themselves as current physical sensations. In this way, if a person turns her attention to these physical sensations in the present, she is, in fact, accessing her past conditionings; she enters the field in which it is possible to change them, or, in the case of Vipassanā meditation, to eradicate them. In this process, one develops a growing awareness of the sensations one experiences, without reacting towards them with craving or aversion, thus depriving the mind of the food necessary for sustaining its process of becoming and forcing it to turn to its stocks of accumulated *saṅkhāras* and "use them up". When these old *saṅkhāras* resurface, they too find their expression in sensations, and if these do not receive a reaction, their respective *saṅkhāras* will be naturally removed from the stockpile of conditionings, and so on and so forth (Hart, 1987).

In this sense, then, Vipassanā is "a kind of fasting of the spirit in order to eliminate past conditioning" (Hart, 1987, p. 105). It offers a process of eradicating instead of repeating (old patterns of reaction) in which the residues of the past surface, due to specific circumstances stimulating them in the present, and can, under certain conditions, be completely annihilated, never to return again. Although very different from the psychoanalytical methods (directly observing the sensations, while keeping in mind their ever-changing, conditioned, and misery-generating nature, as opposed to using free associations and interpretation of transference), and certainly with a different aim (complete eradication, as opposed to modification, improvement, increase of flexibility, and moderation), Vipassanā meditation offers a way "to make conscious" instead of repeating misery-generating, habitual patterns. Bringing something into conscious awareness is possible only in the field in which the past "returns" and manifests itself in the present, the only field in which the past can be directly accessed and exposed to change and, in this case, to eradication.

It is quite interesting to point out that, just as in the context of transference, Freud's "remembering" means "to make conscious", one of the meanings of the Pāli word "sati" is memory, but, when used in the context of Vipassanā, it means "awareness" or "mindfulness".

Either way, the process is not an easy one: that which was imprinted in the past due to a distorted view of reality bound with suffering reappears in the present in some painful form or other. It requires continuous, systematic, and thorough work, since one is only free to the degree in which one has rid oneself of *kammatic* residues accumulated in the mind. In this uncompromising process, each *sankhāra* must surface in order to be uprooted, "until the time comes when the mind is free of all reactions, past and present, liberated from all suffering" (Hart, 1987, p. 106). The process described by Freud and Klein is also uncompromisingly systematic and thorough: according to Freud (1912b), "every conflict has to be fought out in the sphere of transference" (p. 104), and according to Klein (1952), "It is only by linking again and again (and that means hard and patient work) later experiences with earlier ones and vice versa, it is only by consistently exploring their interplay, that present and past can come together in the patient's mind" (p. 437).

*   *   *

Examples of the "new" or "revised editions", as Freud calls them, can be found not only in therapeutic situations, but in any relational sphere of mental life; anywhere they appear, the *samsāric* misery of blindly repeating painful patterns appears along with them. What follows is an example of this painful repetition, evoked under conditions that allowed the man experiencing it to enter a struggle, ultimately allowing him to extricate himself from it. In this example, inevitably, the cessation of a specific *samsāric* repetition and the awareness and understanding that replaced it became attainable by giving appropriate attention to the manifestations of the past in the present; these manifestations, by nature, could have appeared only in the same field in which their related misery-generating complexes were imprinted in the past, and now have resurfaced in circumstances the mind recognised as similar.

Ethan

For Ethan, surrendering to the practice of Vipassanā was especially difficult. In fact, this in itself brought up one of the central issues of his life, or, if you like, one of the first complexes which had to be expressed by his unconscious in the field of transference. I shall refer to his case on two levels: that of external relationships, which were "blanketed in a shroud of transference projections", and that of introspection, which ultimately allowed the unwrapping of this shroud.

On the first level, the Vipassanā technique, the organisation teaching it, and sometimes one teacher or another, served as objects to whom Ethan transferred a certain prototypical experiential pattern. When he first started learning and practising Vipassanā, he felt compelled to do so, as if he had no choice. Something in him felt that there was a sort of profound truth there about himself, a truth he had to face if he wanted to be happy, but that same "something" was split off from him and projected outward, so that even though he was partially aware of the irrationality of it all, he could not shake off the feeling that someone or something external was forcing him to practise Vipassanā. This created a great deal of resistance and conflict within him: he struggled with himself about the need to choose one technique over others, tortured himself with uncertainty about his choice, and was torn between recognising the fruits of his daily practice and the contradiction that existed between it and his alcohol consumption habits, which he was not prepared to renounce. He alternated between being grateful and full of appreciation for the very existence of this method, which had already begun changing his life for the better, and being full of criticism and even anger or contempt toward certain aspects of it. He fluctuated between the extremes of wishing he had never taken this path to begin with, and the desire to progress as far and as quickly as possible on it. He expressed his reservation and anger externally more than once, convinced he was in the right, and seeing clearly.

On the second level, Ethan was fully and directly experiencing the struggle against surrender that was so significantly influencing his life. He reveals,

"Each time I sat down to meditate, I would get extremely restless. I would try to concentrate and scan my physical sensations in an orderly manner, but something inside me was just going wild. Fighting. Struggling. I felt like a baby struggling in his mother's arms because something really feels wrong there, and he just can't let go, surrender, and relax. During the first few courses I attended [he refers to ten-day residential Vipassanā courses, during which the technique is taught and practised], the feeling would become very intense. Even when I wasn't meditating, actually, especially during the breaks, I felt torn up inside. I was being ripped apart by doubts and conflicts. It felt like bloody battles were raging inside me."

It took about four years of daily practice for Ethan's tormenting internal battles to subside. During this time, one of the main conflicts in his life surfaced—a conflict which, up until then, had been transferred to all of his romantic relationships. Like the baby wriggling in his mother's arms, he could not trust his partners to "hold" him properly and to respond to him out of knowledge and sensitivity, and so he struggled, torn between desire and anger, between an intense longing for a relationship and a near-instinctual desire to shake it off, between the wish to go through life with his (current) partner as far and as fast as possible, and the urge (which was usually realised) to abruptly end the relationship and free himself of it, in tormenting pain or with great relief.

It seems, then, that a prototypical pattern had been transferred from his early object relations to his relationships in adulthood, including his relationship with Vipassanā and anyone representing it. Perhaps, as a baby, he could not trust his mother to hold him properly—physically and emotionally—and, therefore, was unable to feel the basic experience in which "everything is all right; I am in good hands, and therefore I can surrender and let go." Due to this, and because of his resulting transferential repetitions, this same experience persisted in his life as it continued and as his love objects changed; that held true for both human objects (romantic partners, teachers) and abstract ones (institutions, technique, theory, teaching). Only this time, with meditation as the experience-evoking object, the re-created prototypical pattern could be fully experienced under conditions that enabled it to start unravelling. The systematic examination of the constantly changing, unpleasant physical sensations accompanying this pattern allowed him to reach deep into his mind, revealing the manner in which his mental life had been operating. The moments in which he managed to maintain a balanced and non-reactive attitude toward these sensations deprived his stream of consciousness of its "food", making it resort to, and "use up", the reservoir of reactive mental residues that was causing his repetitive pattern. Layer after layer of these residues began naturally to wither away. The clear practicality with which the technique was taught, and the decisive moral guidelines accompanying it, along with the lack of dependency-generating figures, or the availability of figures without any personal interest, provided a strong, flexible, and good enough container, allowing the process to unfold. The absence of counterprojections on the part of the objects on to which Ethan projected created a non-reactive echo which returned all his split-off parts back to him (such as the one which supposedly left him no choice and "forced" him to practise), and gave him the time to go through the process for as long as was necessary, without adding any additional, external fuel.

For Ethan, who has since practised Vipassanā happily and whole-heartedly for many years, the unravelling of this particular complex was a profound process that spread through the entire arena of his life. He found a stable, healthy relationship (he is currently married and the father of three), and he is happy and content in his professional life. "It's not as if I suddenly became the calmest and most serene man on the planet. I still have fire inside, a lot of fire! But I no longer have those tormenting conflicts tearing me apart." Nowadays, Ethan's "fire" is mostly invested in his creative work, and is accompanied by joy. Occasionally, his distrust and his struggle against surrender still pop up (when dealing with the medical establishment, for example). Yet, even when they do appear, he is able to recognise them as leftovers from his old familiar mental residues, not as undisputable reality, and, therefore, he does not experience himself as being at the mercy of mighty forces. They do not shake him up as much, and are completely absent from many areas in his life. With regard to the "fire", it is important to point out that what we have here is not sublimation. This is not a simple case in which the same mental energy has been diverted from destructive outlets to more creative and productive ones. Rather, it is a case in which misery-causing patterns, formerly imprinted in the mind, have been largely dissolved and removed, the tormenting conflicts related to them have been settled, and mental energy has started originating from other, healthier mental materials.

Ethan's case clearly demonstrates transferential repetition of an early prototypical pattern. Actually, when we look into it, we find that whenever deep processes occur through Vipassanā, the same mental residues evoked during practice are expressions both of the forces resisting the process, and the opportunity to move through it successfully, both the tendency toward blind repetition, and the possibility of interrupting it and extricating oneself from it. In Shira's case, for example, the denial of suffering served as a force that resisted the practice of Vipassanā, and threatened to discontinue the process: if everything is all right and there is no misery, what is the point of putting so much time and effort into investigating misery and freeing oneself of it? On the other hand, the very practice of turning her attention to the dulled areas of her body (where misery is veiled or hidden) exposed that same complex to examination. Since she repeatedly came back to those body areas, developing the ability to merely witness the non-sensation of dullness without trying to get rid of it and without ignoring it, then the whole mental pattern related to it began unravelling. Joel's severe anxiety resisted the process and threatened to stop it because it was so acute and due to the fact that it was accompanied by an intense urge to escape. None the less, since the urge to escape was ultimately not acted on, the presence of anxiety provided Joel with the opportunity to face all of its aspects and to start freeing himself of it.

With regard to the therapeutic work, the process takes place in the twilight zone between the resistive aspect of transference and its revealing side, and on the seam between the impeding side of countertransference and its illuminating aspect. In the case of Vipassanā meditation, since the effort is invested in sharpening the instrument of observation (i.e., attention) and focusing it on physical sensations, while nurturing a realistic and unbiased attitude towards them, the process takes place to a large degree in ways that bypass the intellect. Either way, whatever surfaces as suffering and delusion has to manifest as such in order to be examined, and the person examining it through the fog of suffering and delusion must be the same person experiencing them. This is the mind, speckled with blind spots of ignorance, which serves as the only instrument with which it can study itself; this is the combination between the sharpening of this instrument and equipping it with direct experiential knowledge about the web-like reality of conditioned arising, which enables the mind to study itself in a way that slowly removes the veils of ignorance from those very blind spots.

CHAPTER EIGHT

The alternative to projection

Projection and its attendant mode of being are associated with a false view of reality and with suffering both for the projector and the recipient of projection. Each of them, however, has some latitude in the actions their minds produce. At each and every moment, in fact, a person is at a crossroads from which two routes fork: the reactive–replicating one, which fuels suffering and blind reactivity in the projector and in the recipient, and the non-reactive one, which helps in breaking through the vicious circle of blindness and misery. The following pages discuss this non-reactive trajectory. I present the mental alternatives to projection's pain-perpetrating way of being, referring to the different perspectives under discussion: Freudian psychoanalysis and object relations theory, on the one hand, and the Buddha's teaching as it is rendered through Vipassanā practice, on the other. I describe the tools each deploys in the attempt to achieve optimal processing of experience components while avoiding the urge to be rid of them, and the possibility of liberation from the circle of reactivity and suffering through a penetrating look into the ever changing and essence-less nature of sensations.

Integration vs. splitting

For Klein, healing involves a process of integration which comes to substitute for the splitting that dominated the psyche hitherto: a split between persecutory objects and idealised ones; a split between different parts and functions of mental life (Klein, 1952), and—according to Racker (1968)—a split, too, between "I" and "you". Splitting, whichever form it takes, is a necessary condition for projection, and, hence, integration offers an alternative psychic foundation from which other mental actions can emerge. In the case of psychoanalysis, this integration can be achieved through the incessant linking between past and present, as it occurs in the analysis of transference (Klein, 1952). The foremost psychological mode leading to splitting and projection is the paranoid–schizoid position, the alternative to which, in which the use of these mechanisms is considerably reduced, is the depressive position. The transition from the paranoid–schizoid to the depressive position involves a shift from focus on self-survival to recognition of dependence on, and care for, the other (Steiner, 1992) and this can only happen on condition that, instead of part-objects, a whole object is recognised. This development requires relinquishing the polarised view as central experience, in favour of the formation of an ability to perceive shades of grey, to experience ambivalence, and to tolerate a reality that also includes grief and loss. This is why it holds the possibility for creating the reflexive space that enables self-contemplation (Ogden, 1986).

A simple illustration of the different modes of conduct implied by these psychological positions can be found in the contrast between the following two patients. The first patient splits the therapist (and, therefore, himself, as well as reality) into her "good" and "bad" aspects. Initially forging an all-good ideal image of the therapist, he projects his hope of recovery and redemption on to it. When something in the external reality fails to unfold exactly as he imagined it in his "all good" illusion, it seems as though a switch in his mind is pressed: in the blink of an eye the entire reality turns inside out and suddenly the ideal therapist is an incarnation of everything bad and negative. Now the patient turns his anger on to the therapist, his frustration and hatred, accusing her of ill intentions or ineptitude. Illusion rules in both states—the "all good" and the "all bad"—and it is strongly felt in the room. Reality, in both cases, is split into its components and rearranged to serve the primitive defences of a fragile psyche which cannot bear the complex nature of the reality on which, to its great dismay, it depends. In both cases, the patient puts his full attention into an object outside himself, but in a projective manner, rather than with the ability to look inside and explore the suffering reflexively. In such a state of mind, it will seem that redemption has to come from the other, and that sabotage and damage, too, originate in him or her; this focus on the other is an egocentric focus: the patient does not perceive a complete person, a feeling, complex subject, and neither is he able to acknowledge his dependence on this person who is not "all good". At the same time, he is unable, too, to recognise how he himself hurts the therapist with the anger, frustration, and hatred he projects on to her.

Another patient, by contrast, who is not under the sway of the paranoid–schizoid position, even if he mildly projects on to his therapist, on the whole sees a complete person, including her imperfections. Most of his effort goes into looking inside himself and exploring internal causes of suffering, and when something unpleasant comes up, he addresses his inner experience and how it interacts with external reality. He has the ability to feel the interdependence between himself and the therapist as that of two people sharing a co-created environment.

These two modes can, of course, appear in a whole spectrum of relationships: between teacher and student, between child and parent (and *vice versa*), between spouses, or between a person and a collective or abstract object such as a religion, an organisation, or a group. From a Buddhist perspective, the reality perception characteristic of the second approach is less distorted and shows a better grasp of the law of *kamma*. Such a grasp manifests itself in a person's recognition of the fact that a destructive act has consequences, that history cannot be rewritten, and that the magical resurrection of a destroyed object is impossible. The result is that one develops responsibility, empathy, and an ability to reflect on death. The depressive mode of being, therefore, represents a higher level of development than its preceding mode, and shows less reliance on splitting and projection. Yet, here too, defences associated with greed and denial can emerge, leading to projective identification (Klein, 1975b). If its typical psychic achievements are to fully unfold, then the depressive position must be processed successfully and, as we shall see, this does not result in a permanent state.

"Open" psychoanalytic states of mind: evenly suspended attention, reverie, and containment

Psychoanalysis attaches key importance to the qualities of the mother's and the therapist's mental positions, to their impact on the infant and its development into a person as well as on the patient and the therapeutic process. These qualities could be harmful when they are supported by mechanisms like splitting and projection with their typical resistance and lack of integration. When they are channelled into a balanced and non-reactive direction, they may, however, assist in undoing suffering.

As early as in Freud's writing, psychoanalysis was preoccupied with the type of attention and processing the therapist should aim for. Freud argued that analysts, in order to do their job properly, should listen non-selectively and non-judgementally with "evenly suspended attention" (Freud, 1912e, pp. 111–112), or, later on, "free floating attention" (Epstein, 1988b, pp. 174–177). This is the mental corollary (on the part of psychoanalysts) of the method of free association (Freud, 1912e), which requires patients to bring anything that comes to their mind into the analytic space, avoiding any filtering or editing. Evenly suspended attention depends on analysts' ability not to allow their expectations and dispositions to determine what they focus on, take in, and perceive:

> For as soon as anyone deliberately concentrates his attention to a certain degree, he begins to select from the material before him; one point will be fixed in his mind with particular clearness and some other will be correspondingly disregarded, and in making this selection he will be following his expectations or inclinations. This, however, is precisely what must not be done. In making the selection, if he follows his expectations he is in danger of never finding anything but what he already knows; and if he follows his inclinations he will certainly falsify what he may perceive. (Freud, 1912e, p. 112)

To expectation and selective attention, Freud also adds another source of interference, which is the wish to significantly affect patients. He presents the analyst with the following stipulation:

> . . . he must turn his own unconscious like a receptive organ towards the transmitting unconscious of the patient. He must adjust himself to

the patient as a telephone receiver is adjusted to the transmitting microphone. Just as the receiver converts back into sound waves the electric oscillations in the telephone line which were set up by sound waves, so the doctor's unconscious is able, from the derivatives of the unconscious which are communicated to him, to reconstruct that unconscious, which has determined the patient's free associations. (Freud, 1912e, pp. 115–116)

But if this organ is to work properly it must be as free as possible from any blockage and interference in the form of the psychoanalyst's (unconscious) resistance to the material:

> . . . if the doctor is to be in a position to use his unconscious in this way as an instrument in the analysis, he must himself fulfil one psychological condition to a high degree. He may not tolerate any resistances in himself which hold back from his consciousness what has been perceived by his unconscious; otherwise he would introduce into the analysis a new species of selection and distortion which would be far more detrimental than that resulting from concentration of conscious attention. It is not enough for this that he himself should be an approximately normal person. It may be insisted, rather, that he should have undergone a psycho-analytic purification and have become aware of those complexes of his own which would be apt to interfere with his grasp of what the patient tells him. There can be no reasonable doubt about the disqualifying effect of such defects in the doctor; every unresolved repression in him constitutes what has been aptly described by Stekel as a "blind spot" in his analytic perception. (Freud, 1912e, p. 116)

So, according to Freud, analysts must aim for a state of mind in which they neither censure or resist any material, nor are guided by their own expectations or wish to influence. Thus instructed not to reject or to prefer certain contents, analysts are in a state of mind that diverges from the psyche's tendency to judge, select, and prefer—the tendency at the roots of mental reaction, splitting, and projection.

Bion's notions of containment and reverie are even more concise and direct psychoanalytic alternatives to projection: when they work well, the subject is able to receive impressions in an open manner and, even if they arouse unpleasant experiences, to digest them without projecting them back. Freud's model implies a communicative aspect of the unconscious, which aims to reach out to, and be interpreted by, some "receptive organ". One person's unconscious, in this model, "broadcasts" to the unconscious of another person who receives the message and processes it into a conscious product: the interpretation. What this model does not explain, though, is how the transmission passes from one unconscious to the other. Detailed and subtle attention is given to this process in Klein's model of "projective identification", which offers one possible explanation as to how one unconscious communicates with another. The elaborated notion and its definition as a concrete interpersonal act by Klein's followers, together with their view on the role of the object of projection, mainly through the notions of reverie and containment, furnish an explanation of how the object of projection receives the transmission and processes it (Brown, 2004). As said, for Bion, an understanding mother will be able to experience the intolerable feelings which her baby is experiencing by means of projective identification and preserve a balanced viewpoint, rather than falling victim to them (Bion, 1959). This idea reflects the intent that the object of projection—whether mother or therapist—receives any experience projected into him or her, no matter how stressful, without turning away from it, without allowing it to cause her or him the same suffering it caused the projector, and without trying to get rid of it by further projection.

It is on this conceptual basis and in the light of extensive discussion of the notion of countertransference that theoreticians have formulated therapists' preferable approach in a variety of ways, stressing various aspects of the issue. It is generally agreed that the therapist should avoid defending him or herself staunchly against the patient's experiences and feelings, and should accept and be tolerant toward them (Ogden, 1979); that he or she should have the capacity of tentatively identifying with the patient's pain, to be temporarily involved and yet, at the same time, be able to transcend it (Grotstein, 1995); that he or she should remain "constant and unaltered" in the face of the patient's movements between different defensive positions, and in the presence of personality parts appearing and disappearing, while not being dragged into enactment (Joseph, 1975); that he or she should be able to absorb the patient's projective identification and suspend interpretation, to empathically acknowledge their experience without claiming responsibility for it, to bear any aggression without collapsing or developing counter-aggression, and generally to act in line with Winnicott's notion of holding and Bion's notion of containment

(Kernberg, 1987). So, all this suggests that the recipient of projection strives to be open to receive the projective identification, yet not produce a counterprojection or other non-integrative behaviour: that is, to be aware of his or her own emerging experience without reacting by enactment. Both psychoanalysis and Buddhism emphasise the need for a combination between openness to impressions and the ability not to act out on them, physically, verbally, or mentally, something which involves mental aptitudes that could be referred to as awareness and equanimity. The Buddhist terms for these mental qualities— whose features and objectives, as will become clear, are not the same as those of psychoanalytic awareness and equanimity—are *sati* and *upekkhā*.

Sati *and* upekkhā

The Buddha defined the establishment of awareness (*satipaṭṭhāna*) as direct observation within the framework of the body and mind themselves of all physical and mental phenomena as they arise and pass away, without craving, aversion, or clinging (DN 22). This state of mind contrasts with the projective mode which rests on the urge to avoid certain materials, on vagueness about their origins and nature, and on the wish to push them away and throw them out instead of dealing with them within the framework of the same body and mind in which they arose. *Sati* practice aims for the subject to perceive the body as mere body, sensation as mere sensation, mind as mere mind, and the contents of the mind as mere contents of the mind, all of them just as they are, without identification, without preference, without judgement or interpretation, without falsifying perception, reactivity, craving, and clinging. The Buddha directs meditators through continuous, systematic, and diligent practice to develop their awareness to such an extent that only "mere understanding along with mere awareness" (DN 22; Goenka, 1998, p. 276) will remain; that is, without even an interpreting or observing subject, without someone who understands or is aware. They will then be able to see things as they are, not through projections or through the self as a point of reference.

The term *upekkhā*, too, suggests that the alternative to perception through the lens of the self is a reality experience divorced from preference or reactivity:

> Upekkha means equanimity in the face of the fluctuations of worldly fortune. It is evenness of mind, unshakeable freedom of mind, a state of inner equipoise that cannot be upset by gain and loss, honor and dishonor, praise and blame, pleasure and pain. Upekkha is freedom from all points of self-reference. (Bodhi, 1998)

This is a state of no pleasure and no pain, of absolute even-mindedness toward them, an absolute non-preference for any one of them. *Upekkhā*, therefore, is not subject to the pleasure principle, in the absence of which the most basic motive for splitting and projection vanishes.

The Buddha proposes a practice that aims for a mode of being which inextricably ties together these two qualities, *sati* and *upekkhā*. When these two join, a mental attitude emerges which is rooted in the gaze penetrating the psycho–physical reality as such, with all its components, transient and essence-less as they are. This attitude reflects a radical acceptance of, and independence from, experience, and it is often described as a form of indifference.

> Rahula [Rāhula], develop the meditation in tune with earth. For when you are developing the meditation in tune with earth, agreeable & disagreeable sensory impressions that have arisen will not stay in charge of your mind. Just as when people throw what is clean or unclean on the earth—feces, urine, saliva, pus, or blood—the earth is not horrified, humiliated, or disgusted by it; in the same way, when you are developing the meditation in tune with earth, agreeable & disagreeable sensory impressions that have arisen will not stay in charge of your mind. (MN 62, translated from the Pāli by Thanissaro Bhikkhu)

To avoid unfortunate misunderstandings, I will briefly pause at the expressions "radical acceptance", "independence", and "indifference" which I just used. What do they—and what do they not—exactly refer to, in the Buddhist context? To put it succinctly, "radical acceptance" refers to the ability of non-preference of the pleasant and non-rejection of the unpleasant. It definitely does not reflect an approach whereby "everything is subjective" and there is no moral good and evil in the world. It holds absolutely no licence to act—physically, verbally, or mentally—in an unethical or destructive manner, or, in other words, in any way that is entailed by the various forms of ignorance, greed, and hate. "Independence" alludes to a condition in which the psyche becomes so stable—so non-reactive, that is—that life's upheavals and the attendant pleasure and pain can no longer perturb it. One no longer suffers, then, from anything, and one's happiness or calm depends no longer on any specific circumstances. "Independence", however, does not refer to people's separateness or autonomy in their relations with the surrounding world. A phenomenon lacking an essential core, the human individual only exists as part of the inter-relations characterising the mental and physical processes that make him into what he is at any given moment in time, and only as a result of his interdependence with his (internal and external) environment. "Indifference", finally, refers to independence from the pleasant and unpleasant, and, hence, to the acceptance of no matter what experience, but it does under no condition point at mundane indifference. Such indifference clashes with the boundless compassion and love entailed by deep recognition of conditioned existence and its associated suffering, a recognition that is achieved through the gradual dissolution of the illusory self's rigid structure. Equipped with this scrupulous reading of these notions, we can now revert to the special mental quality whereby, just like the earth, water, fire, wind, and space "accept" without reaction whatever comes into contact with them, those who cultivate this quality find themselves beyond the pleasure principle: no longer dependent on the nature of sensory experience, whether it is pleasant or not; free of the need to prefer one to the other; free of the need to react to them with craving or with hate.

Suppressing and fuelling: between two extremes

An experience can be pleasant, unpleasant, or neutral, and usually one copes with it at either one of two reactive ends: by suppressing or by fuelling, by turning away from it or by acting it out. Psychoanalytic thought relates to a certain derivative of these fields of action, which is the one that is tied to conflicts and other defensive processes addressing what is intolerable and hard to digest. Buddhism, in this same context, refers to every molecule of mental action, wherever it is concerned with a biased action that approaches the pleasant and unpleasant with craving and aversion, respectively. We know, anyhow, that the attempt to turn away from experience and escape it no matter by what means—repression, denial, splitting, or projection—is bound to fail in the sense that any (unconsciously) manipulated psychic material continues its life in the psyche and goes on leaving its impact. A desire on whose prompt a person acts—say, smoking a cigarette when the wish arises—produces the sensations of pleasure the person was craving, thereby arousing further desire. Unconscious desire, or desire which is not met with direct action to satisfy it, however, also goes on smouldering and accumulating in the mind. Because the mind's deep layers are constantly reacting to the physical sensations associated with the desire in question, they keep evoking it. As a result, the sensations, the desire, and the mental reactions to them continuously multiply in an uncontrollable chain of conditioned becoming. This is why avoidance or suppression, in the general sense of the word, is, at the same time multiplication, also—or even more so—when it occurs covertly, outside the purview of our conscious-ness. Enactment, too, as it manifests in the act of projection, is, on the one hand, related to the attempt not to experience what is difficult to bear, and, on the other, to an involuntary discharge of mental materi-als into the external environment. Thus, enactment reflects both suppression (or avoidance) and fuelling (or discharge), once more illustrating that the two are by no means mutually exclusive.

There is, between these two extremes that blend into one, a middle path whose destiny is different: even-minded observation. Buddhism's so-called "middle path" (which has quite a number of practical as well as doctrinal aspects) does not imply simple complacency or modera-tion, but, rather, refers to an alternative that subverts two dichotomous options, each of which is limited in its own way. In the present context, even-minded self-observation undermines suppression, repression, denial, and other forms of imperviousness by offering full, conscious contact with experience, while equally subverting stimulation and enactment because it does not fuel the flames of desire and hatred towards the sensations these mental actions generate.

A simple case of sexual desire

A married man in his forties told the following simple story: He found himself attracted to a married woman at work.

"Whenever I'd see her or think of her I'd experience desire, that pleasant sensation that starts from a sort of warm throbbing in the loins and spreads through the body . . . I was aware how the sensation would grow stronger when she'd approach me and we talked, and if our eyes met or there was some light physical touch it would explode through my body into currents of pleasure. So, of course, I noticed a wish to have more of this pleasure. To be with her, to be in touch with her, at least in my thoughts and fantasies. When something feels so good, it has the power to take over . . ."

Although it was clear to him, as they were both married, that he was not going to realise any of these desires for her on the physical level, he felt the force of seduction.

"It was as though I was hearing, in my head, a little voice, far away, that said: 'But maybe yes?' Even if I was strong enough not to go with that voice, I still was tempted to 'grab' intimate moments with her, or simply to hold her image in my mind. It was clear to me that all of these things were so seductive because they produced more of that delicious sensation. And, beyond the haze of bliss, I knew that in the end I would only be torturing myself, and perhaps her too, should I let go and allow myself to think of her that way."

On the other hand, he was sufficiently aware of his emotions not to develop negative feelings towards her in the hope that they would protect him against the difficulty of coping with this desire. He liked and appreciated her, and had no intention of avoiding her or discontinuing their friendship.

All he could effectively do was to experience the desire as such. Whenever the sensations of desire arose he felt them and tried to keep his balance on a thin line, avoiding falling either way: to the side that wanted more, that fuelled and amplified, and was very powerful in this case, or to the side that suppressed, that tried to ignore the truth while looking for the woman's unpleasant characteristics, reasons why she actually was not so attractive after all, or by closing himself off to his sensations in other ways.

"I'd watch the sensations as they arose. Sometimes they'd get so intense it was difficult to bear without expressing them in action. And then some moments would pass, with me managing somehow to hold on, balancing on this tightrope, and I'd notice how the sensations would suddenly start subsiding, losing their grip on my mind, eventually to vanish. It took a few such incidents for these sensations to diminish, in terms of their intensity and frequency, but they did eventually lose the power they had over me."

Other people, in their different words and through the lens of their particular personality, describe a similar dynamic through which the desire to smoke, the desire for alcohol or drugs, or their obsession with food abated and eventually dissolved. The more specific the complex, the more simple and efficient it is to cope with but, essentially, the process is similar for complexes that are deeply entrenched and cover more extensive areas of a person's mental life. Buddhist awareness and equanimity are tied to the ability to be alive to experience's different components without producing a mental reaction that is subject to the pleasure principle. When these two join together, they automatically lead to the dissolving and passing away of the pain-inducing experience. In the sense that this process does not involve interpretation, or imagination, or the attempt to understand, it emerges by itself, spontaneously, sidestepping the intellect.

Sarah

Sarah, a forty-five-year-old physician, describes the depression from which she has been suffering most of her life: "My world was bland, had no taste. I had no appetite and all I wanted was to sleep. I felt a heaviness. There was no point getting up in the morning, and I couldn't figure why I should make the effort." Sarah's depressive episodes would come and go, unpredictably, making her feel helpless and impotent.

"Whatever I did to get better or to make it more bearable didn't succeed, and I was walking around with a feeling that nothing was working. It was as though I had absolutely no grip on the situation. As though what's happening doesn't depend on me . . . no connection with me whatsoever. I had nothing to do with getting myself into a depression and I couldn't get myself out of it either. It felt like something that had always been there and would continue forever. Each and every moment seemed like an eternity, followed by another eternity."

Sarah tells how she arrived at her first Vipassanā course full of doubts and misgivings towards the programme, the instructor, and everything "that reeked of spirituality". The spiritual domain, she thought, was divided between "frauds and the suckers who believe them". She maintained this attitude throughout the ten days of the course. While the course was going on, she felt no depression, but she experienced very intense physical burning sensations, as if she was on fire.

"It was incredibly hard. I had all these sensations, I saw my own reactions, and then I noticed a connection which I thought was very peculiar, between my mental activity and the sensations themselves. What's the relation between my back pains, which have to do with a slipped disc and long stretches of sitting, and my thoughts? But there was something there, and it was obvious that the thoughts that were passing through my mind in some cases increased the pain and in others made it grow less."

This discovery was the first crack in Sarah's wall of helplessness, which was at the bottom of her depression. Some time after her first course, she started practising a few minutes every day, faintly hoping it might nevertheless help her—as others had told her—with her daily suffering: the burden of depression as well as the pressures of her professional life, with its heavy responsibility and time schedule. To her great surprise, something inside her started changing, affecting her depression. That initial crack then became a real opening, as the experience of being sentenced without having any say in the verdict was replaced by a new recognition that she could actually do something that would bring real change into her world. She started practising every day and struggled to make the sessions stretch longer. "I still felt as though I was on fire. All of my body was aflame with sensations and my capacity for non-reactive observation was very limited. Every meditation period would start with a sense of depression: that huge weight pressing down on my chest, my throat, my diaphragm. There were other sensations too, which I related to anger and tension, but over and beyond everything there was this heaviness. I'd sense it and then feel how it started dissolving into a mere vibration. I felt I was using Vipassanā like aspirin, and I was hoping that the effect would become antibiotic in due time."

That is what happened, slowly.

"I remember the very powerful experience of waking up one morning and finding that that depressed feeling was no longer there. It simply dwindled, and I didn't even notice. The depression didn't completely disappear but it became a lot less prominent, in terms both of its intensity and the frequency with which it happened. Now, years later, when it comes, I know it will pass after an hour's meditation."

Thus, from a reality in which depression, when it appeared, seemed an eternal presence over which she had no influence, Sarah shifted to a reality marked by a clear understanding of depression as a passing phenomenon which she no longer faced helplessly. Her depression transformed into a sensational–emotional–cognitive compound that did not flood or overwhelm her, and whenever it occurred she could cope with it in a relatively non-reactive manner.

Alongside the overt level of the process, underneath it, another one occurred; it was this level of the process that had led Sarah to look inside and, at some point, find that "my depression is no longer there." This was taking place in the depths of her mind, beyond the intellectual and controlled modes of experience, and only its outcomes testify to its actual occurrence. These are the two inseparably intertwined levels of the process of eradication of the mind's residues: the momentary level, at which the person practises to refrain from reacting with either craving or aversion to what is pleasant or unpleasant, and, thus, not to produce new mental accumulations, and the deep level on which, when reactions are not produced (on the first level) at the given moment, previously accumulated reactions rise to the surface—in this case ones tied to depression—where, unmet by new reactions, they lose their strength, dissolve, and are eradicated.

Awareness and equanimity according to psychoanalysis and Buddhism

Both perspectives, therefore, offer a mental mode that aims to release people from the necessity to react. Developing awareness, the ability to pay attention, and equanimity—the ability of non-reactivity—are a necessary condition for extrication from blind circular dynamics, which, in their absence, functions as a default option. While there are commonalities between psychoanalysis and Buddhism concerning the awareness and equanimity they look for, one should not confuse them as being identical.

Epstein (1988b) compared "evenly suspended attention" to the Buddhist practice of mindfulness (*sati*) that is characteristic of Vipassanā meditation. Attention, in both cases, is directed non-judgementally and non-selectively at the full range of mental phenomena, without exception. For Epstein, evenly suspended attention and

mindfulness, because they suggest directing non-identifying awareness at all mental processes, including logical ones such as formulated
interpretations, help therapists to pinpoint their countertransference
reactions and to avoid interpretations that come to serve their own
ego and are either inappropriate or untimely. He also compares the
state of consciousness in evenly suspended attention to a certain level
of concentration (*samādhi*) mentioned in the Buddhist texts. At this
level of concentration[12] the five hindrances[13]—desire, lust, and
passion; malice, hatred, and anger; dullness, laziness, and sluggish-
ness; restlessness, agitation, and worry; doubt or scepticism—in
whose presence the truth cannot be clearly seen (Nyanatiloka, 1997)
are suspended or suppressed (Mahathera Nauyane, 1994) (only temporarily, at this point, not yet eliminated). This matches, at least to a
degree or superficially, Freud's comment on ". . . the value of self-
imposed blindness to memory and desire, as well as to understanding
and preconception" (Grotstein, 2000, p. 687), and Bion's (1988) call for
psychoanalysts to rigorously train themselves to abstain from them in
their analytic work, while aiming for an optimally receptive state in
which mental activity, memory, and desire are suspended (Bion, 1970).
All this bears out therapists' intention to see the patient and the situation lucidly, without being contaminated or biased by the mental
forces at work in themselves. If this is indeed possible, this suggests
the intention to conduct themselves in a manner originating in direct
contact with reality. So, the question arises, to what extent this can
actually be and how it can be achieved if at all. (I shall discuss this
soon.)

In a similar context, according to Pelled (2005, 2007), the combination of *sati* and *upekkhā* enables a person to take in any impression and
contain it, without resisting it and without the need to evacuate
through enactment. As reverie is "that state of mind which is open to
the reception of any 'objects' " (Bion, 1962b, p. 36), she compares it to
Buddhist meditation, which she proposes to describe as, among other
things, improving the ability for reverie, or as improving the container
so that it will not "be torn apart, on the one hand, or 'suffocate' the
contained, on the other" (Pelled, 2005, p. 117).

> Reverie is a factor that supports everything concerning the reception
> of sense impressions and the associated emotional experience. In
> terms of this relation to the reception of impressions it is identical to

the Buddhist factor of equanimity. In both cases it is defined as being separate from other mental processes active in the course of reactions to sense impressions. This is an openness to whatever happens, free from any resistance or barrier to the received contents. In its turn this openness allows for reaction, but as such it does not constitute a reactive action. (Pelled, 2005, p. 116)

However, in spite of what these concepts have in common, some fundamental differences should be considered. Reverie is a natural function that every healthy-enough mother possesses. Although it is a digestive function, which, at its best, is characteristically open to all mental materials that enter the mind it subserves, it does not have the attribute of fundamental freedom from desire, hatred, or suffering. Neither does it include the infrastructure which Buddhism assumes necessary to allow this freedom: recognition, that is, of the ephemeral, afflictive, essence-less, and conditioned nature of these mental materials, and of the experiences they evoke once they "enter" the mind. So (as earlier chapters have already illustrated), anyone into whom difficult materials are projected experiences mental pain, even when they are able to contain and digest them properly rather than go on projecting them. But *upekkhā*, by contrast, is an absolute zero point between pleasure and pain. Where, in the case of containment and reverie, absence of resistance means right of entry for distressing mental materials (Bion, 1959), in *upekkhā* not only does an open state of mind allow unblocked reception of sense impressions, and not only is the container (or the registering and processing apparatus) strong and elastic enough to manage these impressions and the experiences they arouse without impelling the person to act upon them, but here even the deepest strata of the mind do not produce biased and selective reactions (*saṅkhāra*) and their inherent suffering.

Moreover, as the above indicates, both the objectives as well as the products of these two mental actions differ essentially. The mother and therapist, having processed the baby's and the patient's projections by means of their reverie, will return a transformed and usable version of the unbearable transferred mental material, thus changing "nameless dread" (Bion, 1962b, p. 96) into meaningful mental content. This is how they enable healthy, integrative processing and the gradual internalisation of the functions of containment and reverie themselves. The therapist, similarly, will come up with a certain outcome as the result of cultivating her evenly suspended attention: interpretation. Using her unconscious as a tool that unselectively receives the patient's broadcast (his free associations), the therapist reconstructs the unconscious material from which the latter originate (Freud, 1912e, p. 16). In this case, too, the process generates meaning:

> ... analytic listening is directed in advance towards an eventual interpretation, whose content is not yet known at the time of listening but which gradually takes shape up to the moment when the interpretation has to be formulated to the analysand. (Baranger, 1993, p. 15)

With *upekkhā*, the point is not to transform the raw material into something that can be utilised, and neither is it about generating meaning, or, indeed, generating anything at all. It aims, by contrast, to undo and eradicate, the automatic result of a non-generative, non-cumulative, and non-reactive mental activity.

Digestion and eradication

I would like to expand now on the idea that Vipassanā functions— along with its other aspects—as "a kind of 'fasting of the spirit'" (Hart, 1987, p. 105). Bion argued that the extent to which one is able to bear the unpleasant is in direct proportion to the ability to learn from experience, to be in touch with the truth and know it. One developmental route, from this perspective, involves a transition from the need to evacuate tension (by means of hallucination and projective identification) to the ability to cope with it (Pelled, 2005). I will refer to bearing and coping with the unpleasant as some version—two of which will be presented below—of the alliance between awareness of unpleasantness and the non-aspiration to evacuate it.

Bion (1962b) argued that mental development, just as physical development, depends on an effective digestive system. Awareness and non-awareness depend on the production of alpha-elements by the alpha-function, by means of which the raw materials of experience transform into usable mental components that can be processed in "dream thoughts". For this transformation to happen, a mental digestive system is needed, just as a physical digestive system is needed in order to transform food into something usable. For the baby, this initially occurs via the maternal mental digestive system—her alpha-function—of which reverie is a factor. The mother, who, through projective identification, ingests the infant's experiential raw materials, digests them by means of her reverie. When everything goes well, this function is gradually internalised and installed in the baby, who then becomes equipped with it. If this happens, then he becomes able to use this mental digestive system in the face of the reality he takes in, rather than having immediately to evacuate the raw experiential materials evoked by this encounter with reality, even before they can be thought.

The ability to tolerate frustration, tension, or pain is, in this view, related to digestive processes that are transformative in nature: they make usable what is unusable, and tolerable what is unbearable. When a pain is held in a functional container, this, in itself, is transformative; if the right of difficult materials to gain entry into the psyche is not denied, if the psyche neither rejects nor evacuates them, then primitive components of experience which thought cannot bear transform into ones that can be thought and experienced as meaningful.

The doctrine of the Buddha, as it appears in the Pāli Canon and is applied in the practice of Vipassanā, puts forward another process of digestion. Here, digestion eradicates, and the transformation of suffering is total. The materials held by the Buddhist container, or digested by meditation's digestive system, are not processed for the sake of becoming useful. In the face of the causes of suffering and the accumulations of the *saṅkhāras*, meditation's digestive system consumes, so to speak, rather than digests: it digests reality and consumes the mental residues that cause suffering. While making it possible to absorb and process the components of experience, it eradicates the habitual reactions that lead to the repetitive *saṃsāric* becoming. Transformation, here, is radical: it is a "transformation to zero" that aims to totally annihilate suffering.

Psychoanalytic transformation cannot occur from K to O, to use Bion's concepts, but only from O to K. Knowledge of the truth is not the product of a simple deduction based on sense perception of a phenomenon. Hence, it cannot occur in a saturated space—a space characterised by clinging to knowledge, expectation, desire, and the need to understand—but only in a non-clinging, unsaturated space, where, as expectation, desire, and understanding are suspended, at-one-ment with the unknowable absolute truth evolves (Bion, 1970). Having dwelt in a field with similar attributes, one might say that, in Vipassanā, eradication cannot occur when the desire to eradicate arises in the face of experience. When this is the case, the mind actually generates craving and clinging, which are defined as generative and fuelling actions, not as eradicating actions. Hence, for Bion, in order to know one must not want, not know, and not want to know: instead, one must allow an unmediated encounter with the truth to evolve by itself. In Vipassanā meditation, if one is to eradicate the causes of suffering, one must not want to eradicate distressing experiences, to get rid of them or, in any other manner, coarse or subtle, turn away from them. Instead, one must "contain" them, but in the most extreme sense: not just to bear them, with the help of awareness and non-evacuation, but to fully experience them while absolutely no layer of the mind reacts to them in a way that expresses a mental movement "towards" or "away from".

Bearing or containing suffering, or, in other words, being aware of it without trying to expel it, is not the goal from a Buddhist perspective: this does not suffice to eradicate suffering. Should we, nevertheless, want to claim that they are enough, this will only be possible if we redefine the notions of "toleration", "containment", and "non-expulsion" as referring to the absence of any mental reaction that prefers the pleasant to the unpleasant and, hence, as referring to the non-production of suffering.

This criterion might appear too exacting, too ambitious, even impossible to achieve, but it is precisely where the path of the Buddha leads. For this to happen, it is necessary to take the experience apart, and consider its components—the body and its sensations, the mind and its contents—as objects of observation, so that abstention from reacting to them can be thoroughly practised. If physical sensations are chosen as the main object of observation, then non-reaction is practised specifically toward them, but it naturally and automatically shapes the attitude towards the other components of experience. Through the systematic observation of sensations, whose changing nature becomes a clear and present reality, emerges the recognition of all phenomena as transient, essence-less, and inherently bound up with suffering. This experientially based knowledge gives rise to non-reactivity, the Buddhist equanimity expressing the absence of biased mental movement, whether towards or away from.

Robert

Coping with anger was a key process in the mental life of Robert, a man in his fifties who worked in the media. The anger had many objects: himself, others, various situations, and "the world's chaoticness as a whole". This came together with high expectations of both himself and life and with a deep non-acceptance of any person or situation that did not fulfil them. Towards the outside world, this anger caused him to behave irritably and get into conflict. Robert's anger and non-acceptance complex came to the fore during his first Vipassanā courses, where its characteristic mental components were transferred on to the present figures and situations: He became angry when he failed to experience certain things he had expected to experience, he was annoyed with his "incompetence" and his "bad performance" (which obviously had no real existence, since there is no requirement to achieve anything he had imagined he should achieve in this type of course), and he was full of criticism, resistance, and anger towards the teachers. He often had thoughts, images, and dreams with violent conflictual contents, and they were attended by feelings of anger and offence. Difficult sensations of physical pain came up, and when there was anger in his mind he also noted a feverishness and extreme physical restlessness: "Like very unpleasant currents under my skin, on and off . . . a sort of inner itching . . . like worms swarming about."

The emotional–intellectual–sensational complex Robert was struggling with was tied to aversion, and the powerful unpleasantness that came along with it would automatically arouse further aversion. So, according to the chain of conditioned arising, it fed the continued becoming of aversion with all the specific mental and physical components that, for him, were associated with it. Vipassanā practice aims to subvert this default option as well as the process of the continuous arising of suffering it decrees. To the extent that Robert managed to experience all these components and to maintain equanimity (that is, not generate further hatred, dissatisfaction, or rejection), he stopped fuelling them and this automatically set their eradication into motion. In fact, during his first years of practice, Robert's anger complex gradually shifted from being "a big, shapeless lump" in which the emotional, cognitive, and sensational aspects were all knotted together to becoming more distinct and then falling apart. The intellectual and emotional components gradually subsided—in his meditation hours and in life in general—and, with regard to the sensational aspect, the sensations of pain and restlessness started to dissolve. It is almost needless to say that, in time, his irritability and his interpersonal conflicts also abated.

Yet, the mind is complicated. Residues accumulate over the years, building up layer upon layer: some remain dormant (*anusaya*) and indistinct until the process of observation and investigation develops to a degree of subtlety and depth that allows a light to be cast on them, to shake them up, and raise them to the surface. For Robert, who has been practising steadily for over two decades, such layers came to light after many years. As anger, and the related projective activities, subsided, the presence of the sensational aspect became more pronounced. He said,

"The sensational complex that emerged at this stage seemed totally related to the anger, in a different formation, this time. Physical restlessness increased and became even more extreme. I felt it to the bone . . . A strong tremor and pain started up around my head, as though someone was holding a drill to it. It went on and on. Obviously, anger again arose in me: I couldn't accept it."

It is within the field of suffering, where residues of the past arise in the here and now, that the opportunity for transformation occurs. The deeper and more exacting the emerging residues, the bigger and more far reaching the possibility of freedom held out to the person who copes with them successfully: that is, through awareness and equanimity, non-denial, non-expulsion, and non-production.

When it turns to address the mind's residues, the Vipassanā method moves from the superficial to the deeply buried, from the body's surface inward (though both remain important), and from coarse to subtle.

Robert continued,

"It felt as though I was looking at the wrapping, the outer layer, and now I look at the details, what's inside. The elements of experience (sensational, emotional, and intellectual) started changing at a very fast rate. Everything became so dynamic, as if the 'molecules' of the experiences could be felt. I used to feel there was something homogeneous, definable—but now because of this rapid change everything fell apart into tiny bits. During my meditation hours, I started seeing things as they were, their presences, their true face, and all the minuscule interrelations among them."

In his analytic–synthetic process, Robert's experiential realisation of the impermanence of sensations led to the development of a penetrating view of his mental-material phenomenon, to non-identification with it, and a lessened attachment to it. "The vibrating sensations of that drilling were so powerful and unpleasant, but I knew at the same time that if I reacted with revulsion I would only make things worse. Practice became very demanding because I had to make a big effort, continuously, to stay aware and even-minded. At first I tried to understand: was it fear? Worry? A need to control? At some point it just became whatever it was and stopped being 'mine'. I stopped living in the illusion that I had any control over these sensations and I stopped trying to get rid of them. And that brought relief."

Robert began to take his hard sensations for what they were, without hating or trying to get rid of them. Only then a breakthrough became possible, which further opened the already existing crack in the vicious circle of his specific version of blind reactivity.

"Observing all this molecular spectacle over which I have no control, a sense of calm and well-being arose. Even though, superficially speaking, all the usual vexations stayed the same, I now found myself dwelling in the depth of things, looking at the chaos serenely from the eye of the storm. I'd be there—in the quietness of the eye of the storm—and then again I'd get all stirred up and carried away into chaos, in order, later, to return to peacefulness. I witnessed the hard sensations, the ability to be quiet in their presence and accept them, and also the movement between equanimity and non-equanimity, between the eye of the storm and the whirlpool around it. It created a kind of modesty in me. If I can't control it, then I've got nothing to prove either. There's nothing to pretend. All that remains to be done is to watch how it arises and how it dissolves."

This aspect of meditation appears as follows in the Buddha's words:

> Thus he dwells observing sensations in sensations internally, or he dwells observing sensations in sensations externally, or he dwells observing sensations in sensations both internally and externally. Thus he dwells observing the phenomenon of arising in sensations, thus he dwells observing the phenomenon of passing away in sensations, thus he dwells observing the phenomenon of arising and passing away in sensations. (DN 22, cited in Goenka, 1998, p. 27)

Just as reactive mental activity is engraved on, and influences, a person's mind and life, becoming more deeply entrenched and established the more it is repeated, the same is true for the ability to "merely observe" without reacting: the more frequently it is repeated the more it develops and its influence deepens. So, wherever Robert would react with anger in the past, he now checks within himself and no longer encounters the same old psycho–physical complex. Where in the past there was suffering, irritability, demandingness (of himself as of others) and non-acceptance of what cannot be controlled, there is tranquillity and ease now. The process is not complete yet, and Robert still notices "leftovers" of his old habitual reactions popping up here and there, but they are already absent from most situations, and where they still occur they take a weaker form. The drilling sensation he used to feel, too, has started to subside after a few years of showing up intensively.

Recognising experience as not-I

Robert's breakthrough and the subsequent release were connected to a change of perception he underwent about his type of relationship to his difficult sensations. At some stage, they stopped being "his" sensations and became mere sensations. Buddhism points at a fundamental problematic link between a sensation and identification with it, or between a sensation and the illusory experience of self that distorts the perception of things as they are, leading to mental reactions and suffering. People may relate to their sensations in one of three ways, according to the Buddha's teaching, all of them widely prevalent and all of them misguided: they might identify with the sensations, that is, assume that the sensations they experience are tantamount to who they are; they might wash their hands of them and deny their influence; they might assume it is their "self" that experiences the sensations, that they are the subjects that feel them. With regard to the second and the third way, feeling sensations is a necessary condition for experiencing a sense of self, and so one cannot give up being dependent on them (as long as one experiences oneself as "I"), and neither can one be "the feeling subject of sensations", as this notion is based on the assumption that there is a subject as distinct from one's sensations. In respect of the first possibility, if one identifies with one's sensations or perceives them as defining one's "self", then, since sensations come and go all the time, appear as pleasant, unpleasant, or neutral, and, in any case, are conditioned and bound up with suffering, one will have to accept a matching perception of oneself as such: mutable, particulate, lacking an essential core, conditioned, and constantly changing (DN 15).

Buddhist teaching suggests that a person develops open attention that allows her or him to fully experience every sensation in the first person, while maintaining equanimity as a result of non-identification with it. From this perspective, letting go of reactive activity is tied to the understanding that if the sensation is transient, bound up with suffering and lacking essential selfhood, there is no point clinging to it, developing craving or repulsion towards it, or, in other words, identifying with it and reacting to it. Similarly, if the self is impermanent, bound up with suffering and lacking essential selfhood, then there is no point making the effort to provide it with pleasant sensations and get rid of hard ones on its behalf. So, as the illusion concerning a stable self entity dissipates, no "self" remains to identify with a "sensation". What does remain is a sensation and conscious person whose experiences, however, no longer pass through the filter of his or her self as a point of reference, the filter whose purpose to achieve pleasure and to escape pain distorts the perception of reality it yields. What is left, then, is "mere understanding along with mere awareness", and the clear vision: "This is body!"; "This is sensation!"; "This is mind!"; "These are the contents of the mind!" (DN 22).

This is not exactly the state of affairs in the therapeutic situation. A more dialectic approach is encouraged here: the therapist aims to pass between states in which he or she identifies (temporarily and experimentally) with the transferred mental materials so as to have the most direct possible experience of the patient's inner world, and states in which this identification, as it were, peels away, when he or she grows aware that these materials originate in the patient and not in themselves.

> While listening passively to the patient, the analyst experiences the patient's verbal productions as his immediate sensory perception. They occupy his attention almost exclusively. At that moment the patient's presentations constitute what is presented to the analyst's consciousness and, as a result, he has become identified with the analysand. The analyst thinks and feels like the patient . . .

When the analyst becomes aware that the mood or thoughts he has been experiencing represent commentaries on the patient's material, he has made the transition from simple identification to empathic comprehension. If the analyst fails to take that step and remains in the state of identification, he is sympathetic but not empathic. This is one of the most common factors underlying many forms of countertransference. Thinking with a patient is quite different from thinking about the patient. (Arlow, 1993, p. 1149)

If we attribute the experiences that pass from one person to another in projective identification to the *vedanā* link (the link of sensation), then the object of projection, through the systematic observation of the sensations that arise and pass away, has the option to stop relating to them in a way that leads to identification with them, to feeling subject to them, or, alternatively, to deny them or to disavow their impact. Bion, we may remember, mentioned that the object of projection often finds herself in a state of a temporary loss of insight; Racker spoke about the cruel vicious circle perpetuated by blindness, and Ogden argued that the two parties to projective identification might well find themselves subject to a pseudo-hypnotic type of experience, temporarily subjugated until their individual subjectivity is restored. The Buddhist view on this is that when one is under the influence of perceptual and cognitive distortions, including the distortion that involves the experience of a solid and independent "self", one is "sense-less", or "broken-minded". When, however, these distortions are corrected by means of a realistic way of seeing, then one is restored to one's senses (AN 4.49). Thus, continuous awareness of the arising and passing of a sensation, and shedding misguided assumptions about it and about the self, may get a person out of the quicksands of projective identification and of quasi hypnotic states, restore her senses, and help avoid "drowning in countertransference", or "total countertransference", and uses of non-integrative mechanisms such as splitting and projection. Instead, it becomes possible to process these sensations and to successfully contain them. Staying equanimous, rather than reacting with either craving or aversion, the person will now be outside the cycle of suffering: "containment", here, rather than having a sacrificial quality, will be neutralising–consuming. Thus, the recipient will no longer be hurt by what is projected, or cause the projector the suffering entailed by replication and reintrojection of these mental contents that have become absorbed with fear, hatred, and illusion.

Trembling with the world: the therapist's sensitivity, the meditator's sensitivity, the meditating therapist's sensitivity

The enhancement of awareness is also the enhancement of sensitivity. The therapist aspires to have sharper senses attuned to the patient's communication, whether verbal or non-verbal, whether conscious or unconscious. The effort is to calibrate his subjective apparatus and make it so open and non-selective as to be ready to receive as much as possible of the incoming sensory and mental information. Being a subject himself, whose receptive substrate rests on a specific mixture of complexes, past experiences, and perceptions, the therapist strives to achieve a subtle awareness of his own blind spots, too, of his own Achilles heel and sensitivities, through which an important part of the countertransference manifests itself. In the absence of awareness of these parts, the therapist's sense of the patient will remain anaemic, superficial, and hollow. This type of two-directional awareness— towards what comes in from outside as well as one's own vulnerabilities and blindness—exposes the therapist to pain that must be borne and coped with in a healthy manner.

The meditator aspires to hone his sensitivity to the sensations that arise and pass, pleasant and unpleasant alike, in all parts of the body. In contrast with the workings of the pleasure principle, here the attempt is to develop concentration and awareness so as to be able to take in these sensations in their entirety, with maximum subtlety and depth, not leaving out even the smallest area, not neglecting any sensation, no matter how unpleasant, not keeping any domain or sensation outside the field of investigation. Being a subject, the meditator, whose receptive substrate rests on a specific mixture of complexes, past experiences, and perceptions, experiences in the process all the mental factors tied to these sensations, including those that interfere with investigating one's own, constantly changing, map of sensations. The meditator encounters these factors, which emerge as a consequence of the investigation, and this, in turn, refines his awareness of them. We saw this in the case of Joel, whose intense anxiety came with the urge to escape, threatening his ability to keep going with the process, with Shira, whose sealed body zones, together with her attitude towards them, conspired to keep her suffering out of her own sight, putting at risk her motivation to continue investigating her psyche, and we saw it, too, regarding Ethan, whose basic lack of trust caused him to project his anger and conflicts on to the abstract object of "Vipassanā" and made it extremely hard for him to surrender to the process. For them, as for many others, the very work with these interfering complexes—whose triggering is inherent to any in-depth mental process—is the main work that eventually leads toward transformation and liberation.

Therapists have no other instrument to register themselves and others but their own subjective substrate, riddled as it is with blind spots. Meditators have no other instrument to register their internal reality and its interrelations with the external environment but their own subjective substrate, riddled as it is with blind spots. Although very unlike each other in terms of tools and objectives, both these positions put those who occupy them in a vulnerable place. Those who choose to spend long stretches of time with people who suffer badly expose themselves to mental exchanges with them, and, thus, in a sense they consciously choose to ingest painful materials that might not have been part of them to begin with. However, those who decide to carefully explore themselves, leaving out and eliding nothing, and who are willing to be awake to anything arising in them—do they, too, bring unnecessary suffering upon themselves? In other words: do people who are able to avoid all this actually end up being more free and happy? Are awareness and sensitivity suffering, and is ignorance, really, bliss?

The answer, from the point of view that inspires this book, is no. Many of those who start learning Vipassanā feel how the technique sharpens their sensitivity; alongside those who immediately perceive the advantages of this, there are also others who are taken aback. They are usually people who know themselves to be very sensitive, who have become used to the fact that their sensitivity causes them suffering. Being subject to the same habitual reactive infrastructure that was theirs hitherto, the increased awareness of sensations can indeed lead to increased suffering. But Vipassanā offers precisely this: to break through the old habitual reactive infrastructure responsible for suffering. Joel's intense anxiety and Sarah's "burning" when they started practising Vipassanā were not created by the process. They were manifestations of mental residues that were created in the past, took up residence in their minds, and were brought to the surface in the meditative process. We deceive ourselves when we believe that if only we decide not to lift the stone underneath which there is a scorpion we can pretend there actually is no scorpion. Neglect and turning a blind eye have never really solved a problem.

Calm and equanimity, which are based on low sensitivity, occlude the reactive mental activity that is constantly taking place in the mind's deeper strata and that remains outside conscious awareness until it receives appropriate attention (Hart, 1987). Like the princess with the pea under her mattress in the fairy tale, says Lobel (2014), we are very sensitive to the sensations that arise in us as the result of stimuli in our environment, and not knowing the source of the disturbance does not relieve us from its critical influence. When we look at lack of awareness from the psychodynamic perspective, too, not knowing does not do away with suffering. Quite the contrary: it is not knowing that offers the causes of suffering the opportunity to act powerfully within us and to push us into non-integrative intrapersonal and interpersonal actions. Hence, the difficult self-parts and components of experience that the psyche expels into others rather than becoming aware of them do not actually stop affecting the psyche. Countertransference feelings unaccompanied by awareness produce suffering for whoever experiences them and fuel the suffering of the partner in the process, leading to counter-reactions that perpetuate a blindly vicious circle. Reactions of craving and hatred that are generated, unconsciously, to pleasant and unpleasant sensations alike multiply in the mind, transforming into self-perpetuating harmful residues and habits that are responsible for the creation of suffering and ignorance within the individual and for negative influence on his or her surroundings. Ignorance, therefore, is suffering and by no means bliss.

Yet, not every time mental residues are brought to the surface is a healthy and useful thing. It should happen to those who are capable, when they are capable, and within a context that provides proper holding and tools for the right kind of work with what comes up in the process. In the therapeutic situation, these are the setting, the therapeutic technique, and, especially, therapists' reverie, together with the other professional tools and human capacities they have due to their professional training and personality. In a Vipassanā course, they are the safe physical space, the clear timetable and instructions, the ethical underpinning, as well as the team of people who work on those terms, teachers' holding and, more than anything else, the technique itself, whose key aim is to work with the causes of suffering in an even-minded, non-repressive, and non-eliciting way. From the present angle, then, there are no "excessive" awareness, "excessive" attention to sensations, or "hypersensitivity" wherever the right conditions are provided to people in the right state. However, there can be awareness, attention, and sensitivity lacking a parallel degree of equanimity. Awareness and equanimity are like the two wings of a bird, whose ability to fly depends on both being developed in equal measure, or like the two wheels of a wheelbarrow: when one of them is smaller than the other, the cart will be turning circles around its own axis rather than moving ahead (Hart, 1987). With the proper conditions, the honing of the part of the mind that serves as the instrument for investigating the other parts supports the process whereby mental residues come floating to the surface, making it possible to uproot them, to allow them to arise and be experienced so that they will not arise again in the future.

I referred to the therapist's sensitivity and to the meditator's sensitivity. What about the sensitivity of the meditating therapist? Obviously, here qualities of both positions are included, naturally producing a new therapeutic position. Fleischman (1999), a psychiatrists' psychiatrist and a senior Vipassanā teacher in the method of Goenka, mentions the "wounded healer" syndrome. Wounded healers work on a high professional level. They have enjoyed good training; they are conscientious, knowledgeable, and have a pleasant attitude to patients, but deep inside they are lonely, afraid, anxious, and depressed. Their professional achievements compensate for early deficits, and their generosity at work helps them get some of the human touch they lack. They do not communicate their misery to others, and they have a very hard time finding a therapist whom they feel they can trust enough to receive help. When they do find such a therapist, their progress is slow, leaving the impression that, rather than wanting to be healed, they are in search of being patients in order to participate in a process that affords ongoing attention from a type of adoptive parent who can provide what their original parents, for some reason, were unable to give. The pain of the "wounded healer" is, however, not only a problem, but a source of empathy and insight as well, representing, Fleischman suggests, something essential about healing: the wounded healer experiences, over and beyond personal problems, the pain of pain (Fleischman, 1999).

Suffering often causes people to turn inward. Their personal distress makes them shrink more and more deeply into their egocentric nucleus, as they find it hard to expand their range. With the type of therapist Fleischman sketches, as well as, I believe, with sensitive therapists of other kinds (and, obviously, this is not limited to therapists alone), an inverse process occurs. Suffering their profound personal pain, they, of all people, have the ability to touch the very core of the universal truth concerning suffering as such. Thus, the pain they carry, rather than simply being "blind pain", tightly arranged around their own egocentric nucleus, becomes "noble suffering", suffering which is tied to the recognition of pain as an attribute of existence, which has the strength to push for insight and liberation, which asks for a response that ". . . differentiates true healing from superficial patch-ups and fraudulent elixirs" (Fleischman, 1999, p. 50–51).

The same vulnerability and compassion that led these people to become therapists, as well as their constant exposure to human suffering as a result of their work (Fleischman, 1999), put them in an unusual position. "He who has seen everything empty itself is close to knowing what everything is filled with", wrote the Argentinian poet, Antonio Porchia (1943, p. 3, also cited in Fleischman, 1999, p. 50): such a person is close—close to the threshold, and the question is whether he enters or not.

The suffering of the therapist at this threshold is real, and he needs healing for himself if he is to cross it. Indeed, the healing of his own suffering, too, must be "noble": healing that is not site-specific, not egocentric, not limited to moving from sickness to health or from dysfunction to functionality. This "noble healing" is based on the understanding that suffering can play an enlightening role, and it involves the development of a different perspective on time, on space, and on the close relations people have with whatever is not in concrete and direct touch with them (Fleischman, 1999). Fleischman, who sees himself as a version of this "wounded healer", recounts how Vipassanā practice changed his perspective and his experience. He tells how he began to feel "surrounded by infinities of helpers for my own consternation, and recipients of my skills and affections. Oceans of beings swim at me, reach out to me, count on me to whisper inspiring exhortations in their ears" (Fleischman, 1999, p. 51). Sensitive therapists are set free, in such a process, from their existential solitude. Their pain transforms into insight and their motivating power—which strives for liberation, which breaks forth from isolated egotism into mutually conditioned universality—is realised.

One expression in the Buddha's language for having compassion carries the literal meaning: "trembling with the world", or "quivering" with it.[14] Not unlike others who are not therapists, but often in a different role and in different situations, therapists who follow the footsteps of the Buddha aim to tremble with the world without falling apart. They aspire to respond to the other's mental upheaval with unbiased love and compassion rather than with an egocentric reaction. They aspire to be entirely open to the other's suffering, to let it touch all the strings of their heart without allowing the suffering to become their own or its touch to unsettle the stability of their mind. "Aspire" is, of course, a crucial word here, because often one is not quite capable of achieving this, or might only be able to achieve it in part, or only at times. Yet, this is precisely why they practise awareness and equanimity, and if they do it properly, then they notice how their egocentric reactions gradually subside, compassion and love expand, and the ability to tremble with the world rather than to be crushed by it spreads to ever more remote and more challenging areas of their psyche.

Wholly open, yet not taking into themselves any suffering and experiencing it as their own; trembling yet keeping stable; receptive and soft, yet clear and lucid. A thin, subtle line passes here, hardly perceptible. If one is to move along it and not to collapse, something must help one across the threshold. Something is needed to help one break through loneliness and noble pain. Something must protect one in one's vulnerability. What is this "something"? What helps us to move across, to break through, what protects? The answer, from the perspective of Vipassanā, is this: a person's awareness of the chain of her own mental actions, which lifts the haze of confusion and illusion and brings clarity to the situation—this is what gives protection. The inner compass which enables a careful look into one's overt behaviour for the mental action that directs it—this is what gives protection; one's awareness and equanimity, which increasingly allow one to stay open to suffering without being hurt; one's broad perspective which forges deep connection with the universe; one's vulnerability which grows ennobled; one's sensitivity which, from being contracted, becomes full of compassion—this is what gives protection. One labours to cultivate these and falters, this way and that, and then one goes on. One labours to cultivate them and they, along with the infinities of beings that receive one's skills and love, helping and being helped, accompany one on one's way.

CHAPTER NINE

Is there mental life free from projection?

B oth Buddhism and psychoanalysis propose alternatives to the projective mode of being, and to the immersion in the fog and suffering brought about by blind reactivity. To what extent does each of these approaches consider the possibility of no projection feasible? To what extent does each envision release from the tyranny of the pleasure principle? How profound and fundamental, in other words, is the change the individual can achieve through these practices?

Projection as inherent in mental life: the dialectic nature of the depressive position and the inevitability of countertransference

Psychoanalysis construes projection as a basic mental action. For Freud, it is a feature of human thinking (Ornston, 1978); for Klein (1946), splitting and projection are vital to normal early development; for Bion (1962b) functional (as opposed to pathological; Spillius's 1992) use of projective identification is a necessary condition for the healthy development of thought, the connection with reality, and the ability to process emotion, and for Ogden (1994b), projective identification is indispensable, expressing a human need no less profound than hunger and thirst to form intersubjective constructs ". . . in order to find an exit from unending, futile wanderings in their own internal object world" (p. 105). So, projection is inextricable part of the individual's life. It does not exist in isolation, away from the rest of a person's emotional being; it colours experience rather than constituting the entirety of experience. It constitutes a dimension of everything intersubjective: at times it dominates, and then again it recedes to form a more subtle background (Ogden, 1994b). From this perspective, therefore, projection and projective identification are inherent to mental life, as they are inseparable parts of certain functional strata of it.

Psychoanalysis aspires to help patients acknowledge unacceptable parts of their self which have been split off and projected, to take them back in so that they can be integrated into a more complete self and a richer personality (Klein, 1952; 1975c). As this process moves ahead, anxiety and guilt diminish, love and hate merge in a better way, and, therefore, splitting and repression mellow while the self grows stronger and more coherent. The object's fantastic aspects lose their power, as the gap narrows between objects that seemed persecutory and those that appeared ideal. As fantastic unconscious life becomes less separate from the unconscious part of the mind, it becomes easier to harness for the benefit of the self's activity (Klein, 1952). The subject should, thus, gradually progress from a condition such as that of the patient whose image of his therapist converted in the blink of an eye from "all good" to "all bad"—from ideal to persecutory—to one resembling that of the other patient, who did not tend to massively split and project, and whose ability to contain, to perceive complexity, and to be self-reflexive was relatively high. The sought-for state, then, is a consolidated one: a state in which gaps, splitting, and separation between different mental parts, and between conscious and unconscious, subside, or become attenuated.

The depressive position, as said, is the psychoanalytic alternative considered the more integrated or consolidated, but it is not a static condition. Preferring the notion of "positions" over Freud's idea of developmental stages, Klein (1935) formulated the basis for a dynamic view of the relations between the two positions (the paranoid–schizoid and the depressive). Bion developed this way of thinking

(Ogden, 2004a), and suggested these psychological positions maintain something like a chemical equilibrium (Steiner, 1992). For Ogden (2004a), the two positions (along with a third, autistic–contiguous one), are modes of creating experience or processes of relating to perceived reality; they co-exist in every person, creating, preserving, and negating one another. He argues that every aspect of human experience is produced by the interplay among the various modes of experience, that there is no autonomous depressive entity (Ogden, 2004a), and that a fully developed depressive position is an ideal state, which can never actually be attained (Ogden, 1986). For psychoanalysis, then, one cannot progress to the depressive state irreversibly, without occasional revisits to the paranoid–schizoid position. There is constant movement between the two positions, with neither taking the upper hand permanently or completely. This dynamic can be observed within the span of an hour, or over months and years (Steiner, 1992). Furthermore, splitting and projection are not restricted to the paranoid–schizoid position alone, appearing as they do in the context of depressive mechanisms as well (Klein, 1975b; Steiner, 1992). So, the point is to help one advance from using primitive mechanisms to a way of processing the depressive position which relies less on splitting and projection; still "Complete and permanent integration is . . . never possible. For under strain from external or internal sources, even well integrated people may be driven to stronger splitting processes, even though this may be a passing phase" (Klein, 1975c, p. 233).

Since it does not think in terms of a final release from the paranoid–schizoid mode of experience—and, hence, from splitting and projection—as a feasible objective, psychoanalysis's aims regarding the tendency to project are not absolute. Rather, it purports to lessen and attenuate projections (Klein, 1946),[15] make them less extreme and inclusive, more intermittent, and make it easier to restore previously cast off elements to the personality (Joseph, 1989). It does not aspire to undo them as an everyday or defensive mode of mental operation.

The same also goes, of course, for the therapist. The extensive literature on the subject indicates how complicated it is to try to reach ideal containment, something that involves an incessant struggle against the therapist's inner reactions to the patient's projections. Hypothetically speaking, the therapist should not counterproject on (or into) the patient, but because the former is only human, she is not expected to manage to wholly free herself of this tendency. Psycho-analytic thought, as said, aims for the therapist to be open to any material and to contain it, to properly process it, and to avoid getting drawn into harmful unconscious actions under the pressure of the patient's projected fantasy. But this is considered a rather elusive and short-lived aim that cannot be fully realised: "It must be kept in mind that the idea of 'successful' processing is a relative one and that all processing will be incomplete and contaminated to an extent by the pathology of the recipient" (Ogden, 1979, p. 361). The therapist is doomed to react to the transferred materials—if not in an externalis-ing manner, then at least internally—and to inevitably develop coun-tertransference:

> The transference is always present and always reveals its presence. Likewise countertransference is always present and always reveals its presence, although, as in the case of transference, its manifestations are sometimes hard to perceive and interpret. (Racker, 1968, p. 106)

Moreover,

> Every transference situation provokes a countertransference situation, which arises out of the analyst's identification of himself with the analysand's (internal) objects (that is the "complementary counter-transference"). These countertransference situations may be repressed or emotionally blocked but probably they cannot be avoided; certainly they should not be avoided if full understanding is to be achieved. (Racker, 1968, p. 137)

Countertransference, in this view, is vital in order to gain full under-standing of a patient's world; in any case, given that therapists expe-rience the reality they encounter through their personal, specific complexes or their subjective substrate, which they identify as being "themselves" or "their own", they have no choice but to develop some kind of countertransference. Even if the therapist succeeds in becom-ing a "participant observer" (Grotstein, 1995, following Sullivan), containing the transference and observing it even-mindedly (in psychoanalytic terms), he is, nevertheless, bound to develop counter-transference feelings, "imposed" by projective identification or not. These are expressions of the therapist's own infantile complexes trig-gered in parallel to those of his patients and constantly interacting with them (Grotstein, 1995).

Projection, projective identification, and countertransference, according to psychoanalysis, cannot be sidestepped. Such a view, it may be assumed, is the outcome of the thought that reality cannot but be experienced through the self by way of a reference point, and, hence, that mental activity must be subject, one way or another, to the pleasure principle.

Beyond the pleasure principle: according to Freud, Bion, and what the Buddha taught

The therapist will always be exposed to the direct impact of her patients' projections. Even when initially feeling she faced them even-mindedly, on closer inspection of the event in question, she will discover certain reactions and enactments that might have slipped under her radar at the time (Spillius, 1992). The thought that this is an inevitable reality is tied to the basic assumption that the world cannot be perceived directly and without mediation and must be experienced from a subjective point of view, which is naturally governed by the pleasure principle, relying on definitions and preferences, drives, fears, and desires. Can the receptive apparatus be free of this perspective?

We have seen how Freud instructed analysts to cultivate, in their work, a non-selective state of mind suspending their own inclinations, expectations, and desire to influence. We have also seen how, in his attempt to probe mental life, he discovered the pleasure principle as a central organising force. If so, we might add, therapists' inclinations, expectations, and desire to influence are all tightly woven into the basic mental structure that governs them. To confirm the truth of his claim concerning the tyranny of the pleasure principle, Freud charted cases that were marked by unpleasure and examined whether, from their existence, it was possible to infer that they were "beyond the pleasure principle". He believed that those cases, where unpleasure was caused by the interference of the reality principle, are not "beyond the pleasure principle", as the reality principle stems from the self-preservation instinct and it, too, does not relinquish the seeking of pleasure (Freud, 1920g). Wherever the pursuit of the pleasant is disturbed by neurotic suffering—that is, wherever pleasure cannot be experienced as such (Freud, 1920g)—does not indicate mental activity situated beyond the basic pursuit of pleasure either, but, rather, suggests a conflict obstructing its achievement. Even those cases which Freud introduces under the rubric of "perceptual unpleasure", where unpleasure is triggered because the mind registers the inner pressure created by ungratified drives, or because it perceives something dangerous outside, even those cases do not in the least subvert the pleasure principle's dominance (Freud, 1920g, p. 11). In all of them, direct access to the pleasurable is impeded and this inevitably brings along displeasure or pain, yet none of them suggests mental processes in which the tendency to pursue the pleasurable ceases to exist.

When Freud looks for something "beyond the pleasure principle", he finds it in certain expressions of "repetition compulsion". Rarely observed in its pure form, repetition compulsion is frequently bound up with motivations associated with the ego and the pleasure principle. In the transference, for example, the ego uses repetition compulsion as a means of resistance, as a way, that is, to preserve repression. Since such actions come to avoid pain, they are under the rule of the pleasure principle. Yet, repetition compulsion also includes a component that exists apart from the pleasure principle. This is easy to identify and explain by reference to the phenomenon of dreams that repeat traumatic experiences.

Freud defines traumatic experiences as experiences that have broken through the "protective shield", the dead, inorganic layer situated between inside and outside, which blocks most external stimuli and "absorbs" them in order to prevent their overly intense or engulfing entry into the mind. When a too-powerful experience pierces this envelope, making full impact on the receiving apparatus, this unsettles the system, which now must fulfil the primitive function of controlling the excessive amounts of stimuli and mentally binding them so that they can be disposed of. This acute need temporarily suspends the workings of the pleasure principle. Expectation anxiety and the related hypercathexis of the system increase the capability of binding the massive inflow and, thus, lower the risk of it breaking through the protective shield in the case of a difficult experience. With regard to nightmares that repeat trauma, the point of repetition is to raise the level of anxiety, whose absence, in the original circumstances, contributed to the trauma's occurrence in the first place. Thus, the compulsive repetition of traumatic dreams has a function that does not clash with the pleasure principle but is prior to, and independent from, it (Freud, 1920g).

The mental principle that Freud situates beyond the pleasure principle, therefore, is a more primitive principle. Standing apart from it, this by no means suggests having overcome, or been freed from, it. It may also be noticed that, for Freud, the most perfectly civilised, ethical, beautiful, and intellectual behaviours are the products of repression and sublimation, and that the notion that they are grounded in different instincts—distinguishing human from animal—is nothing but an illusion to him.

> What appears in a minority of human individuals as an untiring impulse towards further perfection can easily be understood as a result of the instinctual repression upon which is based all that is most precious in human civilization. The repressed instinct never ceases to strive for complete satisfaction, which would consist in the repetition of a primary experience of satisfaction. No substitutive or reactive formations and no sublimations will suffice to remove the repressed instinct's persisting tension. (Freud, 1920g, p. 42)

Pelled (2005), accordingly, writes that "Freud's theory of consciousness does not exempt even one mental phenomenon from the domination of the drives" (p. 51). Considering various psychoanalytic theoreticians (Gill, Fairbairn, Greenberg, and Mitchell) who criticised Freud's drive theory and raised alternatives, she finds that

> those who are critical of the drive theory do not offer an escape from the back and forth between pain and pleasure. His opponents protest against the reduction of meaning but find it difficult to come up with a good meta-theoretical alternative. . . . They all debate the significance of human existence *within* the paradigm of the pleasure principle. (Pelled, 2005, p. 51)

One of the more notable exceptions is Bion, who suggested the existence of human experience that is not subsumed under the pleasure principle and, subsequently, the possibility of experiencing reality in an unmediated way (Pelled, 2005), not through the desires of the self and the perceptual distortions they impose. (Pelled mentions both Bion and Erlich (2003), who dealt with the unified experience of "being" as opposed to the instrumental experience of "doing". I believe, especially today, that one might also easily include in this context other theoreticians, such as Ogden and Eigen.)

> The leap forward Bion made, following Freud, specifically, and relative to psychoanalytic thinking in general, can be described in terms of Bion's own key assumption. As against the pleasure principle which dominates the self, there is another principle, the principle of truth. That is to say: the human mind has the capacity to remove itself from the pleasure principle's total domination. This ability does not exist independently of personality traits. It requires tolerance of frustration, of doubt and of the sense of infinity, as well as a great deal of practice, but it exists fundamentally and is always active in the dialectic between knowing the truth and denying it. (Pelled, 2005, pp. 51–52)

Bion (1988) remarked on the illusive influence of memory and desire and urged psychoanalysts to train themselves in avoiding them in their work. In this way he continued Freud's line of thinking about ". . . the value of self-imposed blindness to memory and desire, as well as to understanding and preconception" (Grotstein, 2000, p. 687). He further deepened these ideas by tying them to his concepts of attention, knowledge, not knowing, and truth. For Bion (1970), memory and desire rely on sense impressions and subserve them. They represent what seems to have happened and what has yet to happen, turning them into agents of the perceived past and the wished for future rather than agents of the real and the present. Based on categorical, closed, and saturated knowledge, they do not allow the psychoanalyst to truly experience the patient and to reach knowledge that emerges of its own accord from a non-grasping space of not-knowing (Pelled, 2005). It is no coincidence that the concept of "containment", constituting psychoanalysis's most profound alternative to the projective mode, was first formulated by Bion. Projection is a form of screening, something that separates subject from object and prevents the perception of things as they are. Also, it is a mental activity that throws out what is unpleasant rather than processing it within the framework of one's own body and mind. A mind that is free from desire, expectation, the need to understand, and patterns of the past is also free from projection. This includes the aspect associated with preference and reactivity, the aspect associated with expulsion, and the aspect associated with reality perception and the illusion of a fixed, autonomous self. Pelled (2005) argues that the training Bion proposes in avoiding desire, memory, and understanding represents a renunciation of the sense of self.

> Disowning the pleasure principle from its position requires training until the process is complete. The ego reacts to this process with envy, as it is robbed of pain as well as pleasure, memory and desire, and, eventually, its most precious possession, which in the psychoanalytic paradigm is called "sense of self". (Pelled, 2005, p. 191)

Bion, then, refers to a mode of being with Buddhist affinities, as it aims to transcend the relative and realise the absolute, which is situated beyond the desiring self. The state he describes, without desire, barriers, and projections is, however, an ideal mode of being, referring mainly to the therapist when seated in his or her professional chair, during and between sessions, and one can hardly call it a sustainable alternative that can be applied for any length of time or in any wider context.

The Buddha's teaching, by contrast, has the declared objective of attaining a mode of being that is in direct touch with reality. It shows how one can conduct oneself and function in the world without the intervention of the sense of self in perceived experience (DN 15). It strives for wholly clear vision, removal of the veil of ignorance, the final eradication of the accumulations of habitual reactions, breaking the chain of conditioned arising. It aims at total liberation from subjugation to any mental activity in search of pleasure and avoidant of pain.

> When he sees a form with the eye, he isn't infatuated with pleasing forms, and doesn't get upset over unpleasing forms. He dwells with body-mindfulness established, with an unlimited mind. He understands the liberation through [concentration of] the mind and the liberation through wisdom, where those evil, unskillful mental phenomena cease without remainder. Having thus abandoned compliance and opposition, he doesn't relish any sensation he feels—pleasure, pain, neither-pleasure-nor-pain—doesn't welcome it, doesn't remain fastened to it. As he doesn't relish that sensation, doesn't welcome it, and doesn't remain fastened to it, delight ceases. If delight ceases, clinging ceases. If clinging ceases, [the process of] becoming ceases. If [the process of] becoming ceases, birth ceases. If birth ceases, aging and death cease, along with sorrow, lamentation, physical and mental

pain, and tribulations. Thus ceases this entire mass of suffering. (MN 38: 414).

According to the Buddha's teachings, then, there is a way of attaining a state in which perception is not stained by the preference for pleasure and the aversion to non-pleasure. This is the path leading to release from the chain of *saṃsāra*, from suffering and becoming, and from self-perpetuating repetition.

The profundity of transformation

Buddhism proposes a decisive, fundamental, and absolute solution to counter the projective mode of being and the tyranny of the pleasure principle. In psychoanalysis, though the achievements it seeks are not to be underestimated, the picture regarding the ability to change and to be released from suffering is far less clear and thorough. We have seen that in every person stereotypical patterns emerge, resulting from his or her adopted behaviours, and that through transference they are iterated again and again. Yet, these patterns are not entirely immune to change through new experience (Freud, 1912b). In spite of their repetitive and relatively permanent character, later experiences might have an impact and affect them. As we have seen, the change proposed by psychoanalysis is largely related to the resurrection of these patterns in the realm stretching between transference and countertransference and to the work of integration that is, thus, made possible. For Freud, the potential triumph in the struggle on the transferential plane—that is, the very struggle between the ability to understand and the urge to act—indicates permanent cure (Freud, 1912b). But does this "permanent cure" mean that the "ability to understand" becomes an unambiguous characteristic of the psyche in its entirety, with the "urge to act" no longer featuring at all? The answer is no, from the psychoanalytic or any other psychodynamic perspective. Although change is possible, as well as "cure" (which some, like Bion, stopped seeing as an objective) and the adoption of integrative behaviours instead of behaviours based on splitting, projection, and acting out as principal courses of action, still the latter are never completely rooted out: they remain active in their appropriate psychic strata and make their appearance whenever external and internal circumstances awaken them. Freud's writings, for example, represent the following attitude:

> But whoever understands the human mind knows that hardly anything is harder for a man than to give up a pleasure which he has once experienced. Actually, we can never give anything up; we only exchange one thing for another. What appears to be a renunciation is really the formation of a substitution or surrogate. (Freud, 1908e, p. 145; also in Lazar & Erlich, 1996)

The Buddha's teaching, by contrast, is clearly far more optimistic with regard to a belief in humans' ability to change radically, or, in other words, the change it proposes is more fundamental and essential. From a Buddhist perspective, the above statements are true as long as the individual keeps on blindly rotating within the *saṃsāric* round of conditioned arising. Yet it is wholly possible to renounce this: not merely to abandon "something", but to abandon every object of desire as such; to abandon, that is, desire. This, indeed, is the definition of *nibbāna*, total liberation from the chain of becoming and of suffering: "It is the complete cessation of that very thirst, giving it up, renouncing it, emancipating oneself from it, detaching oneself from it" (SV, p. 421, cited in Rahula, 1959, p. 93).

"Calming of all conditioned things, giving up of all defilements, extinction of 'thirst', detachment, cessation, Nibbana" (SI, p. 136, cited in Rahula, 1959, pp. 36–26).

The Buddha's teachings describe a mental achievement reflected in the ability to take in information from all six sensory spheres without reacting to it. This is possible thanks to the establishment of mindfulness and equanimity, and it eventually leads to the cessation of the chain of becoming and suffering. What this entails is the undoing of the most basic mental conditioning: the conditioning that tends to the pleasant and rejects the unpleasant. So, through Buddhist eyes, change in the mind's very infrastructure and release from subjection to the pleasure principle—no matter how hard—are explicit and attainable objectives. In the course of Buddhist practice, a dialectic takes place between states of equanimity and states of reactivity, as Robert put it well when he described himself as moving back and forth between the eye of the storm and the chaos around it. But the ultimate objective of this path is the absolute and irreversible cessation of *saññā* and *saṅkhāra*, of desire and hatred, of thirst and construction, of biased interpretation and reactive mental activity and, therefore, of projection in its different forms.

The personal stories of Joel, Shira, Mark, Ethan, Sarah, and Robert, illustrated the process of eradication of reactive residues and their consequences. In the Buddha's words, the manner in which they all witnessed the appearance of sensations and the other associated mental components, and the way in which they all observed the gradual, non-intellectual removal of painful complexes from various domains in their lives, is described as follows:

> Whenever aversion is present in him, he understands properly that, "Aversion is present in me." Whenever aversion is absent from him, he understands properly that, "Aversion is absent from me." He understands properly, how aversion that has not yet arisen in him, comes to arise. He understands properly, how aversion that has now arisen in him, gets eradicated. He understands properly, how aversion that has now been eradicated, will in future no longer arise in him. (DN 22, cited in Goenka, 1998, p. 31)

(And the same goes for other mental contents, of course.)

This is the awakening of the accumulations of *saṅkhāras*, the mental residues, the building stones of the "house" that is the "self", the same self whose foundation, addicted to the pleasant as it is, ruled by projection, shrouded in transference, leads us blindly, again and again, through repeated patterns of suffering. This is the process by which, once new reactions of craving and aversion no longer arise, these residues disappear and fade away. When the Buddha discovered the processes whereby these building stones pile up, and when he himself finished undoing them, he said:

> Through countless births in the cycle of existence
> I have run, in vain
> seeking the builder of this house;
> and again and again I faced the suffering of new birth.
>
> Oh housebuilder! Now you are seen.
> You shall not build a house again for me.
> All your beams are broken,
> the ridgepole is shattered.
> The mind has become freed from conditioning;
> the end of craving has been reached.
>
> (Dhp XI 8–9, cited in Goenka, 2006)

Still a long way from the final eradication of craving, but walking the path towards it, all those whose stories were told here seek to reach the bedrock of their mind. Along with many others, they are investigators of the mind, dedicating themselves, minute by minute, to breaking the chain of becoming at the intersection between a sensation and the emergent reaction to it. The already removed layers of anxiety, depression, anger, and doubt have been eliminated, never to return, but since fixation is not stagnation, and since nothing in the mental world is ever static, then as long as their minds still harbour other layers of these same residues, the production of fresh ones will remain their default option. This is why they remain alert to the particular juncture at which they find themselves, a place from which two roads bifurcate: a reactive one which leads to the creation of further sources of suffering, and a non-reactive one which eradicates the aggregates produced along the first track. They see clearly the absence of those layers that were already removed, and feel the resulting relief, happiness, and liberation. They try to keep a clear view of the presence of those layers that were not removed yet, and of the suffering and blindness they carry with them.

This is why Sarah keeps observing the sensations of heaviness in her chest, throat, and diaphragm, directly and without mediation, inside her body, or she keeps observing the sensations of heaviness in her chest, throat, and diaphragm, directly and without mediation, on the surface of her body, or she observes the sensations of heaviness in her chest, throat, and diaphragm, directly and without mediation, both inside her body and on its surface simultaneously. This is why Sarah keeps observing the impermanent nature of the sensations of heaviness: their appearance, their disappearance, their appearance and instantaneous disappearance as they dissolve into mere vibration. When the psycho–physical complex she calls "depression", with its sensations of heaviness, is present in her, she understands very well: "Now there's depression in me and it expresses itself in sensations of heaviness". When the psycho–physical complex she calls "depression", with its sensations of heaviness, is not present in her, she understands very well: "There's no depression in me, and no sensations of heaviness". She understands very well how depression, which has not yet arisen, arises. She understands very well how depression, which has now arisen, is removed. She understands very well how depression, once it has been removed, will not again arise in her.

And this is why Joel keeps observing the psycho–physical complex he calls "anxiety", in unmediated fashion, inside his body: the sudden and very fast plunge from the face downward to the lower belly and the pelvis, the turbulence in stomach and chest, the streams of cold air washing over his arms and legs as all warmth escapes, the lump that presses the throat, the tiny, stinging bubbles moving rapidly through his body, up to his teeth. Or he feels the sensations of the psycho–physical complex he calls "anxiety", directly and without mediation, on the surface of his body as the pores tighten with a shiver, as heat and cold come and go, as the skin of the face and eyes sink. Or he feels the sensations of the psycho–physical complex he calls "anxiety", directly and without mediation, both on the body's surface and within it simultaneously. Thus, Joel keeps observing the impermanent nature of sensations of anxiety, their appearance, their disappearance, their appearance and instantaneous disappearance as they dissolve into mere vibration.

When there is "anxiety" in him with its related sensations, he understands very well: "Now there's anxiety in me which expresses itself in sensations of plunging, turbulence, cold air, a lump, goosebumps and shiver, the skin of face and eyes sinking, and these tiny, stinging bubbles that move fast to the teeth." When anxiety and its related sensations do not exist in him, he understands very well: "There's no anxiety in me, I don't have this complex of sensations of plunging, turbulence, cold air, a lump pressing, goosebumps and shiver, the skin of face and eyes sinking, and these tiny, stinging bubbles that move fast to the teeth." He understands very well how anxiety, which has not yet arisen, arises. He understands very well how the anxiety that has now arisen is removed. He understands very well how anxiety, once it has been removed, will not again arise in him.

Islands of regression

The pull towards regression is a continuous state (Sandler, 1993), with external or internal pressure affecting even those who are relatively mature and have processed their mental materials through years of psychotherapy or meditation. Because at the heart of our habitual mental substructure (as long as it is not thoroughly undone) lies the tendency to pursue the pleasant and the urge to expel the unpleasant, there is always the temptation to project, even for those who spend a considerable part of their personal and professional life refining their ability to "contain" or to remain aware and equanimous. It is a little like someone who decides to put himself on a regime of dieting, exercise, a work or study project, but allows himself an occasional lapse: he eats a piece of chocolate cake, or takes some lazy time off. The same is true for our mind: it is attracted to certain islands of regression and clings to them, as though they were some sweet treat, as if they held true joy, as though they held something to which we are entitled. These are, beyond doubt, the infantile elements that remain alive in us and, equally, expressions of the mental substrate from whose domination it is so hard to escape.

So, we reserve the dubious "right" to be regressive in certain domains of our interpersonal life, with our partner, for instance, or our parents. But this right is not really a right at all, and though it is tempting, it does not hold the slightest happiness. On these islands, not only do we bring suffering upon others, we also—as I hope will have become clear by now—bring suffering upon ourselves and add fuel to our continued revolving through an existence rooted in blindness and leading to *saṃsāric* repetition. What does it take for this inclination to split off the components of reality, this tendency to project them and turn away from them, to subside and eventually cease? The answer is that as the mental layers dissolve, in which the conditioning to react towards the pleasant and the unpleasant with preference and rejection, respectively, reside, the inclination to regress grows weaker and eventually stops.

We might want to picture the sensitive and special—yet universal and, at the same time, so very common—condition of the new mother. We picture her because each and every one of us started life in the arms of (one version or another of) such a mother. We think of her because her situation is nothing but a potent illustration of where we all find ourselves. We think of her because her vulnerability is our vulnerability.

When she becomes a mother, something inside this woman shifts. Much as with all of us, every moment in her life is, anyway, composed of the traces left by her past experiences and mental actions, and the moment shows these—to whoever is willing to see—through both their mental and material fruits. "Synaptic shadows", Siegel (2012, A1–80) calls the neural impressions of past experiences whose influence affects us in the present. "The shadow of the object", Bollas (1987, p. 3)—following Freud—calls the subject's way of recording his or her early experiences of the object, and the traces they leave. "Kammic residues" or "dormant deposits" is what we might call them in Buddhist terms. In the case of the new mother, these past impressions arise sharply, the dark and unprocessed corners of her mind shift this way and that, and she experiences something akin to a second infancy: the roles she now has to assume *vis à vis* her baby, the rawness of the contents that enter her from her baby's tender psyche, and the intensity of her own feelings, the moods and primitive states her mind encounters in facing their archaic versions that dwell deep inside it, all this arouses and resurrects undigested or partly digested materials. Life, at the same time, grows more and more practically demanding as she raises a baby, or maybe two, or maybe three. She is required to cope with all these materials—which thrust her into a second infancy, a second childhood, a second adolescence (and a third, a fourth . . .?)—in a life that is poor on hours of sleep, on time for thinking things over, on space to take a breath.

This mother, what does she do? Where does she put her frustration, her anger, her anxiety, her sorrow? To what extent is she drawn to the islands of regression, and to what extent does she manage to quickly and safely return from them? Does she displace her vexation at her own frustrated needs to her spouse in order not to turn it against her baby? Does she throw herself into work in order not to feel her huge anxiety for this tiny new loved one who completely captivates her? Is she struggling to give her baby what is so very hard to give—that which she never got herself? Does she allow herself to fully experience her baby's own helplessness, and does she become helplessness herself and enact it, or does she manage to transform it?

Tossed into the very centre of a dependency that broaches no denial (a dependency on her spouse, her mother, life around her), she re-experiences all her most primitive, infantile feelings of dependence; her baby's tiniest and most momentous experience alike creates her, creates him, creates her—mindless, many times, and at others straining to open her eyes in the dark and see the obscure patches, her own blind spots, the oblique, forgotten corners of her mind, so that they may not continue to harm. Where is she vulnerable to blindness and oblivion, at their mercy forever, and along with her, her baby; what ability has she to bring these out into the light, investigate them all the way, dissolve and uproot them, disperse their remaining dust in the winds and watch them vanish forever?

How natural it is to shut herself off to this infinite vulnerability that opens up before her like an abyss. How natural it is to be borne down under the weight. How human is this vulnerability, so much the essence of being in this life, and is it not exactly this same vulnerability that calls to bring things out into the light, to investigate all the way, dissolve and uproot, disperse in the winds . . .

My thought goes to the man who would grow all angry and critical and think of these feelings as moral outrage. My thought goes to the process in the course of which this tendency came undone, along with the old world order which had held him in its grip. My thought goes to the sense of renunciation this entailed and the grace of it, too. My thought goes to a woman who managed to free herself from a pattern which led her time and again to choose partners on the basis of the rampant projections she aimed at them, then to discover, each time, after many months of investment and immersion in the relationship, the huge gap between the products of her projections and who those people were in reality. My thought goes to another person, a man, going on eighty, who one day found that he had let go of his harsh and judgemental way of looking at things, something that had been passed on by his father and had dominated his life, and started treating himself and others with an enabling softness—which he hopes to take with him to his deathbed.

And my thought goes to the new mother. I think of her mind, which must, all of a sudden, contain the little one's tender mind. I think of how she yearns, under the pressures of a heavily burdened daily life and the weight of this new demand, to release herself from herself, into another container, larger and stronger than she, whose existence can be taken for granted. I think of her when she finds there is none, there is none like that. That whether whole or in pieces, she will have to maintain and sustain, observing the rhythmic wavelike motion of her mind between strength and its absence, between poise and holding, and the scattering every which way of her content particles. I think of her, myself, of them. I think of her and embrace her inside me.

NOTES

1. Originally: "Sotena saddaṃ sutvā ... pe ... ghānena gandhaṃ ghāyitvā ... pe ... jivhāya rasaṃ sāyitvā ... pe ... kāyena phoṭṭhabbaṃ phusitvā ... pe ..."
   I filled in the *pe* (etc.) with the parts of sentence they stand for.
2. Bion limits the use of the concept to "such content as is suffused with love or hate" (Bion, 1962b, p. 36).
3. This is a fairly rough categorical distinction. A more detailed, exact division of the various possible combinations characterising different perspectives of self and world can be found in the *Brahmajāla Sutta: The All-Embracing Net of Views* (DN 1).
4. The method of conditioned relations (*Paṭṭhāna*) includes twenty-four mental factors. It describes in detail the ways in which these factors interrelate mind-and-matter phenomena. Unlike the method of conditioned arising, this method also refers to the inherent forces of the conditioning states rather than only to the conditioning and conditioned states themselves. There is nothing mystical about these forces: they are simply the specific characteristics that have the power to cause an effect, or to bring about the appearance of any conditioned state (Bodhi, 1993).
5. Transference: The projection of emotional and relational patterns established in the person's past on to his therapist (or others) at a

189

later stage in life. I discuss this phenomenon in the chapter on "Transference and *saṃsāra*".

6. Additional examples of this can, for instance, be found in Winnicott's ideas of the transitional object and the potential space (Abadi, 2003).

7. Introjective identification complements projective identification. It originates in the infant's early relations with the breast and is synonymous with a sadistic–oral internalisation of the breast based on greed (Klein, 1975a; Meissner, 1980).

8. All of the following extracts were originally published in *Subjects of Analysis* by Thomas Ogden (published by Karnac in 1994), and are reprinted with kind permission of Karnac Books.

9. Thanks to my dear brother, Ronny Barnea, at Tel Aviv University's Department of Chemical Physics, who helped me with this part of the work.

10. "Overlapping worlds" refers to the interactive field, discussed in Chapter Five.

11. Grinberg (1962) used the term "projective counter-identification" to indicate those cases where the patient's projections are so intense that any analyst would have reacted to them in the same manner, regardless of his or her specific personality and complexes.

12. *Upacāra samādhi*: the concentration "approaching" the first *jhāna*, coming close to it but still does not enter it (Mahathera Nauyane, 1994).

13. *Nīvaraṇa* (lit. veil, curtain).

14. *Lok'anukampati* (as a compound which functions as a verb) and *lokānukampanā* (as a compound functioning as a noun).

15. Manzano, J., Palacio Espasa, F., & Zilkha, N. (2005), for instance, estimate the intensity and nature of parental projection, thus to establish whether projection is pathological. They use a number of criteria: the degree of aggression and violence of the mother's fantasy as a result of the invasion, and the degree of splitting; the nature of omnipotent control and fusion with the object; the degree to which the mother's self is depleted as a result of the projection; presence of projective identification aimed to prevent communication and awareness, in contrast with normative projective identification which supports empathy.

REFERENCES

Abadi, S. (2003). Between the frontier and the network. *International Journal of Psychoanalysis, 84*: 221–234.

Amichai, Y. (1996). Ibn Gabirol. In: *The Selected Poetry of Yehuda Amichai* (p. 6), C. Bloch & S. Mitchell (Trans.). Berkeley, CA: University of California Press.

AN 4.49. *Vipallāsa Sutta.*

AN 6.63. *Nibbedhika Sutta.*

Arlow, J. A. (1993). Two discussions of 'The mind of the analyst' and a response from Madeleine Baranger. *International Journal of Psychoanalysis, 74*: 1147–1155.

Baranger, M. (1993). The mind of the analyst: from listening to interpretation. *International Journal of Psycho-Analysis, 74*: 15–24.

Barratt, B. B. (2016).Legacies and memorializations in the intergenerational transmission of psychic life: psychoanalytic notes on some of the ways in which sons assume their father's mantle. *Psychoanalytic Review, 103*: 199–219.

Bell, D. (2001). Projective identification. In: C. Bronstein (Ed.), *Kleinian Theory: A Contemporary Perspective* (pp. 125–147). London: Whurr.

Benjamin, J. (2004). Beyond doer and done to. *Psychoanalytic Quarterly, 73*: 5–46.

Berger, S. (2014). Whose trauma is it anyway? Furthering our understanding of its intergenerational transmission. *Journal of Infant, Child & Adolescent Psychotherapy, 13*: 169–181.

Berman, E. (2009). Introduction to "hate in the counter-transference." In: *True Self, False Self: Essays, 1935–1963*. Tel Aviv: Am Oved.

Biderman, S. (1995). *Early Buddhism*. Tel Aviv: The Ministry of Defence.

Bick, E. (1968). The experience of the skin in early object-relations. *International Journal of Psychoanalysis, 49*: 484–486.

Bion, W. R. (1956). Development of schizophrenic thought. *International Journal of Psychoanalysis, 37*: 344–346.

Bion, W. R. (1959). Attacks on linking. *International Journal of Psycho-Analysis, 40*: 308–315.

Bion, W. R. (1961). *Experiences in Groups and Other Papers*. London: Tavistock.

Bion, W. R. (1962a). The psycho-analytic study of thinking. *International Journal of Psycho-Analysis, 43*: 306–310.

Bion, W. R. (1962b). *Learning from Experience*. London: Tavistock.

Bion, W. R. (1970). *Attention and Interpretation*. London: Tavistock.

Bion, W. R. (1988). Notes on memory and desire. In: E. B. Spillius (Ed.), *Melanie Klein Today (Vol. 2): Mainly Practice* (pp. 15–18). London: Routledge.

Bodhi, B. (Ed.) (1993). *A Comprehensive Manuel of Abhidhamma*. Kandy, Sri Lanka: Buddhist Publication Society.

Bodhi, B. (1995). Transcendental dependent arising: a translation and exposition of the Upanisa Sutta. In: *Access to Insight*. Accessed 28 October 2011 at: www.accesstoinsight.org/lib/authors/bodhi/wheel 277.html.

Bodhi, B. (1998). Toward a threshold of understanding. In: *Access to Insight*. Accessed 9 January 2012 at: www.accesstoinsight.org/lib/authors/bodhi/bps-essay_30.html.

Bollas, C. (1987). *The Shadow of the Object: Psychoanalysis of the Unthought Known*. Washington, DC: Library of Congress.

Brodey, W. M. (1965). On the dynamics of narcissism—I. externalization and early ego development. *Psychoanalytic Study of the Child, 20*: 165–193.

Brown, L. J. (2004). The point of interaction, mutuality, and an aspect of the analyst's oedipal conflict. *Scandinavian Psychoanalytic Review, 27*: 43–51.

Buber, M. (2010). *I and Thou*, R. G. Smith (Trans.). Mansfield, CT: Martino.

Chabris, C. F., & Simons, D. J. (2009). *The Invisible Gorilla: How Our Intuitions Deceive Us*. New York: Random House.

Cozolino, L. (2006). *The Neuroscience of Human Relationships: Attachment and the Developing Social Brain*. New York: Norton.

Dhp, XI. 8–9. In: Goenka, S. N. (2006). *The Gem Set in Gold*. Igatpuri, India: Vipassana Reasearch Institute.

Di Pellegrino, G., Fadiga, L., Fogassi, L., Gallese, V., & Rizzolatti, G. (1992). Understanding motor events: a neurophysiological study. *Experimental Brain Research, 91*: 176–180.

DN 1. *Brahmajāla Sutta.*

DN 15. *Mahānidāna Sutta.*

DN 22. *Mahāsatipaṭṭhāna Sutta.*

Doidge, N. (2008). *The Brain that Changes Itself*. London: Penguin.

Einstein, A., Podolsky, B. Y., & Rosen, N. (1935). Can quantum-mechanical description of physical reality be considered complete? *Physical Review, 47*: 777–781.

Epstein, M. (1988a). Deconstruction of the self: ego and "egolessness" in Buddhist insight meditation. *Journal of Transpersonal Psychology, 20*: 61–69.

Epstein, M. (1988b). Attention in analysis. *Psychoanalysis and Contemporary Thought, 11*: 171–189.

Erlich, S. H. (2003). Experience—what is it? *International Journal of Psychoanalysis, 84*: 1125–1147.

Feldman, M. (1992). Splitting and projective identification. *New Library of Psychoanalysis, 14*: 74–88.

Fleischman, P. R. (1999). Healing the healer. In: *Karma and Chaos* (pp. 40–53). Onalska, WA: Vipassana Research Publication.

Forgas, J. P. (1998). On being happy and mistaken: mood effects on the fundamental attribution error. *Journal of Personality and Social Psychology, 75*(2): 318–331.

Fraiberg, E., Edelson, E., & Shapiro, V. (1975). Ghosts in the nursery: a psychoanalytic approach to the problems of impaired infant–mother relationships. *Journal of the American Academy of Child Psychiatry, 14*: 387–421. Reprinted in: *Psychoanalytic Quarterly, 45*: 651 (1976).

Freud, S. (1900a). *The Interpretation of Dreams. S. E., 4–5*. London: Hogarth.

Freud, S. (1901b). The psychopathology of everyday life. *S. E., 6*: vii–296. London: Hogarth.

Freud, S. (1905e). *Fragment of an Analysis of a Case of Hysteria. S. E., 12*: 1–122. London: Hogarth.

Freud, S. (1908e). Creative writers and day-dreaming. *S. E., 9*: 141–153. London: Hogarth.

Freud, S. (1910d). The future prospects of psycho-analytic therapy. *S. E., 11*: 139–152. London: Hogarth.

Freud, S. (1911b). Formulations on the two principles of mental functioning. *S. E., 12*: 213–226. London: Hogarth.

Freud, S. (1912b). The dynamics of transference. *S. E., 12*: 97–108. London: Hogarth.

Freud, S. (1912e). Recommendations to physicians practising psychoanalysis, *S. E., 12*: 109–120. London: Hogarth.

Freud, S. (1912–1913). *Totem and Taboo. S. E., 13*: vii–162. London: Hogarth.

Freud, S. (1914g). Remembering, repeating and working-through (further recommendations on the technique of psycho-analysis II). *S. E., 12*: 145–156.

Freud, S. (1915e). The unconscious. *S. E., 14*: 159–215. London: Hogarth.

Freud, S. (1916–1917). *Introductory Lectures on Psycho-analysis. S.E., 15.* London: Hogarth.

Freud, S. (1917d). A metapsychological supplement to the theory of dreams. *S. E., 14*: 217–235. London: Hogarth.

Freud, S. (1920g). *Beyond the Pleasure Principle. S. E., 18*: 1–64. London: Hogarth.

Freud, S. (1925h). Negation. *S. E., 19*: 233–240. London: Hogarth.

Freud, S. (1927c). *The Future of an Illusion. S. E., 21*: 1–56. London: Hogarth.

Freud, S. (1933a). *New Introductory Lectures on Psycho-analysis. S. E., 22*: 1–182. London: Hogarth.

Goenka, S. N. (1988). *3 Day Course Discourses.* Igatpuri, India: Vipassana Research Institute.

Goenka, S. N. (1990). *The Importance of Vedanā and Sampajañña.* Igatpuri, India: Vipassana Research Institute.

Goenka, S. N. (1998). *Mahāsatipaṭṭhāna Sutta: The Great Discourse on the Establishing of Awareness.* Igatpuri, India: Vipassana Research Institute.

Goenka, S. N. (2010). *Discourses on Satipaṭṭhāna Sutta.* Igatpuri, India: Vipassana Research Institute.

Grand, S., Newirth, J., Stein, A., Baur, A., Itzkowitz, S., Pines, D., Sirote, A., & Sussillo, M. (2009). Violence and aggression in the consulting room. *Psychoanalytic Perspectives, 6*: 1–21.

Grinberg, L. (1962). On a specific aspect of countertransference due to the patient's projective identification. *International Journal of Psychoanalysis, 43*: 436–440.

Grotstein, J. S. (1995). Projective identification reappraised: projective identification, introjective identification, the transference/countertransference neurosis/psychosis, and their consummate expression in the crucifixion, the Pietà, and "Therapeutic Exorcism," Part II: The countertransference complex. *Contemporary Psychoanalysis, 31*: 479–520.

Grotstein, J. S. (2000). Notes on Bion's "Memory and desire". *Journal of the American Academy of Psychoanalysis, 28*: 687–694.

Harari, Y. N. (2015). *Sapiens: A Brief History of Humankind.* New York: HarperCollins.

Hart, W. (1987). *The Art of Living.* Washington, DC: Vipassana Research Insititute & Priyatti Publishing.

Hill, A. L., Rand, D. G., Nowak, M. A., & Christakis, N. A. (2010). Emotions as infectious diseases in a large social network: the SISa model. *Proceedings of the Royal Society B-Biological Science, 277.1701*: 3827–3835.

Hinshelwood, R. D. (1991). *A Dictionary of Kleinian Thought* (2nd edn). London: Free Association.

Horta, B. L., Bahl, R., Martines, J. C., & Victora, C. G. (2007). *Evidence on the Long-Term Effects of Breastfeeding: Systematic Review and Meta-Analyses.* Geneva: World Health Organization.

Iacoboni, M., Koski, L. M., Brass, M., Bekkering, H., Woods, R. P., Dubeau, M. C., Mazziotta, J. C., & Rizzolatti, G. (2001). Reafferent copies of imitated actions in the right superior temporal cortex. *Proceedings of the National Academy of Sciences, 98*(24): 13995–13999.

Iti 50. *Mūla.*

Jeannerod, M. (2001). Neural simulation of action: a unifying mechanism for motor cognition. *NeuroImage, 14*: S103–S109.

Jeremiah 31: 29. In: *The Bible.*

Johansson, R. E. A. (1979). *The Dynamic Psychology of Early Buddhism.* London: Curzon.

Jones, E. (1946). A valedictory address. *International Journal of Psychoanalysis, 27*: 7–12.

Joseph, B. (1975). The patient who is difficult to reach. In: E. B. Spillius (Ed.), *Melanie Klein Today (Vol. 2): Mainly Practice* (pp. 41–51). London: Routledge, 1988.

Joseph, B. (1985). Transference: the total situation. *International Journal of Psychoanalysis, 66*: 447–454.

Joseph, B. (1989). Projective identification: clinical aspects. In: J. Sandler (Ed.), *Projection, Identification, Projective Identification* (pp. 65–76). London: Karnac.

Joseph, B. (2001). Transference. In: C. Bronstein (Ed.), *Kleinian Theory: A Contemporary Perspective* (pp. 181–192). London: Whurr.

Kernberg, O. F. (1987). Projection and projective identification: developmental and clinical aspects. *Journal of the American Psychoanalytic Association, 35*: 795–819.

Klein, M. (1930). The importance of symbol-formation in the development of the ego. *International Journal of Psychoanalysis, 11*: 24–39.

Klein, M. (1935). A contribution to the psychogenesis of manic-depressive states. *International Journal of Psychoanalysis, 16*: 145–174.

Klein, M. (1946). Notes on some schizoid mechanisms. *International Journal of Psychoanalysis, 27*: 99–110.

Klein, M. (1952). The origins of transference. *International Journal of Psychoanalysis, 33*: 433–438.

Klein, M. (1975a). Some theoretical conclusions regarding the emotional life of the infant. In: M. M. R. Khan (Ed.), *Envy and Gratitude and Other Works 1946–1963* (pp. 61–93). London: Hogarth Press and the Institute of Psycho-Analysis.

Klein, M. (1975b). On identification. In: M. M. R. Khan (Ed.), *Envy and Gratitude and Other Works 1946–1963* (pp. 141–175). London: Hogarth Press and the Institute of Psycho-Analysis.

Klein, M. (1975c). Envy and gratitude. In: M. M. R. Khan (Ed.), *Envy and Gratitude and Other Works 1946–1963* (pp. 176–235). London: Hogarth Press and the Institute of Psycho-Analysis.

Kramer, M. S., Aboud, F., Mironova, E., Vanilovich, I., Platt, R. W., Matush, L., Igumnov, S., Fombonne, E., Bogdanovich, N., Ducruet, T. J. P., Chalmers, B., Hodnett, E., Davidovsky, S., Skugarevsky, O., Trofimovich, O., Kozlova, L., & Shapiro, S. (2008). Breastfeeding and child cognitive development: new evidence from a large randomized trial. *Journal of the American Association of Psychiatry, 65*(5): 578–584.

Laird, J. D., & Bresler, C. (1992). The process of emotional experience: a self-perception theory. *Emotion. Review of Personality and Social Psychology, 13*: 213–234.

Larson, R. W., & Almeida, D. M. (1999). Emotional transmission in the daily lives of families: a new paradigm for studying family process. *Journal of Marriage and the Family, 61*: 5–20.

Lassmann, W. (2013). Intergenerational transmission of influence and family pattern: some French perspectives. *British Journal of Psychotherapy, 29*: 75–97.

Lazar, R., & Erlich, H. S. (1996). Repetition compulsion. *Psychoanalysis and Contemporary Thought, 19*: 29–55.

Lewis, T., Amini, F., & Lannon, R. (2001). *A General Theory of Love.* New York: Vintage.

Lobel, T. (2014). *Sensation: The New Science of Physical Intelligence.* New York: Atria.

Lotz, M. (1991). Projective identification on different levels. *Scandinavian Psychoanalytic Review, 14*: 19–38.

Mahathera, N. A. (1994). Anapana sati: meditation on breathing. In: *Access to Insight* (Legacy Edition). Accessed 14 September 2014 at: www. accesstoinsight.org/lib/authors/ariyadhamma/bl115.html.

Manzano, J., Palacio Espasa, F., & Zilkha, N. (2005). *The Narcissistic Scenarios of Parenthood*. Tel-Aviv: Bookwarm.

Mauss, I. B., Gross, J. J., Ferrer, E., John, O. P., Shallcross, A. J., Troy, A. S., & Wilhelm, F. H. (2001). Don't hide your happiness! Positive emotion dissociation, social connectedness and psychological functioning. *Journal of Personality and Social Psychology*, 100(4): 738–748.

Meissner, W. W. (1980). A note on projective identification. *Journal of the American Psychoanalytic Association*, 28: 43–66.

Meltzer, D. (1983). *Dream-Life: A Re-Examination of the Psychoanalytic Theory and Technique*. London: Karnac.

Meltzer, D. (2008)[1978]. *The Kleinian Development*. London: Karnac.

Mitchell, S. A., & Black, M. J. (1995). *Freud and Beyond: A History of Modern Psychoanalytic Thought*. New York: Basic Books.

MN 38. *Mahātaṇhāsaṅkhaya Sutta*.

MN 62 (2006). *Mahārāhulavāda Sutta*, T. Bhikkhu (Trans.). Access to Insight. Accessed 19 March 2016 at: www.accesstoinsight.org/tipitaka/mn/mn.062.than.html.

Money-Kyrle, R. E. (1956). Normal counter-transference and some of its deviations. *International Journal of Psychoanalysis*, 37: 360–366.

Moore, D. M. (1995). Projective and introjective identification in a couple therapy case study: a hermeneutical examination. Dissertation submitted to the faculty of the Virginia Polytechnic Institute and State University in partial fulfilment of the requirements for the degree of Doctor of Philosophy in Family and Child Development: Virginia.

Nathanson, D. L. (1986). The empathic wall and the ecology of affect. *Psychoanalytic Study of the Child*, 41: 171–186.

Nummenmaa, L., Glerean, E., Hari, R., & Hietanen, J. K. (2013). Bodily maps of emotions. *Proceedings of the National Academy of Sciences*, 111(2): 646–651. Accessed 26 December 2015 at: www.pnas.org/content/111/2/646.full.

Nyanatiloka (1997). *Buddhist Dictionary: Manual of Buddhist Terms and Doctrines* (4th revised edn). Kandy, Sri Lanka: Buddhist Publication Society.

Oddy, W. H., Kendall, G. E., Li, J., Jacoby, P., Robinson, M., de Klerk, N. H., Silburn, S. R., Zubrick, S. R., Landau, L. I., & Stanley, F. J. (2010). The long-term effects of breastfeeding on child and adolescent mental health: a pregnancy cohort study followed for 14 years. *Journal of Pediatrics, 156*(4): 568–574.

Ogden, T. H. (1979). On projective identification. *International Journal of Psychoanalysis, 60*: 357–373.

Ogden, T. H. (1986). *The Matrix of the Mind: Object Relations and the Psychoanalytic Dialogue*. Oxford: Rowman & Littlefield.

Ogden, T. H. (1994a). The analytic third: working with intersubjective clinical facts. *International Journal of Psychoanalysis, 75*: 3–19.

Ogden, T. H. (1994b). Projective identification and the subjugating third. In: *Subjects of Analysis* (pp. 97–106). London: Karnac [reprinted Lanham, MD: Rowman & Littlefield, 2004].

Ogden, T. H. (2004a). *The Primitive Edge of Experience*. Lanham, MD: Jason Aronson.

Ogden, T. H. (2004b). On holding and containing, being and dreaming. *International Journal of Psychoanalysis, 85*: 1349–1364.

Ornston, D. (1978). On projection: a study of Freud's usage. *Psychoanalytic Study of the Child, 33*: 117–166.

Payutto, P. A. (1995). *Dependent Origination: The Buddhist Law of Conditionality*, B. Evans (Trans.). Thailand: Buddhadhamma Foundation.

Pelled, E. (2005). *Psychoanalysis and Buddhism: On the Human Capacity to Know*. Tel Aviv: Resling.

Pelled, E. (2007). Learning from experience: Bion's concept of reverie and Buddhist meditation: a comparative study. *The International Journal of Psycho-Analysis, 88*: 1507–1526.

Platek, S. M. (2003). Contagious yawning: the role of self-awareness and mental state attribution. *Cognitive Brain Research, 17*: 223–227.

Porchia, A. (1943). *Voices*, W. S. Merwin (Trans.). Port Townsend, WA: Copper Canyon, 2003.

Racker, H. (1968). *Transference and Countertransference*. International Psycho-Analytic Library, 73:1–196 [reprinted London: Hogarth Press and the Institute of Psycho-Analysis, 1988].

Rahula, W. (1974). *What the Buddha Taught* (2nd and enlarged edn). New York: Grove.

Rapaport, D. (1944). The scientific methodology of psychoanalysis. In: M. M. Gill (Ed.), *The Collected Papers of David Rapaport* (pp. 165–220). New York: Basic Books, 1967.

Raz, J. (2006). *Zen Buddhism: Philosophy and Aesthetics*. Israel: The Ministry of Defence.

Rhys Davids, T. W., & Stede, W. (Eds.) (1921–1925). *The Pāli Text Society's Pāli–English Dictionary*. Chipstead: Pāli Text Society. 8 parts (738 pp).

In: *Digital Dictionaries of South Asia*. Accessed 7 May 2015, http://dsalsrv02.uchicago.edu/cgi-bin/philologic/getobject.pl?c.2:1:503.pali.

Rizzolatti, G., Fadiga, L., Fogassi, L., & Gallese, V. (1999). Resonance behaviors and mirror neurons. *Archives Italiannes de Biologie, 137*: 85–100.

Rumi (1995). Sometimes I forget completely. In: *Selected Poems* (p. 47), C. Barks (Trans.). London: Penguin.

Sadeharju, K., Knip, M., Virtanen S. M., Savilahti, E., Tauriainen, S., Koskela, P., Åkerblom, H. K., Hyöty, H., & the Finnish TRIGR Study Group (2007). Maternal antibodies in breast milk protect the child from enterovirus infections. *Pediatrics, 119*(5): 941–946.

Safran, J. D. (1999). Faith, despair, will, and the paradox of acceptance. *Contemporary Psychoanalysis, 35*: 5–23.

Sandler, J. (1993). On communication from patient to analyst: not everything is projective identification. *International Journal of Psychoanalysis, 74*: 1097–1107.

Sandler, J., Meissner, W. W., Kernberg, O., Tarnopolsky, A., Solan, R., Braun, A., Berner, W., Shoshani, M., & Oosterhuis, E. (1989). Discussion of Otto F. Kernberg's paper. In: J. Sandler (Ed.), *Projection, Identification, Projective Identification* (pp. 117–131). London: Karnac.

Schrödinger, E. (1935). Discussion of probability relations between separated systems. *Mathematical Proceedings of the Cambridge Philosophical Society, 31*: 555–563.

Schrödinger, E. (1950). What is an elementary particle? *Endeavour*: 109–116.

Segal, H. (1957). Notes on symbol formation. *International Journal of Psychoanalysis, 38*: 391–397.

Segal, H. (1998). 'The importance of symbol-formation in the development of the ego'—in context. *Journal of Child Psychotherapy, 24*: 349–357.

Shabad, P. (1993). Repetition and incomplete mourning: the intergenerational transmission of traumatic themes. *Psychoanalytic Psychology, 10*: 61–75.

Shaw, J. (2014). Psychotic and non-psychotic perceptions of reality. *Journal of Child Psychotherapy, 40(1)*: 73–89.

Shepperd, J., Malone, W., & Sweeny, K. (2008). Exploring causes of the self-serving bias. *Social and Personality Psychology Compass, 2*(2): 895–908.

Siegel, D. J. (2012). *Pocket Guide to Interpersonal Neurobiology: An Integrative Handbook of the Mind*. New York: Norton.

SN 5.7. *Upacālā Sutta*.

SN 22.59. *Pañcavaggiya* [*Anattalakkhaṇa*].

SN 56.11. *Dhammacakkappavattana Sutta*.

Spillius, E. B. (1992). Clinical experiences of projective identification. *New Library of Psychoanalysis*, 14: 59–73.

Spillius, E. B., Milton, J., Garvey, P., Couve, C., & Steiner, D. (2011). Projective identification. In: *The New Dictionary of Kleinian Thought* (pp. 126–146). Hove: Routledge.

Steiner, J. (1992). The equilibrium between the paranoid–schizoid and the depressive positions. *New Library of Psychoanalysis*, 14: 46–58.

Symington, J. (1985). The survival function of primitive omnipotence. *International Journal of Psychoanalysis*, 66: 481–487.

Thera, N. (1998)[1949]. *Abidhamma Studies: Buddhist Explorations of Consciousness and Time*. Boston, MA: Wisdom.

Tomkins, S. S. (1995). The quest for primary motives: biography and auto-biography of an idea. In: E. V. Demos (Ed.), *Exploring Affect: The Selected Writings of Silvan S. Tomkins* (pp. 27–63). Cambridge: Maison des Sciences de l'Homme and Cambridge University.

VIS. *The Path of Purification (Visuddhimagga): The Classic Manual of Buddhist Doctrine & Meditation*, B. Nāṇamoli (Trans.). Kandy, Sri Lanka: Buddhist Publication Society, 1991.

Waska, R. (2013). Working to understand our role in the patient's mind: countertransference and the problems of immersion. *British Journal of Psychotherapy*, 29(4): 466–480.

Wender, L. (1993). Two discussions of 'The inner experiences of the analyst' and a response from Theodore Jacobs. *International Journal of Psychoanalysis*, 74: 1136–1139.

Winnicott, D. W. (1949). Hate in the counter-transference. *International Journal of Psychoanalysis*, 30: 69–74.

Winnicott, D. W. (1960). The theory of the parent–infant relationship. *International Journal of Psychoanalysis*, 41: 585–595.

Wollheim, R. (1993). *The Mind and its Depths*. Cambridge, MA: Harvard University Press.

Yarom, N. (2010). *Body Stories: On Silent Psychic Experiences Breaking Out in the Body*. Israel: Modan.

INDEX